Human Rights and Persons with Disabilities in Nigeria

Laws, Policies, and Institutions

Adonis & Abbey Publishers Ltd
St James House
13 Kensington Square,
London, W8 5HD
United Kingdom

Website: http://www.adonis-abbey.com
E-mail Address: editor@adonis-abbey.com

Nigeria:
Suites C3 – C6 J-Plus Plaza
Asokoro, Abuja, Nigeria
Tel: +234 (0) 7058078841/08052035034

British Library Cataloguing-in-Publication Data
A catalogue record for this book is available from the British Library.

ISBN: 9781913976026

Human Rights and Persons with Disabilities in Nigeria
Laws, Policies, and Institutions

Halima Aliyu Doma, Ph.D

ADONIS & ABBEY
PUBLISHERS LTD

Dedication

This book is dedicated to the memory of my late father, Dr. Aliyu Akwe Doma, who taught me to respect human dignity and to value education.

Preface and Acknowledgements

This book is the product of my doctoral thesis which was completed in 2017 at the University of Jos. Enhancements have been made to reflect changes in legislation and other developments regarding disability issues in Nigeria. I must further place on record that neither this book nor my interest in exploring disability rights would have been conceived had I not interned at the National Human Rights Commission, where I witnessed the frustrations of numerous persons with disabilities who dared to approach the Commission for the protection and/or enforcement of their rights. The arduous task of navigating through available laws, institutions, personnel, and prejudices to enforce these rights is an experience I will never forget.

With an estimated 25 million disabled persons in Nigeria, about one in every eight Nigerians live with at least one form of disability. Like many other countries, Nigeria is signatory to various international treaties and domestic regulations which necessitate the protection and promotion of the rights and interests of persons with disabilities. Notwithstanding the foregoing, evidence suggests that the vast majority of disabled persons in Nigeria are poor and unable to access important public services and opportunities including education, healthcare and employment.

I have written this book to emphasize the importance of human rights in the specific context of disability, and the extent to which law can improve the plight of persons with disabilities. In particular, the legal and institutional structures that seek to enhance the position of persons with disabilities in Nigeria are considered , following which an assessment is made on the adequacy of these laws and institutions in addressing the phenomenon of disability discrimination which continues to prevail within Nigeria.The book ultimately canvasses for a holistic consideration and protection of the Human Rights of Persons with Disabilities giving special attention to the unique vulnerability of women, children, and elderly persons with disabilities; and the urgent need to integrate disability issues in National Planning.

Although originally conceived as a guide for students, researchers, activists, and policy makers in the fields of Human Rights Law and Disability Studies (in Nigeria and beyond), I expect that the book will also be useful for those who encounter persons with disabilities on a regular basis.

My appreciation goes to staff of the National Human Rights Commission who encouraged me to join the disability rights campaign, and availed me some useful contacts and materials to undertake this research. I also appreciate all the persons with disabilities who I encountered in the course of the research for sharing their stories, and aspirations with me.

A debt of gratitude goes to other wonderful people who were instrumental to the production of this book. While space will not permit me to fully acknowledge everyone, I wish to specially thank my supervisor, Professor Dominic Asada for his patient guidance throughout the period of my doctoral research, and for creating time to painstakingly review this manuscript. I am also grateful to members of the University of Jos Law Faculty for enriching the quality of this book by reading my seminar papers, engaging in vibrant discussions, and offering different insights on human rights, disability and society.

The unquantifiable encouragement of my esteemed teachers and senior colleagues: Professor Jamila Nasir, Professor Dakas C.J Dakas (SAN), Professor Tawfiq Ladan, and Professor Yemi Akinseye-George (SAN) cannot be left unappreciated. I have also benefitted greatly from the moral and intellectual support friends: Chinwe, Muhammad, Jamila, Bridget, Phokoo, Abraham, and Abdul-Wahab. Each of them was mandated to either critique or edit parts of this book.

My deepest gratitude goes to my family for their unparalleled support. I am especially grateful to my husband Abubakar Idris Kutigi, and my children Maryam, Adam and Hauwa for their unwavering patience. I am equally grateful to my dear parents for constantly encouraging me and giving me the opportunities that have made me who I am today.

Above all, I am thankful to Almighty Allah, without whom this undertaking would not have been possible.

Table of Contents

Table of Cases

Table of Statutes

List of Acronyms

AD	Anno Dominium
ALDIN	Association of Lawyers with Disabilities in Nigeria
ARI	African Rehabilitation Institute
ASCEND	Association for the Comprehensive Empowerment of Nigerian with Disabilities
AU	African Union
BC	Before Christ
CAMA	Companies and Allied Matters Act
CCD	Centre for Citizens with Disabilities
CRA	Child Rights Act
CRC	Child Right Convention
CRC	Convention on the Rights of the Child
CRPD	Convention on Rights of Persons with Disabilities
CWD	Children with Disabilities
DNA	Deoxyribonucleic Acid
DPI	Disabled Peoples International
DPOs	Disabled Persons Organisations
DWIN	Deaf Women in Nigeria
	Eds Editors
FRN	Federal Republic of Nigeria
HRC	Human Rights Committee
ICCRP	International Covenant on Civil and Political Rights
ICESCR	International Covenant on Economic, Social and Cultural Rights
ICF	International Classification of Functioning
ICIDH	International Classification of Impairments, Disabilities and Handicaps
ICT	Information and Communication Technology
INEC	Independent National Electoral Commission
JONAPWD	Joint Association of Persons with Disabilities
LDA	Lunatics Detention Act
MEND	Movement for the Empowerment of Nigerian with Disabilities
NGOs	Non-Governmental Organisations
NHRC	National Human Rights Commission
NNAD	Nigerian National Association of the Deaf
OAU	Organisation of African Unity

13

PWD	Persons with Disabilities
RCAD	Resource Centre for Advocacy on Disability
SA	South Africa
	DPWDSecretariat of the African Decade of Persons With Disabilities
SCIAN	Spinal Cord Injury Association of Nigeria
UBE	Universal Basic Education
UDHR	Universal Declaration on Human Rights
UK	United Kingdom
UN	United Nations
UNESCO	United Nations Educational, Scientific and Cultural Organisation
US	United States
VAP	Violence Against Persons
WHO	World Health Organisation

CHAPTER ONE

Global Picture of Disability

1.1 Introduction

Globally, on a daily basis, many persons are confronted with one form of disability or the other. This condition may occur as a result of various factors ranging from malnutrition, disease, environmental hazards, natural disasters, traffic and industrial accidents, civil conflicts, and war. Also, some disabilities are as a result of medical negligence, while others are due to birth defects. Disabilities are not ascribed to a particular class, gender, or religion; anybody can be a victim any time. In countries with life expectancies of over 70 years of age, people spend an average of 8 years, or 11.5% of their lifespan living with disabilities or impairments[1].

The World Bank estimates that approximately one billion people or 15% of the world's population have a disability (making it arguably the world's largest minority group), and 80% of these people live in developing nations. If families of persons with disabilities (PWDs) are included, then at least 25% of the world is directly affected by disability[2]. As the world population grows, the number of PWDs is also increasing. Notably, there is a two-way link between poverty and disability. It is estimated that 20% of the world's poorest people have some kind of disability, and a high increase in the number of PWDs is prevalent in most developing countries. This is compounded by the poor economic situation, lack of health capacity in the rural areas (where a majority of

---

[1] *Ibid.*
[2] World Health Organization (WHO) & World Bank (2011) *World Report on Disability* <http://www.who.int/disabilities/world_report/2011> accessed 24/3/16.; See also *Disability and HIV/AIDS* (World Bank: 2004) <htt://www.worldbank.org/>accessed 24/3/16.

the population live), and the entrenchment of traditional religious beliefs marginalising persons with disabilities as a burden on society[3].

In its World Health Report on Disability, the World Health Organisation divides human beings into two groups; those with impairments and those without. The report states that one in six to seven of the world's population is disabled[4] and further presents this very stark fact: *across the world people with disabilities have poor health outcomes, lower education achievements, less economic participation and higher rate of poverty than people without disabilities[5]*.

Similarly, the UN Handbook for Parliamentarians on the Convention on the Rights of Persons with Disabilities and its Optional Protocol assesses the situation in this manner:

> As the world's population grows, so does the number of persons with disabilities. In developing countries, poor medical conditions during pregnancy and at birth, the prevalence of infectious diseases, natural disasters, armed conflict, landmines and small-arms proliferation cause injuries, impairment and lasting trauma on a large scale. Traffic accidents, alone, result in millions of injuries and disabilities each year among young people. In developed countries, those born after the Second World War are living longer, which means that many of them will eventually live with a disability later in life[6].

Most human rights instruments often involve the requirement for "equal rights". The idea embodied in the expression is that the rights conferred on all human beings are equal irrespective of physical or mental status, race, religion, social or political standing. In other words, PWDs must enjoy the rights stipulated in any legal instrument, which the state may

---

3   Biegon, J., "The Promotion and Protection of Disability Rights in the African Human Rights System", in Grobbelaar-du Plessis, I., & Van Reenen, T., Aspects to Disability Law in Africa (Pretoria: SA: Pretoria University Law Press) 2011, p.53.

4   World Health Organization (WHO) & World Bank World report on disability (2011) 29; See also Report of the Special Rapporteur on Torture And Other Cruel, Inhuman Or Degrading Treatment Or Punishment' A/HRC/22/53(11 May, 2013) <http://www.ohchrc.org/Documents/HRBodies/HRCouncil/RegularSession/Session22/A>accessed 9/7/14.

5   Ibid.

6   From Exclusion to Equality: Realizing the rights of persons with disabilities, Handbook for Parliamentarians on the Convention on the Rights of Persons with Disabilities and its Optional Protocol,<http://www.ipu.org/PDF/publications/disabilities-e.pdf >accessed 17/02/15.

accord to other able persons. Flowing from above, therefore, equality in law precludes discrimination of any kind. Regrettably however, the absence of context and public education on matters relating to disabilities makes the public to remain uninformed about the moral framework and philosophical underpinnings of any existing legal 'instruments on disabilities.

Thus, notwithstanding existing staggering statistics, PWDs are often overlooked by society in many parts of the world. They are neglected, excluded and forgotten even in matters that directly affect them, which ordinarily would require their opinion and input. A lot of government policies and legislation neglect to take them into account[7]. In situations where they are taken into account, the laws, policies and practices that address them are rooted in charity rather than rights, thereby perpetuating dependency rather than promoting independence. This attitude places the disabled at a disadvantage in society because not only are they marginalised but also there is no proactive adaptation to ensure that they function as part of the society[8]. The perception that a person with disability is not a full member of society pervades the entire system, which includes potential sexual and physical abuse[9]. The level of abuse and social exclusion is perpetuated from childhood all the way through adult life. For example, the disabled child may be excluded from education because he or she is seen as incapable of benefitting society[10]. The same problem is experienced if he desires gainful employment. This is because his disability is deemed as undermining his capability for employment. Consequently, employment is considered as unsuitable, or

---

[7] The Convention on the Rights of Persons with Disabilities (CRPD), in its preamble, not only recognizes the fact that the majority of persons with disabilities live in conditions of poverty but also calls for addressing the negative impact of poverty on persons with disabilities. UN General Assembly 'Convention on the Rights of Persons with Disabilities', adopted 24 January 2007, A/RES/61/106 (CRPD) Preamble.

[8] Lansdown, G., 'Disabled Children in South Africa: Progress in Implementing the Convention on the Rights of the Child' (being a paper on the rights of disabled children),<http://www.daa.org.uk/uploads/pdf/SA%20Childrens%20report%20.pdf> accessed 27/10/16.

[9] Biegon, opcit p.54.

[10] Chataika, T., McKenzie, J.A., Swart, E., &Lyner-Cleophas, M., 'Access to Education in Africa: Responding to the United Nations Convention on the Rights of the Persons with Disability' *Disability &Society* Vol. 27, Iss. 3, 2012pp. 385-398.

if employment is given then reasonable adaptation is not even considered[11]. Thus, perceptions of disability have a negative effect on the individual's capability of having a fulfilled life.

It is right to assert that PWDs have since time immemorial been victims of human rights violation and social exclusion[12]. Aristotle, a brilliant philosopher is quoted to have pronounced as far back as 355 BC that, "Those who are born deaf become senseless and incapable of reason[13]." Again, PWDs were among the earliest victims of the Nazi concentration camps to which the United Nations Human Rights machinery largely owes its existence[14]. At the onset of World War II, Adolph Hitler ordered widespread "mercy killing" of the sick and disabled. Code-named *Aktion T4,* the Nazi euthanasia program was instituted to eliminate "life unworthy of life." Under this program, about 250,000 people with intellectual or physical disabilities were systematically killed from 1939 to 1941.

In most parts of the world, cultural beliefs and practices have always been discriminatory towards the disabled. Many cultures ascribe disability to sin of individual families or generations, which must be atoned for. In such cultures,persons with disabilities are often stigmatized, and thereby subjected to all manner of dehumanizing treatment and psychological abuse. For instance, in Zimbabwe, the word used for disability is *'chirema',* which literally translates to "useless". In Brazil, the term is *'perna',* which is slang for an affliction that comes as punishment[15]. These few examples demonstrate the extent of ill treatment and marginalization that

[11] Kanter, A.S., 'The Promise and Challenge of the United Nations on the Rights of the Persons with Disabilities' *Syracuse Journal of International Law and Commerce* Vol. 34, 2007, p. 287.

[12] Dube. A., "Disability Rights Protection Under the African Human Rights System in the Light of the Convention on Persons Living with Disabilities" (Deutschland: LAP Lambert Academic Publishing GMBH & Co. KG, 2002) p. 1.

[13] Disability History Timeline, <htt://www.disability history.org/timeline-new.html>accessed 5/7/14.

[14] Quinn, G., and Degener, I., "Human Rights and Disability: The Current Use and Future Potential Use of the United Nations Human Rights Instruments in the Context of Disability" p. 33 in Dube, A. 2002.

[15] Charlton, J., "Nothing About Us Without Us", (Nerkeler: University of Califonia Press, 2000) p. 35. He stressed that dehumanization of people through use of language (as just one obvious example) has a profound influence on consciousness. That other oppressed peoples are constantly told by the dominant culture what they cannot do and what their place is in society.

PWDs have always faced, ranging from denial of rights to non-allocation of social resources.

Fortunately, there is no existing law anywhere in the world that excludes PWDs from the enjoyment of their rights as human beings. In the past, there was little or no interest towards the plight of the disabled. Recent decades however, have witnessed considerable improvement in the perception of disability worldwide, and recognised disability rights as human rights. Indeed the UN General Assembly's adoption of the Convention on the Rights of Persons With Disabilities in December 2006 was hailed as a milestone, marking a paradigm shift from treating disability as a mere welfare issue to treating it as a human rights issue[16]. Thus, the rights of PWDs are well established internationally, and all the shortcomings we are witnessingis simply denial of such rights. In other words, persons with disabilities are simply deprived of their rights, especially in developing nations of the world, including Nigeria, which is the focus of this book.

1.2 Disability in Nigeria

Nigeria has the largest population in Africa with an estimate of 200 million people, and out of this numberabout 25 million people suffer from some form of disability[17]. The United Nations project that the overall population of Nigeria will reach about 401.31 million by the end of the year 2050. By 2100, if current figures continue, the population of Nigeria will be over 728 million.Naturally, the population of PWDs is expected to surge as the nation's population rises.

Available research suggests that men are more likely than women to be disabled in Nigeria, and that sight and mobility impairments are the most common forms of disability[18]. Furthermore, a 2005 study by the Leprosy Mission Nigeria found that, out of 1,093 respondents, 37

---

[16] Dakas, C., "Nigeria's Obligations Under the International Convention on the Rights of Persons With Disabilities," in The Rights of Persons With Disabilities, E. Azinge and C. Ani,(eds.), NIALS Abuja, 2011 pp.1-33.

[17] World Health Organisation, *World Disability Report* (2011)<who.org> accessed 15/6/2020.

[18] Smith, N., 'The Face of Disability In Nigeria: A Disability Survey In Kogi and Niger States' *The Journal of Disability, CBR and Inclusive Development*, Vol. 22, No.1, 2011, p 35-40.

percent struggled with visual impairments, 32 percent had limited mobility, 15 percent had reduced hearing and the majority of people surveyed—61 percent—were unemployed because of their disability.

Like many countries, Nigeria is State Party to various international treaties and domestic regulations which confer the duty to promote and safeguard the rights and interests of PWDs[19]. For instance, the African Charter on Human and People's Rights 1981 was ratified by Nigeria on 22 June 1983, and enacted into domestic law in 1983[20]. Various provisions of this Charter can be interpreted as conferring on Nigeria a duty to protect persons with disabilities from discrimination[21].Nigeria also ratifiedthe African Charter on the Rights and Welfare of the Child 1990[22], which emphasises the non-discrimination of children with disabilities and also provides a specific duty to introduce special safeguards to protect children who are physically or mentally disabled[23]. These positive obligations extend to ensuring access to education, employment, recreation, social life and public highways and buildings.[24]

Nigeria further ratified both the United Nations Convention on the Rights of Persons with Disabilities and its Optional Protocol on 30 March 2007 and 24 September 2007 respectively[25] and as such is under a duty to "promote, protect and ensure the full and equal enjoyment of all human rights and fundamental freedoms by all persons with disabilities, and to promote respect for their inherent dignity.[26]" Like the other instruments discussed above, this Convention provides for a general duty of non-discrimination[27] (accompanied by a carefully crafted and highly detailed definition or test for discrimination[28]), the right of equal access to public services[29], the right to dignity and freedom from degrading

---

[19] Chapter Fourcontains a detailed analysis of the legal framework for protection of PWDs.,which includes international, regional, and domestic instruments.

[20] African Charter on Human and Peoples' Rights (Ratification and Enforcement) Act 1983.

[21] Perlin, M.L., "International Human Rights and Mental Disability Law: When the Silenced are Heard" (London: Oxford University Press) p.55.

[22] ratified on 23 July 2001.

[23] African Charter on the Rights and Welfare of the Child 1990, Article 13(1).

[24] Ibid, Articles 13(2) and (3).

[25] The Convention entered into force on 3rd May 2008.

[26] UN Convention on the Rights of Persons with Disabilities 2008, Article 1(1).

[27] Ibid, Article 3(b).

[28] Ibid, Article 2.

[29] Ibid, Article 3(e) and (f).

treatment[30] and the duty to promote the social and economic integration of PWDs in society[31]. This Convention also introduces a duty for State Parties to raise awareness of and, ultimately, respect for PWDs within society.[32]

Undoubtedly, it would be unfair to say that Nigerians are insensitive to the plight of people living with disability because Nigeria's attempt towards legislating disability issues predates the United Nations Convention on the Rights of Persons with Disabilities. As far back as 1993, Nigerian Military Government enacted the Disability Decree 1993, which sought to establish a comprehensive framework for the protection of the rights of PWDs and the promotion of access to safeguards and services[33]. It also provided a policy restatement of the government's duty to prohibit discrimination on the grounds of disability and to promote the social and economic integration of persons with disabilities.[34] Unfortunately, this legislation was never activated.Nevertheless with the return to civil rule, more assertive attempts were made over the years. On 13th July 2016, a bill titled "Discrimination against Persons with Disabilities (Prohibition) Bill, 2016" was passed by the Senate, to end discrimination against PWDs, and to establish a National Commission that will cater for their needs[35]. Prior to its passage, the senators expressed their hope that the Bill would be expeditiously assented to by President Buhari's administration but the Bill failed to secure Presidential Assent subsequently. A similar Bill titled "Nigerians with Disability Bill, 2016" was also passed by the House of Representatives and both houses are expected to harmonise the Bills before they are sent to the President for assent. Finally, the long struggle to have a federal disability law in the country bore fruit on the 23rd of January 2019, when President Muhammadu Buhari signed into law, *The Discrimination Against Persons with Disabilities (Prohibition) Act, 2018* (hereinafter, the Disabilities Act or

---

[30] Ibid, Articles 15, 16 and 17.

[31] Ibid Article 3(c) and (d).

[32] Ibid. Article 8.

[33] This statute promotes access to legal services, voting, telecommunications, sports and recreation, social services, transportation, housing, vocational training and employment, education, and healthcare.

[34] Disability Act 1993 *Section 2(1)*.

[35] The Bill is sponsored by Sen. Francis Alimikhena (APC:Edo), and was presented for first and second reading in October and December, 2015 respectively.

the Act) . Specifically, the Act proscribes any form of discrimination against persons living with disabilities, provides for the full integration of persons with disabilities into the society, and establishes the National Commission for Persons with Disabilities.

Aside the Discrimination Against Persons with Disabilities (Prohibition) Act, 2018, a few states in the country like Plateau, Bauchi, Ekiti, Lagos and, recently, Nasarawa have demonstrated pragmatic commitment to address the plight of the PWDs by enacting specific legislations to protect and enhance their welfare within the State[36]. However, available reports have shown that these laws are not being implemented presently, owing to the absence of budgetary and administrative commitment required to implement the laws[37]. Thus notwithstanding obligations to extant international and domestic instruments, evidence suggests that the vast majority of PWDs in Nigeria continue to suffer violations, rejection and discrimination. Many of them live in poverty and are unable to access important public services and opportunities including education and healthcare[38]. Access to employment continues to be a problem even where the disabled applicants are more qualified than their non-disabled counterparts[39]. Likewise, it is difficult for them to participate in poverty reduction or social protection programmes in the form of cash or kind transfers from government and development agencies. Furthermore, very little information is available about the use and impact of social assistance for poor, disabled people and their households in Nigeria[40].

---

[36] Joint National Association of Persons With Disability Website<http://jonapwd.org>accessed 23/2/18.

[37] Angelo Dube, Disability Rights Protection Under the African Human Rights System: In Light of the Convention on Persons With Disabilities (Germany: Lambert, 2012) p.49.

[38] Smith, N., "The Face of Disability In Nigeria: A Disability Survey in Kogi and Niger States" The Journal of Disability, CBR and Inclusive Development, Vol. 22, No.1, 2011, pp. 35-46.

[39] MAARDEC, The Plight of Disabled Nigerians and the Need for Mass Enlightenment (2013) <http://www.maardec.net>accessed 11/05/2013.

[40] Marriot, A., and Gooding K., "Social Assistance and Disability in Developing Countries" (West Sussex:Sight Saver International, Hayward's Health, 2007) p.4. There are several barriers to accessing social assistance such as limited public information, physical inaccessibility, bureaucracy and means test which may unfairly exclude disabled people who face high cost of living associated with disability.

Another critical problem is that PWDs in Nigeria are often not given the opportunities to voice their peculiar concerns and participate in policies that directly affect their lives, nor are they given the chance to suggest solutions to their problems. Thus, PWDs remain socially and economically ostracized, elicited by the prevailing perception that they require charity and welfare rather than human rights protection, *per se*[41].

Recent studies[42]also indicate that policy makers (international, regional, national) attempting to design and implement more inclusive disability policies are doing this on a background of scanty information, inadequate data and hardly any coordination of activities. At present, information and data on disability are scarce, unreliable and scattered among organizations and institutions around the country, making it extremely difficult to conduct research necessary to fully understand the status of PWDs, develop cost-effective disability policies and strategies, or evaluate the cost-effectiveness of competing approaches.

Notably, there has always been some subsisting legislation relevant to disabilities in Nigeria. However, these laws are not disability-specific and thus remain scattered pieces of legislation that are not responsive to the needs of PWDs. Although the successful enactment of Discrimination Against Persons with Disabilities (Prohibition) Act, 2018, has become a ground-breaking achievement towards ensuring the rights and wellbeing of PWDs in Nigeria, we anticipate that there is bound to be some implementation challenges eventually[43].

As *bonafide*citizens of Nigeria, PWDs possess innate human rights and they are entitled to exercise and enforce their civil, social, political, and economic rights. However, they are unable to enjoy these rights despite the superficial protection afforded by several laws and institutions. In light of the subsisting gap between the legal theory and practical reality of

---

[41] Lang, R., and Upah, L., Disability Scoping Study in Nigeria (DFID, Nigeria 2008), p.6.

[42] Metts, R. L., Disability Issues, Trends and Recommendations for the World Bank. SP Discussion Paper No. 0007, Washington DC, World Bank 2000, p 55.

[43] Such challenges could be due to limited conceptual understanding and awareness; inadequate or inappropriate institutional arrangements; a general lack of capacity; and perhaps, lack of allocated fiscal resources and commitment by government, and agencies responsible for such implementation. In this regard, Nigeria can gain immensely from the experiences of other countries that have effective legislation and policy implementation regarding disability, not using them merely as case studies or examples but as standards to be emulated.

the plight of PWDs in Nigeria, it can be said that little attention has been paid to examining the challenges of protecting the rights of PWDs in Nigeria.Research is therefore required to addressthe following pertinent questions: (1) What is the relevance of human to the wellbeing of PWDs in Nigeria? (2) Is the existing legal regime adequate and effective? If not, what are the deficiencies? (3) Is the existing institutional arrangement adequate and effective? If not, what are the deficiencies? (4) Are there other factors militating against the protection of the rights of PWDs in Nigeria? (5) What measures can be taken to ensure that PWDs can effectively enjoy these rights, and participate in mainstream society on equal basis with others?

Hopefully, this book will provide answers to these pertinent questions- and many others.

CHAPTER TWO

Conceptual Foundationof Disabilities

This chapter explores the conceptual foundation of disabilities. It explains the meaning of disabilities, from both legal perspective and layman's understanding, by considering specific theories, viewpoints or ideas. The chapter thus discusses the history, types, and causes (which vary as widely as the types) of disabilities. It identifies four models of disability, which have over time shaped public policy and attitude towards disability, and gives a description of the impact of disability on the individual, family, and society.

2.1 Meaning of Disability

Disability is a relative construct, and what is considered a disability in one country may not be perceived and labelled as such elsewhere since individuals and states define disability in different ways. Disability can be construed in relation to several interpretations and understanding of the phenomenon and conceptual framework. Thus, there are various definitions of disability, depending on national social legislation and cultural standards[44].Some of these definitions are discussed as follows:

> The American Heritage Medical Dictionary defines disability as a disadvantage or deficiency, especially a physical or mental impairment that prevents or restricts normal achievement[45]. The Oxford Dictionary of Law defines a disabled person as a person who has a physical or mental impairment, which has a substantial and long-term effect on his ability to carry out day-to-day activities[46].The foregoing definitions are drawn from distinct fields[47]; however, it is noted that the word "impairment" reflects in all the definitions and is therefore key to the

---

[44] This makes it more difficult to establish reliable data on the number of persons affected.

[45] The American Heritage Medical Dictionary (Houghton Mifflin Company, 2007).

[46] Elizabeth A. Martin (ed.), Oxford Dictionary of Law, 6th Edition, (Oxford University Press 2004).

[47] Medicine, and Law respectively.

idea of disability.

The World Health Organization (WHO) defines disability in a three-fold manner that distinguishes among impairment, disability and handicap[48]. The organization defines "impairment" as any loss or abnormality of psychological, physiological or anatomical structure or function. It then defines"disability" as any restriction or lack (resulting from an impairment) of ability to perform an activity in the manner or within the range considered normal for a human being. It further defines "handicap" as a disadvantage for a given individual, resulting from an impairment or a disability, that prevents the fulfilment of a role that is considered normal (depending on age, sex and social and cultural factors) for that individual. The term is also a classification of circumstances in which disabled people are likely to find themselves.

The above definition of disability has been criticized by some disability rights activists as being tooconfusing, and not providing adequate guidance for policy makers since it doesnot fully reflect contemporary understanding of disability issues – particularly the requirement to address both individual needs (such as rehabilitation and technical aids) and the shortcomings of society which puts obstacles in the way of disabled people participating fully. For instance, Kaplan considersthe definition to be aimed at perpetuating the imbalances caused by contemporary social organization, which takes little or no account of people who have physical impairments', and this excludes their activities[49].

In light of this criticism the WHO developed the International Classification of Functioning (ICF) in 2002, in an attempt to integrate both the social and medical models of disability[50]. The ICF, which also calls for the elimination of distinctions, explicitly or implicitly between health conditions that are 'mental' or 'physical,'does not override the original concepts. However, it reworks the definition from being concerned with the consequences of disease to one concerned with

---

[48] WHO Health topics /Disabilities < http://www.who.int/topics/disabilities/en/> accessed 23/4/15.

[49] Kaplan,D., 'The Definition of Disability'<http://www.accessiblesociety.org/topics/ demographeics-indentiy/dkaplaripaper.htm>accessed 22/6/15.

[50] International Classification of Impairments, Disabilities and Handicaps (ICIDH), General World Health   Organization, 1980 <http://www.who.int/classifications /icf/en/> accessed 25/5/15.

human functionality and health, therebyemphasizing functional status over diagnoses.The new ICF focuses on analysing the relationship between capacity and performance. If capacity is greater than performance then that gap should be addressed through both removing barriers and identifying facilitators. Thus, the new system is not just about people with traditionally acknowledged disabilities diagnostically categorized but about all people.

The United Nations Convention on the Rights of Persons with Disabilities 2006 (CRPD) defines persons with disabilities thus:

> Persons with disabilities include those that have long-term physical, mental, intellectual or sensory impairments, which in interaction with various barriers may hinder their full and effective participation in society on an equal basis with others[51].

It is noted however, that the above UN definition falls short of being generally acceptable because of the word "long-term". It fails to take cognizance of the fact that there could always be a short-term disability.

The UK Equality Act defines disability as, "A physical or mental impairment that has a 'substantial' and 'long-term' negative effect on your ability to do normal daily activities"[52].

Another definition, as given by the Americans with Disabilities Act (ADA), states:

> An individual with disability is a person who has a physical or mental impairment that substantially limits on or more major life activities, or has a record of such impairment, or is regarded as having such impairment[53].

According to the Nigerians With Disability Decree, a"Disabled person" is:

> A person who has received preliminary or permanent certificate of disability to have condition which is expected to continue permanently

---

[51] Article 1.

[52] UK Equality Act 2010, (Section 6) < http://www.legislation.gov.uk/ukpga> accessed 6/715.

[53] Golden (1978) cited in Abang, T., The Exceptional Child-Handbook of Special Education (Fah Educational Books, 2005) p.17.

or for a considerable length of time which can reasonably be expected to limit the person's functional ability substantially, but not limited to seeing, hearing, thinking, ambulating, climbing, descending, lifting, grasping, rising, any related function or any limitation due to weakness or significantly decreased endurance so that he cannot perform his everyday routine, living and working without significantly increased hardship and vulnerability to everyday obstacles and hazards[54].

It is noted that the Decree does not concisely address in details the protection of PWDs; however, there are some phrases used in the Decree that infer disabilities that are known, related, or ascribed to the military. This implies that the Decree seems to promote the welfare of members of the Nigerian Armed Forces whose disabilities may be as a result of armed conflict or while in the line of duty. Furthermore, and interestingly, it is noted that this law is not included in the 2004 Laws Of The Federation, which is the authoritative compendium of laws validly enacted in Nigeria as at 2000. Consequently the decree remains a subject of controversy among writers with some arguing that it was never passed in the first place[55]. This writer is however of the view that the complete exclusion of this law from the Laws of the Federation is a clear indication of the societal attitude (including policy makers) towards disability issues in Nigeria.

From the foregoing, it is deduced that as legal frameworks are enacted in different ways in different countries resulting in different experiences, so also the definitions of disabilities. Thus, this researcher's definition of disability is:

> Any severe or chronic injury of function resulting from disease, accident or congenital defect; and a person is considered as having disability when they find it difficult to see, learn, walk, talk, hear or perform other functional activities.

---

[54] Nigerians With Disability Decree 1993, (Section 3)
<http://digitalcommons.ilr.cornell.edu/cgi/viewcontent.cgi?article> accessed 6/71
[55] See Ayodele Atsenuwa, 'Legal and Institutional Mechanisms For Protecting Persons With Disabilities In Nigeria', in E. Azinge And C. Ani (Eds), *The Rights Of Persons With Disabilities*, NIALS 2001, p.127.

2.2 Meaning of Impairment

Impairment is defined as any deviation from the norm, which results in defective function, structure, organization or development of any part of the body[56]. Mercer and Barnes provide a concise and accessible introduction to the concept of disability[57]. They define impairment as the functional limitation within the individual caused by physical, mental or sensory impairment, while disability is the loss of limitation of opportunities to take part in the normal life of the community on an equal level with others due to physical and social barriers. The authors saythat the presence of impairment does not mean automatic transfer to the status of being a disabled person except where social barriers exclude that individual from participation in daily life activities. Thus, we can say that a person with visual impairment becomes disabled when his environment requires visual performance, which is impossible for him. An impaired person need not be disabled or handicapped[58]. A person's performance may be reduced as a result of a significant physical problem, such as the loss of an arm, or loss of a legor eyesight. However, a person with visual impairment becomes disabled only when his environment requires visual performance, which is impossible for him.

According to the World Health Organization International Classification of Impairments, Disabilities, and Handicaps[59]; impairment may be:

a. Physical: Such as affecting ambulation, coordination, speech and vision;
b. Mental: For instance, affecting ability to think, remember and comprehend, or general learning ability;
c. Social: Such as affecting ability to communicate and establish relationships with other people.
d. Emotional: Such as affecting self-esteem, self-acceptance, or mental health;

---

[56] *Opcit*, n 12 above.
[57] Barnes C, and Mercer G. (eds.), '*The Social Model of Disability and the Majority World*', (Leeds: The disability Press, 2005) pp. 1-16.
[58] *Ibid.*
[59] A Manual of Classification Relating to the Consequence of Disease (Geneva: WHO, 1980).

e. Occupational: Such as affecting vocational or home making ability.

It is however, noted that the WHO classification is not exhaustive, as there are other classifications of disability, depending on (national) social legislation and cultural standards. This has made it difficult to establish reliable data on the number of persons affected. Although the figure most frequently cited is that of one billion PWDs in the world, published by WHO, which corresponds to approximately 15% of the global population, the prevalence in developing and industrialized countries diverges widely due to different reference systems and the lack of registration systems. Whereas industrialized countries have a percentage of persons with recognized disabilities of between 8 and 20%, often the developing countries only acknowledge much lower percentages officially because what is considered a disability in one country may not be perceived and labelled as such elsewhere.

2.3 Meaning of Handicap

It is pertinent to equally define the term handicap. Handicap means the disadvantage imposed by the impairment on the individual as he functions in his environment[60]. Handicap describes the social and economic roles of impaired persons that place them at a disadvantage compared to other persons[61].

Disabled Peoples International in 1981 defined handicap as a person's inability to carry out his or her function as a result of a disability. In other words, handicap is a condition or state that makes a person unable to function or perform a task. Disability results in handicap. Consequently, disability becomes a handicap when an amputee is unable to carry out the functions of the arm, or does that with great difficulty[62]. It is worthy of note that every handicapped person has a disability but not every person with disability is handicapped. Obviously, the degree

---

[60] The word handicapped is thought to come from a game that involved a "cap in the hand," and it has the contemporary meaning of assigning extra weight (a handicap) to better performers to "level" a playing field and enhance wagering. Unfortunately, the word conjures up the negative image of a person with disabilities begging in the street. In most instances today, the person-first with disabilities is preferred over the term handicapped.

[61] Disabilities Right <http://www.un.org/disabilities>accesed 22/3/15.

[62] World Health Organization (WHO) Document, 1980 page 29.

and type of disability determines the type of programme and services that should be provided for the individual. In other words, PWDs are given protection based on the type of disability they suffer.

Flowing from the foregoing definitions, it is noted that although the terms impairment, disability, and handicap are sometimes used interchangeably, they are not synonymous, though one may lead to another. Impairment refers to the loss or reduced function of a particular body part or organ (e.g., a missing limb), while disability exists when impairment limits a person's ability to perform certain tasks (e.g., walk, see, add a row of numbers) in the same way that most persons do. A person with a disability is not handicapped, however, unless the disability leads to educational, personal, social, vocational, or other problems. For example, if a child who has lost a leg learns to use a prosthetic limb and thus functions in and out of school without problems, then such a child is not handicapped in terms of functioning in the physical environment.

Notably, language plays a key role in understanding disability,particularly how people with disabilities are talked about in places like the media or in everyday conversations. There is no doubt that the use of language and words describing people with disabilities has changed over time.In recent years, there has been ongoing debate over the proper words to use when talking to, referring to, or working with the Disability Community. The subject is whether to use 'person-first language', or 'identity-first language'. The person-first language is where the person comes before the disability such as a 'person with a disability' or 'person with autism'. Proponents of this view argue that using disability as a descriptor ('deaf person', 'autistic person')places emphasis on the disability, which is undesirable because having a disability does not define or describe PWDs in anyway. They are just like everyone else, except that they happen to have a disability.The idea behind person-first language is that it puts the person first – it's about seeing the person, not the disability.

On the other hand, proponents of the"identity-first language" say that the disability comes before the person such as 'disabled person' or 'autistic person'. Their argument is that disability is a diverse cultural experience and essential identifier; and that you cannot see the person without the disability.

Disrespectful language can make people feel excluded and can be a barrier to full participation. Therefore, the use of the terms "handicapped," "able-bodied," "physically challenged," and "differently abled" is discouraged. It is preferable to use language that focuses on their abilities rather than their disabilities, and person-first language is considered by many to be the most respectful and appropriate to refer to them . Therefore the proper term to use is "person with disability".

2.4 Meaning of Discrimination

Discrimination largely refers to any bias or prejudice resulting in denial of opportunity, or unfair treatment regarding selection, promotion, or transfer[63]. It is unequal treatment provided to one or more parties on the basis of a mutual accord or some other logical or illogical reason, such as on the grounds of age, disability, ethnicity, origin, political belief, race, religion, sex, etc. or factors which are irrelevant to a person's competence or suitability[64].

The CRPD defines discrimination on the basis of disability under Article 2 as:

> Any distinction, exclusion or restriction on the basis of disability which has the purpose or effect of impairing or nullifying the recognition, enjoyment or exercise, on an equal basis with others, of all human rights and fundamental freedoms in the political, economic, social, cultural, civil or any other field. It includes all forms of discrimination, including denial of reasonable accommodation.

Furthermore, The Human Rights Committee (HRC) (which monitors the implementation of the International Covenant on Civil and Political Rights (ICCPR)) in General Comment 18 on non-discrimination has defined discrimination as:

> any distinction, exclusion, restriction or preference which is based on any ground such as race, colour, sex, language, religion, political or other opinion, national or social origin, property, birth or other status, and which has the purpose or effect of nullifying or impairing the

---

165BussinessDictionary<http://www.businessdictionary.com/definition/discriminatio n.html#ixzz44Tm7tRhA>accessed 29/3/16.

[64] *Ibid.*

recognition, enjoyment or exercise by all persons, on an equal footing, of all rights and freedoms.

'Distinction' naturally includes exclusion, restriction or preference; while 'impairing' includes nullifying; and 'enjoyment' covers exercise; and 'human rights and freedoms' include entitlements, interests, rights and freedoms contained in the provisions of a human right treaty. Therefore, the definition of non-discrimination that captures the three elements ('distinction/exclusion', 'impairing' and 'right') entails differentiation based on a prohibited ground such as disability that impairs the enjoyment of a human right. Thus, it is important to note that discrimination based on disability can be caused by discomfort or misguided pity that occurs in an overprotective and patronizing behaviour. An illustrative case in this regard is *Cleburne v Cleburne Living Centre*[65].In this case, Cleburne Living Centre, Inc. (CLC) submitted a permit application seeking approval to build a group home for the mentally retarded. The city of Cleburne, Texas refused to grant CLC a permit on the basis of a municipal zoning ordinance. CLC then sued the City of Cleburne on the theory that the denial of the permit violated the Equal Protection rights of CLC and their potential residents.The case went all the way to the Supreme Court, which asserted the following relevant to the discussion on causes of discrimination based on disability:

> As the history of discrimination against the retarded and its continuing legacy amply attest, the mentally retarded have been, and in some areas may still be, the targets of action the Equal Protection Clause condemns. With respect to a liberty so valued as the right to establish a home in the community, and so likely to be denied on the basis of irrational fears and outright hostility, heightened scrutiny is surely appropriate.

Furthermore, in a comparable case: *Alexander v. Choate*[66], the US Supreme Court held that discrimination against PWDsis usually the result of 'benign neglect' resulting from indifferent attitudes rather than affirmative hostility.

---

[65]   *473 U.S. 432 (1985).*
[66]   469 U.S. 287 (1985).

Under international law, states are enjoined to take measures that curb both direct and indirect discrimination against all persons, including persons with disabilities[67]. Overt/direct discrimination here refers to a situation where the differential treatment is expressly mandated in the law or policy or where the differential treatment is based on a prohibited ground of discrimination. For example: A law, which proscribes blind or deaf students from being admitted into public schools, constitutes direct/overt discrimination on the basis of disability. On the other hand, indirect/covert or hidden discrimination arises where a law or policy serves the aim or has the effect of giving advantage to a particular group or imposing a disadvantage on a particular group[68]. For example, if a school admits a blind student but fails to provide learning materials in a format that the student can read (either in Braille or using text to speech software), that would amount to indirect discrimination against the student by the school.

Discrimination may also be expressed as '*De jure*' or '*De facto*'. While *De jure* discrimination refers to differential treatment that is imposed by law, *De facto* discrimination occurs when state agencies discriminate in practice but not necessarily designed by law. The term *de facto* discrimination involves a pattern of discrimination that is significant enough to produce statistical disparities between groups in a manner consistent with the imbalances that are produced by *de jure* discrimination.[69] An example of *de facto* discrimination is where a state, instead of funding public schools to be able to provide education to students with disabilities, funds a few special schools. The consequence is that education becomes segregated and only few students with disabilities are able to access education. While such a state may not have a law stating that "students with disabilities do not have a right to education", the end result is that students with disabilities do not access education on an equal basis with others.

---

[67] Committee on Economic, Social and Cultural Rights (CESCR) General Comment 5, paras 14.

[68] CESCR General Comment 20, paras 10.

[69] *Ibid, paras 12.*

2.5 Meaning of Equality

It has been expressed that theoretically, equality and non-discrimination represent the same idea and can be seen as simply the positive and negative assertions of the same principle[70].Thus, formal or juridical equality excludes indirect discrimination. It requires that individuals in like situations should be treated equally, based on the appearance of similarity without regard to the broader context within which such treatment occurs)[71]. It disregards the physical elements that cause certain groups to fall behind the rest of society. In other words, the formal conception of equality (which is also referred to as the sameness approach or symmetrical approach) excludes indirect discrimination[72]. It guarantees consistency in treatment (procedural equality) and fails to consider content of treatment (substantive equality) despite any unequal results that may flow from it[73]. This model of equality was the general global standard before the adoption of the Universal Declaration of Human Rights. Formal equality is included in such instruments as the International Covenant on Civil and Political Rights (ICCPR) and the International Covenant on Economic, Social and Cultural Rights (ICESCR), which have open-ended non-exhaustive anti-discrimination clauses.

By contrast, substantive equality requires that the life chances of a person is not weakened by obstacles beyond his control, which usually form prohibited grounds of discrimination. In many cases, substantive equality may be achieved at no cost but by simply changing priorities and modifying policies and rules. However in some cases, additional costs must be incurred in order to achieve substantive equality. For example, while the law must provide all people with equal entitlements to education, more effort is required in order for the 'equal entitlement' to translate to actual access to education for learners with disabilities. In this case, it becomes necessary to invest additional resources towards

---

[70] Bayefsky, A.F., 'The Principles of Equality and Non-discrimination in International Law' [1990] (II) (1/2), pp.1-34

[71] Arnardóttir, OddnýMjöll, A Future of Multidimensional Disadvantage Equality? The UN Convention on the Rights of Persons with Disabilities: European and Scandinavian Perspectives (Martinus Nijhoff 2009), pp. 41-66.

[72] *Ibid.*

[73] *Ibid.*

ensuring that schools are accessible and that learners are provided with the required expert teachers, study materials and accommodation. Substantive equality therefore entails equality of results and equality of opportunity in recognizing thatseemingly identical treatment can, in practice, advance inequality because of past or ongoing discrimination or differences in access to power and resources.

2. 6 Exceptional Children

It is pertinent at thisstageto define some concepts relatedto children with disabilities, which we will come across in many parts of this book. One of such is "exceptional children". The word "exceptional" means having much more than average intelligence, ability, or skills[74].The term exceptional child therefore means a child whose intelligence, ability, or skills do not fall within the ordinary average range. This includes children who experience difficulties in learning as well as those whose performance is so superior that modifications in curriculum and instruction are necessary to help them fulfil their potential[75]. Thus, exceptional children is an inclusive term that refers to children with learning and/or behaviour problems, children with physical disabilities or sensory impairments, and children who are intellectually gifted or have a special talent. The physical attributes and/or learning abilities of exceptional children differ from the norm (either below or above) to such an extent that they require an individualized program of special education and related services to fully benefit from education. They are markedly different from most children in one or more of the following ways:they are mentally retarded, gifted, learning disabled, emotionally disturbed, physically handicapped, or have disordered speech or language, impaired learning, or impaired sight[76].

---

[74]The American Heritage Dictionary of the English Language, 4th Edition (Houghton Mifflin Company 2004) <http://dictionary.reference.com/browse/exceptional> accessed18/6/15.

[75] Hallahan, D.P., and Kauffman, J.M., Exceptional Children: Introduction to Special Education (USA: Eaglewood, 1982) pp.11-18.

[76] *Ibid*, p.25.

2.7 Special Education

The need to define the term'special education' is imperative in this research because the groups PWDs undergo either general education or special education. While most people are more familiar with general education, special education is a relatively new and specialized area of study. Special education is:

> The education of children and adults who have learning difficulty because of different sorts of handicaps; blindness, partial sightedness, deafness, hardness of learning, mental retardation, social mal adjustment, physical handicap and others due to circumstances of birth, inheritance social position, mental and physical health patterns, or accident in later life. As a result, few children and adults are unable to cope with the normal school class organization and methods. It further provides that there are also the especially gifted children, who are intellectually precocious and find themselves insufficiently challenged by the programme(s) of the normal schools[77].

Rogers[78] depicts special education as an area within the framework of general education that provides three major contrivances: appropriate facilities, specialized materials, and teachers with specialized training for children considered handicapped.This definition seems to be more acceptable though not comprehensive as special education benefits exceptional children as well as adults[79].

Okeke[80]states that exceptional children have significant defects that inhibit normal functioning which marks them out for special education programmes, services and facilities. She further classified exceptional persons as the mentally retarded, thebehaviourally and emotionally disturbed, the learning disabled, the physically/health impaired, the learning impaired, the visually impaired, the speech and communication disordered, and the gifted/talented.

---

[77] Document of the Federal Republic of Nigeria on National Policy on Education 1981.

[78] See Rogers et al (1968) Special Education.

[79] '12m Nigerians living with learning disability', *The Punch* (5/6/14)<http://www.punchngr.com> accessed 21/2/15.

[80] Okeke, B.A. Essentials of Special Education (Afro-Orbis Publication Ltd: 2001) 23-24.

Special education therefore entails specially designed instruction, which meets the unique needs of an exceptional child. These needs include special materials, teaching techniques, equipment, and/or facilities that may be required. For example, visually impaired children may require teaching materials in large print or Braille; learning impaired children may require hearing aids and/or instructions in manual communication; physically handicapped children may need wheelchairs, ramps, and a variety of equipment available only in special medical facilities; and gifted children may require access to working professionals and their environs. Furthermore, related services such as special transportation, psychological assessment, physical and occupational therapy, medical treatment and counselling may be required if special education is to be effective[81].

The major advantage of special education is that it gives every child the opportunity to get through school, and at his own pace. However, the challenge is that of funding. Special education is very expensive, and not all schools are well prepared to equip the students or teachers with the necessary materials and facilities that areneeded- especially in developing countries like Nigeria where funding the regular schools remains a constant challenge. There is also a shortage of teachers trained in the area of special education. Another disadvantage is that students who require special education are often teased, and made to feel stupid by their peers. Perhaps owing to these challenges, some disability rights activists are now agitating for inclusive education for all[82].

2.8 Mental Retardation

There are various understanding by various groups as to the meaning of mental retardation. For instance, physicians describe mental retardation as brain damage or biological malfunction in the individual's make up, which results in an IQ measured as below 70 to 75 and significant delays or deficiencies in at least two areas of adaptive skills[83]. Psychologists define mental retardation as a condition diagnosed before age 18, usually

---

[81] *Ibid, p.24.*

[82] Avoke, M.K., and Others, *Issues in Special Education* (Accra North: The City Publisher, 1998).

[83] Definition of Mental Retardation<http://www.medicinenet.com/script/main/art> accessed 18/315.

in infancy or prior to birth, which includes below-average general intellectual function, and a lack of the skills necessary for daily living[84]. When onset occurs at age 18 or after, it is called dementia. Mental retardation is also known as intellectual disability[85], and levels of intellectual disability vary greatly in children –from a very slight problem to a very severe problem. Children with intellectual disability find it difficult to communicate to others what they need, and can hardly take care of themselves. Again, mental retardation could slow the development of a child. For example, it could take longer for a child with intellectual disability to learn to speak, walk, or eat without help, and they usually have trouble learning.

---

[84]'Mental Retardation,'*PsychologyToday*<https://www.psychologytoday.com/conditions/mental-retardation>accessed 15/3015.

[85] Tidy Colin, *'General Learning Disability'*<*Patient.info*>accessed 18/315.

CHAPTER THREE

History, Types and Models of Disability

This section historicises the concept of disability, and considers the types and models of disability. The impact of disability and the trauma it presents to the victims is also discussed.

3.1 Historical Perspectives of Disability

It is no gain saying that disability affects the whole universe. Therefore the origin of disability is diverse, with different writers holding contrary views. Throughout history, everything relating to disabilities was attributed to evil; andPWDs were ignored, hidden and cursed[86]. When made visible, they became subjects of exhibitions and objects of ridicule and were labelled with many names such as fools, demons, and animals. Ultimately, they suffered untold trauma stemming from the negative attitude they received from other people, which were mainly shaped by cultural prejudices and traditional stereotype of their various communities[87]. However today, science has proved the assertions of the past wrong as people have become aware of different causes of disabilities[88].

Prior to the 19th century, PWDs were generally deprived of human love and dignity, and were rather subjected to inhuman treatment by society. In the African context, societal perceptions and treatments of PWDs within cross-cultural settings was a medley of varying hues that reflect intolerance, hatred, love, fear, reverence, and devotion. In many traditional African societies, any form of disability was considered a punishment visited upon the family by the gods or ancestors as a result of past offences.

---

[86] Society has been 'dealing' with the problem of people with disability by placing them in institutions or prisons and by sterilizing women and girls as an acceptable treatment.

[87] Avoke, *Opcit*, n 83 above.

[88] History shows that ignorance, neglect, superstition and fear are social factors that have exacerbated isolation of persons with disabilities.

Hence in these societies, PWDs were generally treated poorly.[89] Some of these negative treatments start from birth, with the parents and the traditional birth attendants' plan to silently eliminate handicapped babies. For instance in some communities in Northern Nigeria, PWDs are expected to beg for a living and society is encouraged to be charitable towards them, while in the Eastern part of the country, the Igbo's treat persons stricken with leprosy as outcasts. In some communities in Kenya and Zimbabwe, a child with a disability is a symbol of a curse befalling the whole family. Such a child is considered a "shame", hence the rejection of the child by the family and the rejection of the family by the community. Among the Ashanti of Central Ghana, traditional beliefs precluded men with physical defects, such as amputations, from becoming chiefs. This is evident in the practice of dethroning a chief if he acquires epilepsy[90]. To the Lobis in the Wa district of Ghana, blindness was considered as an offence against the gods. Such people are mocked and disregarded in the society.

By contrast, the Alago people of North Central Nigeria consider the wellbeing of a person with disability as the collective responsibility of all his family members, and such an individual does not lose any rights or privileges within the extended family circle on the basis of disability[91]. Among the Chagga in East Africa, the physically disabled were perceived as pacifiers of the evil spirits. Hence, care was taken not to harm them. Among the citizens of Benin Republic, constables were selected from those with obvious physical handicaps, and in some communities, children born with anomalies were seen as protected by supernatural forces, and were believed to bring good luck to the community[92]. Also, the Ga from Accra region in Ghana treated the feeble-minded with awe, owing to the belief that the retarded were the reincarnation of a deity.

The history of disability in other parts of the world is no different. For instance, the Spartans used to leave the handicapped in the wild to be devoured by animals. Among the Greeks, the sick were considered inferior and individuals with special educational needs were excluded

---

[89] Chomba Wa Munyi, 'Past And Present Perceptions Towards Disability: A Historical Perspective,' [2012] (32) (2) *Disability Studies Quarterly*.

[90] Sarpong, P., Ghana in Retrospect: Some Aspects of Ghanaian Culture (Accra: Tema Publishing Corp, 1974).

[91] Interview with Madaucin Doma, Elder Ali Akwe on 15 March 2016 in Doma Town.

[92] B.A. Wright, Physical Disability: A Psychological Approach, (Harper and BON, 1960).

from national policy on militarism and total fitness for all[93]. Again, in some European countries, PWDs were not regarded as being fit to live, and those allowed to live were either used as royal jesters, or held solely for the purpose of tasting the food placed before royals to guarantee that such food was poison-free[94]. Even the most knowledgeable people then, were not devoid of prejudices against PWDs. Often quoted is a discriminatory statement, attributed to Aristotle, that "those who are born deaf become senseless andincapable of reason"[95], while Platorecommended that the deformed offspring of both the superior and inferior be put away in some "mysterious unknown places"[96]. Also a theologian and sociologistEiesland sees disability as denoting an unusual relationship with a god and that a person with a disability is either divinely blessed or dammed, the defiled evildoer or the spiritual superhero[97]. The great astronomer, Tycho Brahe was said to have kept persons with mental retardation as close companions in the hope that their muttering would give him divine revelation[98]. The magnitude of hatred towards the disabled by even prominent leaders of thought explains why societal perceptions on disabilities during this period encouraged rejection, subjection and total neglect of PWDs, even by their immediate families.

The Medieval period witnessed a tremendous relief regarding human altitudes towards PWDs. Early Christian doctrine introduced the view that disease is neither a disgrace nor a punishment for sin but, on the contrary, a means of purification and a way of grace[99]. It brought the message of compassion and protection to PWDs. For instance, it is narrated in the Holy Bible that the disciples saw a man who was blind

---

[93] Blanck, P. and Others, Disability Civil Rights and Policy, (Thomson West, 2004) p. 2.
[94] *Ibid.*
[95] Disability History Timeline<http://www.disabilityhistory.org/timeline-newhtml>accessed 20/6/15.
[96] Plato, The Republic: Concerning The Definition of Justice, (380 B.C.) <http://classics.mit.edu/Plato/republic.html> accessed 1/4/16.
[97] Eiesland, N.L, The Disabled God: Towards A Liberatory Theology of Disability (Abingdon Press, 1994), p.70.
[98] Catherine Slater, 'A History of Mental Disability 1000AD to 2000AD: From Idiocy to Intellectual Impairment' <http://caslater.freeservers.com/disability3.htm>accessed 1/4/16.
[99] R. G. Barker and Others, *'Adjustment to Physical Handicap and Illness: A Survey of the Social Psychology of Physique and Disability'* (New York: 1953).

from birth and asked Jesus, 'Rabbi, who sinned; this man or his parents that he was born blind?' Jesus answered, 'neither this man nor his parents sinned'[100]. It is further narrated that Jesus blessed the deaf and the dumb[101]. The above perspective discredits the claim that disabilities occur as a result of sin as envisaged by some people[102]. Islam also preaches compassion and love for PWDs and encourages giving assistance and protection to the handicapped. It emphasizes the notion of social responsibilities and duties to provide such individuals with their basic needs such as food, safety, care and shelter. As indicated, the Holy Qur'an states:

> There are not upon the blind [any] constraints, nor upon the lame, nor upon the ill, nor upon yourselves when you eat at your [own] houses or the houses of your father or the houses of your mother or the houses of your brothers or the houses of your sisters or the houses of your father's brothers or the houses of your father's sisters…[103]

The foregoing paragraphs have revealed that, historically, the most consistent feature in the treatment of PWDs in most societies is the fact that they were categorized as "deviants rather than inmates by the society."[104] Consequently, many persons living with one form of disability or the other as well as their families were ostracized and excluded from mainstream community life. Worse still, they were not allowed to marry or be married in many African societies, as it was believed that such restrictions would limit the level of contamination, since disability was considered a curse. Essentially, the reasons for the inhuman treatment meted on PWDs were orchestrated by superstitious belief, ignorance and

---

[100] John 9:1-3, The Holy Bible (Revised Standard Version) <https://www.biblegateway.com/versions/Revised-Standard-Version-RSV-Bible> accessed 29/3/16.

[101] *Ibid*, Mark 7:32.

[102] However, during the 16th century, Christians such as Martin Luther and John Calvin (both leaders of the 16th Century Reormation) suggested a contrasting view by preaching that evil spirits possessed the mentally retarded and other persons with disabilities. Thus, these men and other religious leaders of the time often subjected people with disabilities to mental and/or physical pain as a means of exorcising 'evil spirits'.

[103] Quar'an 24:61, The Holy Quar'an (English Translation by Muhammad Alli) <http://www.aaiil.org/text/hq/trans/ma_list.shtml> accessed 29/3/16.

[104] Lippman, *UNESCO Braille Courier*, (1972) p.89, UNESCO.

fear of contamination. Again, since human beings were valued for their economic input, PWDs were regarded as incapable of economic participation and contribution, hence, their neglect by the society[105].

One might ask, has there been a considerable attitudinal change towards PWDs in the modern era? There is no gainsaying that in most parts of the world including Nigeria (which has a population of 25 million PWDs)[106] the disabled are still looked down upon, even by some family members, friends and relatives. However, this does not suggest a total lack of improvement because, in the contemporary African setting, there has been a gradual attitudinal change towards PWDs, but a lot needs to be done in the area of protecting their rights through legislations and policies that would ensure that they are totally included into mainstream society[107].

It must be stated here that remarkable effort was made in 1998, in Mexico at the Fifth World Assembly of the Disabled Peoples International (DPI), of the African Decade of Disabled Persons, which was formally adopted in Africa as part of the Cape Town Declaration in January 1999[108]. The Declaration states that priority should be given to issues pertaining to disabilities and such issues should be allocated specific funding in government budgets; that enforceable and implementable disability legislation and policies should be evaluated and monitored; that self-representation of PWDs should be promoted in all structures of government; and that the United Nations Standard Rules should be incorporated into national legislation across the region. In the next chapter, we are going to establish whether Africa has recorded any development regarding the Cape Town Declaration. This is in line with the fact that there is no generally acceptable definition of some words, especially, the precise word, "disability". The changing perceptions on disability also attributes to lack of a comprehensive definition of disability.

---

[105] Dube, A., Disability Right Protection Under the African Human Rights System (Germany: Lambert Publishing Co., 2007) p.1.

[106] World Report on Disability, 2011 < http://www.who.int/disabilities/world_report /2011> accessed 24/3/16.

[107] 'Autism: Experts say disability laws will improve access to treatment', *The Punch* (6/4/13) http://www.punchngr.com>accessed 22/2/15.

[108] Report in Disabled Peoples International (DPI) official publication of 1999, vol. 6 p.1.

3.2 Types of Disabilities

Disability is an encompassing term, which could be easily understood when categorized. Hence, the need for the following categorization to it:

3.2.1 *Physical Disability*

This type of disability occurs when there is a restriction of movement or agility due to neuromuscular disorder of the circulatory, respiratory and nervous system in such individual. It affects a person's ability to use their upper or lower body. Physical disability is a generic term that encompasses a wide range of conditions. Such conditions include spin bifida, muscular dystrophy or cerebral palsy or it could be a condition acquired at any state including post-accident, tumour or stoke[109].Spinal bifida and/or Hydrocephalus is a neural tube defect in the development of the spinal column. It can cause nominal or complete paralysis of the spinal cord. About 80% of the people with spinal bifida also have hydrocephalus.

Physical Disability also includes limb abnormalities, which may be congenital or traumatic affecting one or more limbs. This can be partial or total. Upper limb abnormalities affectyoung person's arms and hand (most young children who suffer from the above abnormalities can hold objects even when parts of their arms and hand are missing or misshapen), while Lower limb abnormalities affectyoung persons' legs or feet thereby requiring adaptive footwear, or the use of a wheel chair, which is usually associated with tiredness[110].

3.2.2 *Learning/IntellectualDisability*

This is a situation where the affected individual finds it extremely difficult in a normal learning environment.Usually, the individual involved has a very low ability to perform his/her daily life activities, and exhibits a below-average intellectual capacity. It includes intellectual disabilities, which relateto difficulties with thought process, learning,

---

[109] Resource file for Special Educational Needs Physical Disability Available at Physical Disability can be described as long term usually lasting a life time and is seldom static so changing needs should be revised often.

[110] The UK Loss Information Centre< http://www.himblosinformationcentre.com> accessed 20/316.

communicating, remembering information and using it appropriately, making judgments and problem solving[111]. Closely related is the cognitive disability, which affects a person's thought process, personality and memory,this type of disability is usuallyas a result of a genetic disorder, or brain injury.

3.2.3 *Sensory Disability*

This affects vision or hearing of such individual[112]. There are hundreds of thousands of people that suffer from minor to various vision disability or impairment. These injuries can also result insome serious problems or diseases like blindness and ocular trauma, to name but a few. Some of the common vision impairment includes scratched cornea, scratches on the sclera, diabetes-related eye conditions, dry eyes and corneal graft[113].

Hearing disabilities affect people that are completely or partially deaf (Deaf is the politically correct term for a person with hearing impairment).People who are partially deaf can often use hearing aids to assist their hearing. Deafness can be evident at birth or occur later in life from several biologic causes, for example Meningitis can damage the auditory nerve or the cochlea[114].

It is noted that the most common form of disability is the physical. Some people may have more than one disability and may experience additional disadvantages to adequate service provision due to factors such as culturally and linguistically diverse background.[115]

3.3 Causes of Disability

There are different triggers of disabilities, which include medical history, infectious diseases, accident and injuries, andmental disorders. They are discussed as follows:

---

[111]Document of Australian Disability Services Commission<http://www.health.wa.gov.an/.../training-package/fcommand/disability.pdf> accessed 22/3/16.
[112]*Ibid.*
[113]*Ibid.*
[114]*Ibid.*
[115]*Ibid.*

1. Medical History: These include chronic-degenerative illnesses. For instance neoplasm, arthritis,spondylitis, diabetes mellitus, and heart diseases.
2. Infectious Diseases: These are short-term diseases, which could occur as a result of epidemics as the name implies.
3. Accident and Injuries: These are disabilities which occur as a result of road or other types of accidents which could result in damages of parts of the body, for example damage to legs, hands, or other parts of the body.

Furthermore, physical disability, which is the most prominent type of disability,[116] is caused mainly by the following: trauma, illness, and genetic and congenital disorders.

a. Trauma: It is an accident that occurs after birth, which results in physical disability. Examples are arm or leg amputation, traumatic brain injury and others.
b. Illness: Some illnesses are on their own a disability while some lead to disability. For instance, someone who has meningitis and failed to receive adequate treatment is at the risk of suffering from brain tumours, polio, deafness or brain injury.
c. Genetic Disorders: This is as a result of the DNA inside the body. This form of disorder presents itself at birth, and is usually the leading cause of intellectual disability. It is noted that intellectual disability, though not a genetic condition, is caused by genetic mutation. Foetal alcohol syndrome and fragile syndrome also occur prior to birth and can cause intellectual disabilities.

It is important to note that in some cases, the causes of disability are unknown. Furthermore, disabilities may be genetically or environmentally determined. Hence, a genetically determined disability is usually inherited from the parents while an environmentally determined disability could be as a result of accident, injury, disease or infection. For instance, acquired brain injury, spinal cord injury and diabetes[117].

It is observed that poverty is another cause of disability. This is because poverty limits access to health services, which may result in disability especially in situations where dormice diseases are not adequately treated resulting in one form of disability or the other. Again,

---

[116] *Ibid.*
[117] *Ibid.*

poverty makes people more vulnerable to disability and, on the other hand, disability deepens poverty. Another prominent and contemporary cause of disability is violence, civil war, and terrorism. For instance, the current Boko Haram insurgency ravaging the North Eastern States of Nigeria is bound to ultimately increase the population of PWDs in the country because victims of armed conflict are largely prone to physical disabilities. Violence and rape also cause mental health complications and psychotic diseases or disturbances among victims of war.

3.4 Models of Disability

The history of disability across the world has ultimately been characterized by a progressive development of four models namely medical, charity, social, and human rights models, which are briefly discussed below:

3.4.1 *The Medical Model*

The medical model of disability, which is also known as the "individualized model"or the "deficit model", began to develop in the nineteenth century, along with the enhanced role of the physician in the society. The model is grounded on the idea that since many disabling conditions have medical roots PWDs are expected to benefit considerably under the direction of the medical profession.[118] Thus, under this model, PWDs are defined by their illness or medical condition. They are disempowered on the basis of medical diagnosis used to regulate and control their access to social benefits, housing, education, leisure, relationships and employment. This model promotes the view of a person with disability being dependent and needing to be cured or cared for, and it justifies the way in which disabled people have been systematically excluded from society[119].

---

[118] Parson, T., 'The Sick Role and the Role of the Physician' [1975] (53) *Health and Society*, pp. 257-278.

[119] Amudson, R., '*Against Normal Function*' [2000] (31) *Studies in History and Philosophy of Biological and Biomedical Sciences*, pp. 33-53.

3.4.2 *The Charity Model*

Driven largely by affecting appeals of charity, this model treats PWDs as helpless victims needing 'care' and 'protection'. The model relies largely on the goodwill of benevolent humanitarians for 'custodial care' of the PWDs (rather than justice and equality) and creates an army of powerless individuals dependent on either arrangements maintained by these benevolent individuals who are outside of the mainstream development, and State sponsored charities or mechanisms of social support like special schools and protection homes for PWDs.

In the core of this model, disability is perceived as a disqualification for claiming the right of social resources, which ensures the exclusion of PWDs from social arrangements and public services, and justifies their exclusion from mainstream education and employment.

3.4.3 *The Social Model*

This model of disability is a reactive and progressive approach of the Medical Model. In the 60s, individuals with disabilities started demanding for civil rights. This movement advocated that disability be framed in a manner where disability is understood in how barriers affect individuals' equal rights. In 1983, a disabled academic Mike Oliver coined the phrase "social model of disability"[120]. A fundamental aspect of the social model concerns equality and strongly believes in the phrase "Nothing about us without us". The social model of disability is based on a distinction between the terms "impairment" and "disability". Impairment is used to refer to the actual attribute (or abnormality) of a person, whether in terms of limbs, organs or mechanisms, including psychological. It addresses issues such as under-estimation of the potential of PWDs to contribute to the society by enhancing economic values if given equal rights, suitable facilities and opportunities.

---

[120] Oliver, M., 'The Individual and Social Models of Disability'; Paper presented at Joint Workshop of the Living Options Group and the Research Unit of the Royal College of Physicians <leeds.ac.uk > accessed 12 /3/16.

3.4.4 *The Human Rights Model*

The human rights model of disability gives an important dimension of human culture, and it affirms that all human beings regardless of their disabilities have certain rights, which are inalienable. This model builds upon the spirit of the Universal Declaration of Human Rights, 1948, according to which: 'All human beings are born free and equal in rights and dignity'.Consequently, society has to change to ensure that all people including people with disabilities have equal possibilities for participation. Also, laws and policies need to ensure that these barriers created by society are removed. The Rights-based Model states that support in these areas is not a question of humanity or charity, but instead a basic human right that any person can claim. The two main elements of the rights-based approach are empowerment and accountability. Empowerment refers to the participation of PWDs as active stakeholders, while accountability relates to the duty of public institutions and structures to implement these rights and to justify the quality and quantity of their implementation[121].

Although various models of disabilities are discussed above, it is contended that having a strict black and white view of disability strategy in form of models of disability is ultimately counter-productive, because adopting a single model could preclude the fact that other models might have things to offer. Since the rights based model of disability is relatively new, the competing models remain the medical model and the social model.While the formeris concerned with disability as an individual health condition that needs high medical attention, which is vital to an improved quality of life, the latter is concerned with social barriers and restrictions of opportunities. Both concerns are important, therefore there is need to develop a hybrid of the models, in order to fully utilize their benefits. However, retrogressive models such as the charity model should be entirely rejected.

---

[121] Handicap International Handbook on PRSP (1999), <http://www.making-prsp-inclusive.org/en/6-disability/611-the four models.html> accessed 15/3/15.

3.5 Impact of Disability

Disability comes with economic, political, psychological and social implications.Therefore, theimpact of disability is experienced at the individual, family and community levels[122].

3.5.1 *Impact of Disability on the Individual*

Nobody wishes to suffer any form of disability. This is because disability is a hindrance to social and economic benefits. It sometimes leads to rejection of the individuals by their immediate environment. Disability is both a cause and a consequence of poverty. A report has it that about 80% of the world population of PWDs live in low-income countries and experience social and economic disadvantages and deprivation of rights[123]. It is not in doubt that most of the developmental initiatives ignore the need of PWDs[124], and they often suffer exclusion from the mainstream of society. It is not worthy that majority of persons with disabilities get along with other family members[125]. They also relate to their peers, with disabilities more than those without disabilities. Theyfacerejection, by the society and sometimes by their immediate family. Some parents even deny them basic education.InNigeria, PWDs suffer marginalization and exclusion. Lang and Upah[126] rightly observed that:

> Nigerians living with disabilities are no better off when compared with others living in other parts of the developing world, in terms of the challenges they face. They are poor, marginalized and excluded.

---

[122] Alexa Josephine, *Social Impact of Disability*< http://www.ehow.com/info_ 8363316> accessed: 19/5/15.

[123] *Ibid.*

[124] *Ibid*; see also The UN Convention on the Rights of Persons With Disabilities, which emphasizes the importance of mainstreaming disability issues for sustainable development.

[125] *Ibid.*

[126] *Lang, R. and Upah, L., Scoping Study; Disability issues in Nigeria*,<https://www.ucl.ac.uk/lc-ccr/downloads/scopingstudies/dfid_nigeriareport>accessed 23/415.

They further noted that despite the declaration of full participation in the disability agenda of the United Nations by the Nigerian government; Nigerians with disabilities are still faced with these challenges[127]. The marginalization and exclusion suffered by PWDs are due to social attitudes and prejudice. Worst still, they are regarded as parasites, or passive recipients. PWDs are not easily integrated into society. They are regarded and treated as odd members of the society rather than equal members with equal rights and opportunities. Hence they are forced to live in perpetual fear, shame and rejection. Society often relegates PWDs to the background, and they are regarded as being recipients of charity rather than equal and productive members of society. As a result of this, they suffer exclusion from education, employment and other developmental agendas. Another major issue is employers' discrimination against PWDs. Most employers turn them away and reject them even if they have the best qualifications and skills required for the job.

PWDs suffer all manner of violence and abuse that may be physical, sexual, verbal or emotional. Other forms of abuse include neglect, withholding support, financial abuse and manipulation of medication. They experience these challenges in places like schools, workplace, and health services[128]. These abusive actions eventually impede and militate against their active social inclusion within contemporary society.

3.5.2 *Impact of Disability onthe Family*

Parenting children with disabilities (CWDs) poses a great challenge to the parents involved. The mothers in that situation bear the bulk of responsibility as the primary care givers because it is tasking and requires time and skills. Sometimes, parents of CWDs also suffer discrimination, marginalization, exclusion and rejection. Some societies or communities see them as being the cause of their children's disabilities, and they are accordingly stigmatized. The parents' resources are stressed and strained because of the high cost involved in taking care of their disabled child.The family finance is stressed as a result of special diets, special equipment, special medication, and learning aids. It is noteworthy that the needs of parents caring for children or adult family members with

---

[127] *Ibid.*

[128] PWDs are often sexually molested as a result of their condition.

disabilities are often forgotten and overlooked. This situation is more pronounced in poor families where parents cannot afford to give the special child quality health care as required. Parents in such situations are always in perpetual regret, in addition to suffering physical and emotional stress that eventually affects their health and emotions. This is because CWDs are equally valued members of their families, who grow in loving relationships with their parents and other family members. Parents strive to see their children happy and safe. Yet it is noted that meeting the basic needs of CWDs is sometimes very difficult. On the other hand, parents of CWDs testify that they learned special skills in the course of taking care of such children and have learnt to look at life in different ways[129].They testified that their experiences as mothers of children with disabilities have made them better people, increased their awareness of a wide range of issues and taught them to look at the world and other people differently. They equally believed that they have been given greater insights, learned acceptance, become more sensitive to others' differences, learned new talents, and gained a sense of fulfilment. It is worthy of note that the responsibilities which other parents are able to share with the community, neighbours and society are often borne exclusively by parents of PWDs[130]. Some of these parents testify and describe their experiences as deeply rewarding and satisfying, finding a "new appreciation for life" through their relationship with their children, and becoming stronger and more resilient to life's difficulties.[131] Invariably,parentsofpersons with disabilities have no option than to accept the condition with joy and live by it. For what one cannot change that he accepts.

3.5.3 *Impact of Disability on the Society*

It is evident that society does not favour people with disabilities. Nigeria is no exception as PWDs continue to grapple with problems of discrimination, rejection and denial. They experience economic and social deprivations. Suffice to point out that some countries do not have any legal instrument protecting PWDs thereby denying them their rights.

---

[129] The Roeher Institute Study (2000), '*Beyond the limits: Mother's Caring for Children with Disabilities'.*

[130] *Ibid.*

[131] *Ibid.*

Equally, in countries, where such rights exist, the test remains the problem of enforcement. In Nigeria, for instance, most of the developmental policies and initiatives often ignore the need of PWDs. However, the CRPD[132] emphasizes the importance of mainstreaming disability issues for sustainable development. Generally, in Africa and in Nigeria in particular, PWDs are often relegated to the background despite the indisputable fact that there is ability in disability. The fact that an individual is with disability does not in totality make him/her unproductive. There are professionals such as lawyers, doctors, engineers, economists, and teachers with disabilities. Unfortunately, because of their condition, they are being relegated to the background as second-class citizens. They are not given the opportunity to contribute to society and their talents die with them. Both government and private establishments discriminate against them in terms of employment. In some cases, people with disabilities are more qualified for a job but are denied because of their condition. The economic efficiencies of PWDs are often neglected and rejected by the society.

Worthy of note is the fact that many people are becoming disabled day after day. With an estimate of over 25 million people with disabilities[133], disability is both a cause and a consequence of poverty in Nigeria. The above figure is alarming and calls for concern. Since people with disabilities are denied job opportunities, the economy of Nigeria is restricted as a result of the steady increase in the number of PWDs, who are often not allowed to contribute their quota towards national development[134].

In 2015, the UN set up the Sustainable Development Goals, and the first of them is to "eradicate extreme poverty for all people everywhere by 2030". Nigeria is among the 189 countries that adopted the Sustainable Development Goals (SDGs), and by so doing promised to

---

[132] UN Convention on the Rights of Persons with Disabilities, 2006. See also the World Health Assembly Resolution 5823 of May 2005<www.who.int/disabilities /publications/darworld-report-concept..pdffile.>accessed 23/4/15.

[133] Disability and HIV/AIDS, *Opcit*, n 1 above.

[134] See Halima Doma Kutigi and Chinwe Kate Okoli, "Lest We Forget the Place of Persons With Disabilities in National Planning and Development: Nigeria in Context" in, Advancing the Frontiers of Law and Justice: Essays in Honour of Professor Dakas C.J. Dakas, SAN, F.M Kwede and T.M. Ngufuwan (eds) pp.405-425.

reduce extreme poverty and its major consequences[135]. To achieve this globally, 90 people need to leave poverty every minute to eradicate poverty totally by 2030; and to achieve this in Africa, 57 people have to leave every minute; and in Nigeria, 12 people per minute. Nigeria has one of the world's highest economic growth rates[136], yet over 80 million Nigerians (about 42.4% of the population) live below the poverty line[137]. This is even worsened by the rising rate of overpopulation,[138] which needs to be addressed now, rather than in 2030. In view of the significant population of PWDs in Nigeria, and the additional barriers they face, one wonders if the SDGs can really be achieved without impacting their lives by not only including them in all government policies and programmes, but also giving them the opportunity to contribute to society. Worthy of note is the fact that many people are becoming disabled day after day. With an estimate of 25 million people with disabilities; it is obvious that disability is both a cause and a consequence of poverty in Nigeria. The above figure is alarming and calls for concern.

PWDs possess rights which they are entitled to exercise. They also present veritable potential in terms of human resources that no serious nation can affordto neglect. The case of Nigerian Paralympics team, which won several medals in London Paralympics Games in 2012, shows the extent to which PWDs can contribute to the overall progress of the country.There istherefore need for government to think more of PWDs as assets who are capable of offering to the society the very talents they are endowed with rather than seeing them as a heavy burden. Thus the interest of PWDs is best served with developing and adopting disability law and policy that is based on a hybrid of the different models of disability which will not only address medical and administrative issues of disabilities, but also capture the impact of structural factors and environment. There is also a more pressing need for attitudinal change

---

[135] UN Convention on the Rights of Persons with Disabilities, 2006. See also the World Health Assembly Resolution 5823 of May 2005<www.who.int/disabilities/publications/darworld-report-concept...pdffile.>accessed 23 April 2018

[136] Averaging 7.4%, according to the Nigeria economic report released in July 2014 by the World Bank

[137] Daily Post< http//dailypost.ng/2016/09/05/Nigeria-one-poorest-countries-world-80m-living-poverty-line-un-report>accessed 22 August 2018.

[138]Kobini<www.konbini.com/ng/lifestyle/nigeria-will-replace-us-worlds-3rd-populous-country-2050>accessed 22August 2018.

and total acceptance of PWDs into the society as human beings with equal rights and privileges as contained in the various international and national legal instruments. We intend to analyse such legal instruments in the next chapter, in order to bring to the fore the incontestable rights of people with disabilities.

CHAPTER FOUR

The Legal Framework for Protection of the Rights of Persons with Disabilities in Nigeria

This chapter considers the legal framework for the protection of persons with disabilities in Nigeria (under domestic, regional, and international headings), and assesses the impact and adequacy of these laws in protecting the rights and interests of persons with disabilities.

The United Nations Charter affirms that "Universal respect for, and observance of, human rights and fundamental freedoms for all without distinction" is essential. This principle of universality is reinforced by the values of equality and non-discrimination, which are assimilated in The Universal Declaration of Human Rights (UDHR)[139].Although not legally binding on any state or person, the Declaration is of great significance as an agreed statement of the common standard of achievement for all peoples of all nations.[140]Accordingly, its principles are central to the existence of most constitutions of the world, and the rights and freedoms contained therein have been articulated in many other international instruments[141].

Disability rights are not new rights *per se*; rather, they bring poignancy to human rights that already exist but have been historically denied, neglected or marginalised. Thus, disability rights reaffirm that people with disabilities are entitled to the respect of their inherent dignity and of all human rights and fundamental freedoms on an equal basis with others.[142]The rights of PWDs like other individuals are enshrined in the 1999 Constitution and other local legislations. Furthermore, Nigeria has adopted certain regional and international instruments which affect the

---

[139]   Adopted by the General Assembly of the UN on 10 December 1948.

[140]   Statement of Eleanor Roosevelt as Chairman of the UN Committee on Human Rights, New York Inauguration of the UN Assembly, 1948.

[141]   The UDHR together with the ICCPR and the ICESCR constitute the International Bill of Human Rights.

[142]   Preamble to, and article 1 of, the CRPD.

rights of PWDs either specifically or generally; hence, such instruments are also deliberated on. Underlying the regional and international framework is a fundamental distinction between rights that are legally enforceable entitlements and those that are not.[143]Thus, the most important instruments are the ones Nigeria has ratified, because they define legal obligations that have been agreed to formally, and are therefore binding. It is important to elucidate here that the domestic application of Regional and International Human Rights Norms in Nigeria is guided by provisions of Section 12 of the Constitution of the Federal Republic of Nigeria, which clearly compels that no treaty between Nigeria and any other State shall have the force of law unless it is domesticated. Even then, in *Abacha v Fawehinmi*[144], the Nigerian Supreme Court held that a domesticated treaty is subordinate to the Nigerian Constitution. In the words of Ogundare, JSC (who delivered the lead judgment):

> No doubt, Cap. 10 [the African Charter on Human and Peoples' Rights as domesticated by Cap. 10] is a statute with international flavour. Being so, therefore, I would think that if there is a conflict between it and another statute, its provisions will prevail over those of that other statutes for the reason that it is presumed that the legislature does not intend to breach an international obligation. To this extent I agree with their Lordships of the court below that the Charter possesses "a greater vigour and strength" than any other domestic statute. But that is not to say that the Charter is superior to the Constitution as erroneously, with respect, was submitted by ... learned counsel for the respondent. Nor can its international flavour prevent the National Assembly, or the Federal Military Government before it remove(sic) it from our body of municipal laws by simply repealing Cap. 10[145].

It is however submitted that in spite of the Supreme Court's subordination of domesticated regional and international human rights instruments to the Nigerian Constitution (as Ogundare JSC points out), these instruments, given their regional/international flavour, are superior to conventional Acts of the National Assembly in the hierarchy of norms

---

[143] Bickenbach, J. 'Disability Human Rights Law and Policy', in G. Albrecht, K. Seelman, and M. Bury (eds) *Handbook of Disability Studies* (Beverly Hills: Sage., 2000).

[144] *Abacha & Others v Fawehinmi*(2000) 6 N.W.L.R 660 at 228.

[145] *Ibid*, at 289.

in the Nigerian legal system[146]. Furthermore, scholars[147] have underscored the fact that a State cannot rely upon or plead the provisions of its municipal law or deficiencies in that law before an international judicial, arbitral or similar body in answer to a claim against it for an alleged breach of its obligations under international law[148]. Correspondingly, a municipal court, which defers to municipal law, notwithstanding an inconsistent rule of international law, itself, acts in breach of international law and will, as an organ of the State, engage the international responsibility of that State[149]. Hence, before an international tribunal, a respondent State cannot plead that its municipal law (not even its constitution) contains rules which conflict with international law. It cannot also plead the absence of any legislative provision or of a rule of its internal law as a defence to a charge that it has broken international law[150].

---

[146] Dakas C., 'Activism, Ignorance or Playing to the Gallery?: Untying the Knots of the Jurisprudence of Nigerian Courts on the Domestic Application of International Human Rights Norms', in I. I. Gabriel (ed.), *New Vistas in Law* (Jos: New World Publishers Ltd., 2000), pp. 398-454.

[147] Dakas C., *Judicial Reform of the Legal Framework for Human Rights Litigation in Nigeria: Novelties*
and Perplexities' being an enlarged and updated text of an earlier invited paper delivered at a training organised by the national secretariat of the Nigerian Bar Association (NBA), at Osogbo, OsunState, on February 21, 2012<Dakas-Judicial Reform-Legal Framework of Human Rights Litigation.pdf> accessed 12/4/15.

[148] Under Article 27 of the Vienna Convention on the Law of Treaties, "a party may not invoke the provisions of its internal law as justification for its failure to perform a treaty". However, this rule is without prejudice to Article 46 of the Convention which is to the effect that "a State may not invoke the fact that its consent to be bound by a treaty has been expressed in violation of a provision of its internal   law regarding competence to conclude treaties as invalidating its consent unless that violation was manifest and concerned a rule of its internal law of fundamental importance". A violation is said to be manifest "if it would be objectively evident to any State conducting itself in the manner in accordance with normal practice and in good faith": Vienna Convention on the Law of Treaties, 1969, *reprinted* in 8 I. L. M. 679 (1969).

[149] The attitude of Courts regarding the domestic application of Regional and International Human Rights Norms in Nigeria is extensively considered in the next chapter of this book.

[150] *Opcit,* n 244 above.

4.1 Domestic Framework for the Protection of the Rights of Persons with Disabilities in Nigeria

4.1.1 *The Constitution of the Federal Republic of Nigeria 1999*

The Constitution of the Federal Republic of Nigeria 1999, which is the basic law of Nigeria that guarantees legal security for all its citizens, operates a bifurcated regime of human rights. While Chapter IV makes provision for "Fundamental Rights" to every person (including the disabled), which are clearly justiciable, Chapter II makes provision for "Fundamental Objectives and Directive Principles of State Policy", (which forms the basis of economic, social and cultural rights), but expressly makes them non-justiciable[151].In specific terms, Chapter IV embodies civil and political rights (which are primarily libertarian in character) and, in the generational paradigm of human rights discourse, formsthe bedrock of first generation rights. These rightsinclude: The Right to life; Right to dignity of the human person; Right to personal liberty; Right to fair-hearing; Right to privacy and family life; Right to freedom of thought, conscience and religion; Right to freedom of expression and the press; Right to freedom of movement; Right to freedom from discrimination; Right to acquire and own immovable property anywhere in Nigeria; and the Right against compulsory acquisition of one's property without compensation[152]. To guarantee the rights enumerated above, the Constitution specifies a special procedure for the enforcement of these Rights by the Courts[153].

In addition to the provisions on fundamental human rights, the Nigerian Constitution, under Section 15 prohibits discrimination based on religion, status, or ethnic or linguistic association. However, it is noted that the Constitution does not include disability as a ground for discrimination. In other words, if a person with disability suffers any form of discrimination as a result of his disability, he cannot invoke this right under the Constitution. The needs of the disabled and the other difficulties they face on a daily basis could be ameliorated through the inclusion of disability in the list of protected cases in the Nigerian

---

[151] Section 6(6)(c).

[152] See generally Sections 33 to 46, Constitution of the Federal Republic of Nigeria, 1999.

[153] The Fundamental Human Rights (Enforcement Procedure) Rules, 2009.

Constitution. This gesture would reinforce to the Nigerian people the government's commitment to ensuring that disability should not be used to deny a person's benefits or opportunities.

Chapter II of the Nigerian Constitution, on the other hand, makes provision for economic and social objectives, and obliges the State to direct its policy towards ensuring that the economic system is not operated in such a manner as to permit the concentration of wealth or the means of production and exchange in the hands of few individuals or group. Thus, every citizen is entitled to the opportunity for securing adequate means of livelihood as well as adequate opportunity to secure suitable employment; conditions of work are just and humane; suitable and adequate shelter and food; reasonable national minimum wage; old age care and pensions; and unemployment, sick benefits and welfare of the disabled are provided for all citizens[154]. Furthermore, Section 13 imposes a "duty and responsibility" on "all organs of government, and all authorities and persons, exercising legislative, executive or judicial powers, to conform to, observe and apply" the provisions of Chapter II of the Constitution.

Remarkably, Section 6(6)(c) of the same Constitution, seemingly restricts the application of this obligation, by providing that judicial powers "shall not...extend to any issue or question as to whether any act or omission by any authority or person...is in conformity with the Fundamental Objectives and Directive Principles of State Policy set out in Chapter II of this Constitution." Thus, one of the recurrent themes in political and legal discourse in Nigeria has always been the propriety or otherwise of the non-justiciability of economic, social and cultural rights[155]. However, modern trends in human rights jurisprudence favour the justiciabilityof ratified human rights instruments which recognize socio-economic rights of citizens and also statutes that have been enacted to actualize provisions under Chapter II[156]. Thus, in *Attorney*

---

[154] Sections 16 and 17, Constitution of the Federal Republic of Nigeria, 1999.

[155] See *Archbishop Anthony Olubunmi Okogie & Ors v Attorney General of Lagos State (1981) 2 NCLR 337;*

and *A.O. Adewole & Ors v AlhajiJakande & Ors (1981) 1 NCLR 262.*

[156] Such enactments include the Nigerian Education Bank Act, the Child's Right Act 2003, the Compulsory, Free, Universal Basic Education Act 2004, the Independent Corrupt Practices and Other Related Offences Commission Act, 2000, the Freedom of Information Act 2011 etc.

General of Ondo State v Attorney General of the Federation &Ors[157], the Ondo State Government challenged the constitutionality of the enactment of the Corrupt Practices and Other related Offences Act under whichthe Independent Corrupt Practices and Other Related Offences Commission (ICPC) was established to fight corruption throughout the country, including through the prosecution of alleged offenders. The Supreme Court, per Uwaifo JSC, justified the enactment of the Act on the basis of the Fundamental Objectives and Directive Principles of State Policy. Borrowing from Indian jurisprudence, he declared as follows:

> [Every] effort is made from the Indian perspective to ensure that the Directive Principles are not a dead letter. What is necessary is to see that they are observed as much as practicable so as to give cognizance to the general tendency of the Directives. It is necessary therefore to say that our own situation is of peculiar significance. We do not need to seek uncertain ways of giving effect to the Directive Principles in Chapter II of our Constitution. The Constitution itself has placed the entire Chapter II under the Exclusive Legislative List. By this, it simply means that all the Directive Principles need not remain mere or pious declarations. It is for the Executive and the National Assembly, working together; to give expression to any one of them through appropriate enactment as occasion may demand.

Similarly, in *AG Lagos State v AG Federation*[158]the Supreme Court held that the National Assembly was competent to enact the Federal Environmental Protection Agency Act[159] for the protection of the environment, in furtherance of Chapter II. These two cases represent an alternative route via which Chapter II could be judicially enforced.

4.1.2 *Other Laws Relevant to Persons with Disabilities in Nigeria*

In addition to the Constitution, many laws that deal with diverse issues in society also contain components that apply to PWDs either generally or specifically.These legislations are generally discussed in this section.

---

[157] (2002) 9 NWLR (Pt 772) 2.
[158](2003) 15 NWLR (Pt 842) 113, 175.
[159]Federal Environmental Protection Agency (Amendment) Act 1992.

The Universal Basic Education (UBE) Programme was introduced in 1999 by the Federal Government of Nigeria as a reform programme aimed at providing greater access to and ensuring quality of basic education throughout Nigeria. The Universal Basic Education Act (2004) defines Universal Basic Education as early childhood care and education[160]. The UBE Programme objectives include ensuring an uninterrupted access to 9-year formal education by providing free and compulsory basic education for every child of school-going age. The UBE programme is designed to remove distortions and inconsistencies in basic education delivery and to reinforce the implementation of the National Policy on Education. It is also to provide greater access to basic education and ensure its quality throughout the country. According to the Implementation Guidelines for the UBE[161], the scheme stresses the inclusion of girls and women and a number of underserved groups, including the disabled. These will reduce the menace of dropping out of school and improve the acquisition of literacy, numeracy, life skills and other values for lifelong useful living.

A commendable feature of the UBE Programnmeis its emphasis on Curriculum diversification and relevance to effectively and adequately cover individual and community needs and aspirations. Thus the programme provides for special needs education[162].

Unfortunately, however, the depressing reality is that, in Nigeria, many children with disabilities are unable to attend school, and when they enrol it is often in special schools which segregate them from their peers and offer fewer opportunities. Thus, school for most disabled children remains a nightmare of discrimination and disrespect, with badly designed curriculum, poorly trained teachers, and inaccessible facilities. Strong arguments have been made for inclusive education, which reflects the principles of the CRC, and welcomesall children without discrimination into ordinary schools, which provideall the support that is required by the disabled child such as communication aids, sign language

---

[160] Section 15(1) UBEC Act 2004.

[161] Implementation Guidelines for the Universal Basic Education (UBE) Programme (2000), Federal Ministry
of Education, Abuja.

[162] Revised National Policy on Education, 6th Edition (2013), Sec 7: Special Needs Education (Nigerian
Educational Research and Development Council, Abuja).

teachers, and study materials on tape or in Braille[163]. This researcher concurs that a disabled child would benefit most from inclusive education as this will best prepare them to face the challenges of the larger society.

The Armed Forces Pensions Act[164]defines "disabled" as meaning physical or mental injury or damage, or loss of physical or mental capacity.[165] It further provides that a serviceman shall be regarded as disabled for the purposes of this section, if the termination of his service is necessitated or accelerated by an injury or condition due to war service. The section also deals with the award of pensions and gratuities of disabled servicemen[166].

Section 342 of the Companies and Allied Matters Act[167]provides for directors 'report, which shall among other things contain a fair view of the business of the company and its subsidiaries during the year and their positions at the end of it. Part III of the fifth schedule of the Act, titled 'Employment of Disabled Persons', provides for reports on matters and activities that relate to the employment, training, and advancement of PWDs[168].

This provision makes it clear that every company in Nigeria is mandated to have and make clear provisions and arrangement for the sustained employment of PWDs, and the welfare of disabled employees. Needless to say, the rate of unemployment among disabled Nigerians is a clear indication of the degree of compliance to this law.

Similarly, the Consumer Protection Council Act[169] recognizes the right to PWDs to special assistance. Thus it provides that where a consumer (or a person having an interest in a matter) is an illiterate or is subject to any physical disability and thereby unable to write, the clerk or other official working with the State Committee shall cause such consumer's statement to be written at no cost to such consumer[170].

A comprehensive provision for compensation is provided under the Employees Compensation Act (2011) for any death, injury, disease or

---

[163]   Avoke*Opcit*, n 155 above.
[164]   Armed Forces Pensions Act (Chapter A23 Laws of the Federation of Nigeria 2004).
[165]   *Ibid*, Section 9(1)
[166]   *Ibid*, Section 9(2).
[167]   CAMA (Chapter C20 Laws of the Federation of Nigeria 2004).
[168]   Companies and Allied Matters Act, Section 7 (a-c).
[169]   Chapter C25, Laws of the Federation of Nigeria 2004
[170]   Consumer Protection Council Act, Section 6(2).

disability arising out of or in the course of employment and for matters connected therewith.[171] Interestingly however, while the Act recognizes various forms of disability, it is silent on the issue of mental disability.

The Child Rights Act (CRA) domesticates the survival, development, protection and participation rights of children guaranteed under the UN Convention on the Rights of the Child and that of the African Union Charter on the Rights and Welfare of the Child.[172] Section 3 of the Act also affirms the rights in Chapter IV of the Constitution of the Federal Republic of Nigeria, 1999, and includes in successive sections other rights specific to the child. The CRA also gives teeth to the various state legislations dealing with specific aspects of child protection such as the prohibition of child hawking, child begging, child trafficking and labour, female genital mutilation, child marriage, and other harmful practices.

The CRA does not specifically mention disabled children, although S. 16provides for "children in need of special protection". However, no definition is given for the children referred to therein. Again, S. 50 (1) (d), which makes a feeble attempt to incorporate disabled children, covers only children with mental or severe physical disabilities.

The right of PWDs to participate in the process is recognized under the Electoral Act[173]. It makes allowances for them to participate effectively. Thus, Section 56(1) provides that a person with disability can be accompanied to the polling unit by any person of his choice who, with the permission of the Presiding Officer, can make exception to the requirement of secret balloting by allowing such escort to assist the disabled voter to make his mark. Section 56(2) of the Act further provides for suitable means of communication such as Braille, large embossed prints or electronic devises or sign language interpretation or off site voting where necessary.

It is observed that INEC was receptive to consultations with disability organisations and developed various innovations, thus significant improvements were made in the involvement of PWDs during Nigeria's 2015 elections[174]. Nevertheless, unlike women and youth

---

[171] *Ibid*, long title.
[172] Child Rights Act, 2003, Section (1).
[173] See Electoral Act 2010
[174] Final Report of The EU Election Observation Mission, Nigeria General Elections 2015<http://eeas.europa.eu/nigeria/docs/eu-eom-nigeria-2015-final-report_en.pdf>accessed 3/6/16.

groups, PWDs are yet to have significant representation in the parties' decision-making structures and are hardly ever favoured as candidates for elective or appointive positions in either the party or the government. The reluctance of political party leaders to include PWDs in party affairs is often based on the misconception that PWDs face the challenges of mobility, financial resources, and conflict of interest with other PWDs.On a positive note however, in the 2015 general elections, several PWDs were successively elected into various positions across the country.

The Violence Against Persons Act (VAPP) is an improvement on the Penal and Criminal Code in relation to violence[175]. The Act was passed into law in a bid to eliminate violence in private and public life; prohibit all forms of violence, including physical, sexual, psychological, domestic, harmful traditional practices; discrimination against persons and to provide maximum protection and effective remedies for victims and punishment of offenders[176]. The Act contains ample provisions that cover most of the prevalent forms of violence in Nigeria today, which include physical violence; psychological violence; sexual violence; harmful traditional practices; and socio-economic violence[177]. The Act does not only ensure that the violators are brought to justice, but also that the victims are adequately compensated, re- integrated into the society and given the necessary support and protection.

Furthermore in addition to fundamental rights provided for under Chapter IV of the Nigerian Constitution, the Act entitles victims and survivors of violence to comprehensive medical, psychological, social and legal assistance by accredited service providers and government agencies or non-governmental agencies providing such assistance; information on the availability of legal, health and social services and other relevant assistance and the readily afforded access to them[178].

---

[175] Violence Against Persons (Prohibition) Act (2015). The National Agency for the Prohibition of Trafficking in Persons (NAPTIP) is named as the service provider.

[176] Under the VAPP Act, rape, spousal battery, forceful ejection from home, forced financial dependence or economic abuse, harmful widowhood practices, female circumcision or genital mutilation, abandonment of children, harmful traditional practices, harmful substance attacks] such as acid baths, political violence, forced isolation and separation from family and friends, depriving persons of their liberty, incest, indecent exposure, and violence by state actors are punishable offences.

[177] Section 44, Violence Against Persons (Prohibition) Act, 2015.

[178] *Ibid*, Section 38(1) (a)-(c).

Although the VAPP does not specifically allude to PWDs, it is believed that the Act will bring reliefand effective remedies to millions of victims (including those with disabilities) who have suffered violence, in one form or the other, in silence without recourse to justice or rehabilitative, psychological or social support for their recovery and reintegration.

The major drawback in relation to this law is its limited application to the Federal Capital Territory, Abuja[179] as only the High Court of the Federal Capital Territory Abuja empowered by an Act of Parliament has the jurisdiction to hear and grant any application brought under the Act[180]. Duplicity of laws is another major downside of the Act given that most of the crimes stipulated in the VAPP are provided for in the existing criminal laws and also there are provisions for liberty of the citizen in Sections 35, 40, and 41 of the Constitution.

4.1.3 *Legislative Initiatives on Establishing Disability Specific Laws in Nigeria*

In addition to the enactments discussed above, it is important to state here that successive governments in Nigeria have over the years attempted several legislative initiatives in response to the plight of PWDs. For instance,the Nigerians with Disability Decree was enacted in 1993, which established a comprehensive framework for the protection of the rights of PWDs and the promotion of access to safeguards and services. Specifically, it sought to promote access to legal services[181], voting[182], telecommunications[183], sport and recreation[184], social services[185], transportation[186], housing[187], vocational training and employment[188], education[189] and healthcare[190]. It also provided a policy restatement of the

---

[179]   *Ibid*, Section 47.
[180]   *Ibid*, Section 27.
[181]   The *Nigerians with Disability Decree 1993, Section 14.*
[182]   *Ibid, Section 13.*
[183]   *Ibid, Section 12.*
[184]   *Ibid.* Section 11.
[185]   *Ibid*, Section 10.
[186]   *Ibid*, Section 9.
[187]   *Ibid*, Section 7.
[188]   *Ibid* Section 6.
[189]   *Ibid* Section 5.

government's duty to prohibit discrimination on the grounds of disability and to promote the social and economic integration of persons with disabilities, thus:

> Disabled persons shall be guaranteed treatment as equals to other Nigerians for all purposes in the Federal Republic of Nigeria. Accordingly it shall be the duty and responsibility of organs of government and of all authorities and persons to adopt and promote policies that will ensure full integration of the disabled into the mainstream of the society.[191]

Interestingly, it is noted that the present status of this law is unclear. Its omission from 2004 Laws of The Federation (which is the authoritative compendium of laws validly enacted in Nigeria as at 2000)remains a subject of controversy among researchers, with some arguing that it was never passed in the first place[192]. We are therefore of the view that the complete exclusion of this law from the Laws of the Federation of Nigeria simply implies that it no longer exists. This further confirms the general perception of disability by the Nigerian society (including policy makers) that disability issues are simply not important.

Relatedly, two significant Bills for persons with disabilities were introduced at the National Assembly in year 2000, namely (1) A Bill for an Act to Provide Special Facilities for the Use of Handicapped Persons in the Public Buildings and (2) A Bill for an Act to Establish a National Commission for the Handicapped Persons and to Vest it with the Responsibility for Their Education and Social Development and for the Connected Purposes. Nothing significant came out of these Bills. Again, a Bill was passed in 2012 making it a criminal offence for employers (whether individual or corporate) to discriminate against disabled employees or applicants in Nigeria[193].

At the state level, some states have demonstrated pragmatic commitment to the plight of the PWDs by enacting specific legislations

---

[190] *Ibid* Section 4.
[191] *Ibid*, Section 2(1).
[192] See AyodeleAtsenuwa, 'Legal and Institutional Mechanisms for Protecting Persons With Disabilities in Nigeria', in E. Azinge And C. Ani (Eds), *The Rights Of Persons With Disabilities*, NIALS 2001, p.127.
[193] GAATES, 'Nigeria Passes Law On Discriminating Against Persons With Disabilities', <http://globalaccessibilitynews.com/2012/04/30/nigeria-passes-law-on-discriminating-against-persons-with-disabilities/> accessed 11/6/13.

to protect their rights and interests. Way back in 1981, the Plateau State Government enacted the Plateau State Handicapped Law, 1981. The law stipulates inter alia, that education of children with handicaps is compulsory and provides for the rehabilitation needs of adults with handicaps. We are however not aware about the level of implementation of this relevant piece of legislation.

In 2003, Lagos State enacted a law captioned "the Disabled Persons Welfare (Enhancement) Law, 2003 of Lagos State". The law seeks to enhance the welfare of PWDs within the State. Available reports show that this law is not being implemented presently. Also recently, the same Lagos State Government enacted a law the Lagos State Special People's Law 2011 to ensure inter-alia that people living with disabilities in the state are given equal rights in all social services, employment, political and educational facilities. The law also safeguards them against discrimination and guarantees their right to access information, conducive socioeconomic environment, and access to special education and public transportation facilities.

Remarkably, after almost 20 years of struggle, the Discrimination Against Persons with Disabilities (Prohibition) Act, 2018 was finally passed by the National Assembly for domestication and assented to by the President. The Actprohibits any form of discrimination against PWDs,curb the abuse in all forms of Nigerians with disabilities, and promote the respect of their rights. Although the Act contains innovations, it remains to be seen how the provisions when tested eventually, would fare.[194] Thus, in spite of the social rights guaranteed under our laws, most PWDs live off begging on the city streets, because access to employment continues to be a problem even where the disabled applicants are more qualified than their non-disabled counterparts[195].

---

[194] To date, the National Commission for Persons with Disabilities has not taken off, transport is not free for the disabled, national news and official broadcasts do not provide sign language for interpretation in accordance with, and it has been difficult in the circumstance of our electoral process for the disabled to exercise their rights to vote and be voted for.

[195] MAARDEC, 'The Plight of Disabled Nigerians and the Need for Mass Enlightenment'<http://www.maardec.net/THE%20PLIGHT%20OF%20DISAB LED%20NIGERIANS%20AND%20T>HE%20NEED%20FOR%20MASS%20 ENLIGHTENMENT.html>accessed 11 May 2013.

4.1.4 *Discrimination Against Persons with Disabilities (Prohibition) Act, 2018 (the Disabilities Act or the Act)*

Section 57 of the Act defines disability to include "long term physical, mental, intellectual or sensory impairment which in the interaction with various barriers may hinder full and effective participation in society on equal basis with others" and discrimination to be "differential treatment and its verbs and infinite form, discriminate, to discriminate have the corresponding signification".

Section 1 of the Act expands the rights of persons not to be discriminated against by prohibiting discrimination against persons with a disability on the grounds of their disability by any person or institution in any manner or circumstance. To this end, the Act criminalizes discrimination against a person with disabilities, as it is an offence liable upon conviction, to six months imprisonment or a fine of ₦100,000 (One Hundred Thousand Naira) or both imprisonment and a fine, for an individual. For a body corporate, it will be liable upon conviction to a fine of ₦1,000,000 (One Million Naira)[196]. Notably, whilst the Act criminalizes the discrimination ofPWDs, it allows the victim of such discrimination to institute a civil action against the offender without prejudice to any acquittal or conviction. Thus, the Act allows for both civil and criminal liability.

A commendable provision of the Act is the requirement for the Ministry of Information and Culture to raise awareness about the law and other disability issues[197].

a. Additional Rights and Protections under the 2018 Act

Other privileges afforded persons with disabilities under the Act include: priority in queues[198], the protection of the Government in light of their vulnerability in risky situations and humanitarian crisis,[199] and priority in the provision of accommodation where this is provided by schools, employers, service providers, government, organizations, etc.[200]

---

[196] Section 1 (2) of the Disabilities Act.

[197] Section 2, *Ibid.*

[198] Section 26(1) of the Act, a person who contravene this provision will be liable upon conviction to imprisonment for a term of 6 months or a fine of N50,000 or both.

[199] Section 25 of the Act.

[200] Section 27 of the Act.

Contravention of this provision is also an offence, liable on conviction to a fine of N50,000.00 (fifty thousand Naira) or a term of six months imprisonment or both. Of equal importance is thatPWDs have "the right to work on an equal basis with others and this includes the right and opportunity to gain a living by work freely chose or accepted in a labour market and work environment that is open"[201]. This means that employers are under a duty to ensure that all persons irrespective of their disability are afforded the opportunity to apply for work and gain employment and the decision to not employ a person with disability should not be based on the disability. Where a person contravenes this provision, he is liable on conviction to a minimum nominal damage of N250,000 (two hundred and fifty thousand Naira). In the case of a company, it will on conviction be liable to nominal damages of a minimum of N500,000 (Five hundred thousand Naira). Further, principal officers of the company in violation will also be liable to N50,000 (fifty thousand Naira) in damages. These damages are payable to the affected person with the disability. The Act imposes an obligation on all employers of labour in public organisations to have persons with disability constituting at least 5% of their employment.

b. National Commission for Persons with Disabilities

The Act establishes the National Commission for Persons with Disabilities (the Commission). The Governing Council (the Council) of the Commission is vested with the power to amongst other things[202], liaise with the public and private sector and other bodies to ensure the peculiar interests of PWDs are taken into consideration in every government policy, programmes and activity. They are also empowered to receive complaints from persons with disabilities on the violation of their rights; issue insignia of identification for PWDs; support their rights to seek redress in court, investigate, prosecute and/or sanction in appropriate cases violations of the Act and ensure research, development and education on disability issues andPWDs.

---

[201] Section 28 of the Act.
[202] Section 37 of the Act

4.2 Regional Legal Framework for the Protection of the Rights of Persons with Disabilities in Africa

The African regional human rights system is the youngest in the world. This regional system was initiated under the former Organisation of African Unity (OAU), which was mainly concerned with independence for African States from colonialists. The African Union (AU) succeeded the OAU in 2000 with the adoption of the AU Constitutive Act. Conscious of the specificities of the African continent[203], African States have adopted a number of Conventions for the protection and promotion of human rights in Africa.

Under the African System, three bodies are most relevant to human rights protection, viz the African Commission[204], the African Court on Human and Peoples Rights[205] and the African Committee on the Rights of the Child[206]. Despite their general nature, these regional instruments contain specific references to persons with disabilities, and fight against the discrimination they are subjected to. They also make provisions for the disabled specifically in the areas of education, vocational training, employment, health care and leisure. Hence African States have the obligation to implement the provisions of these regional instruments, which include taking legislative and administrative measures that favour persons with disabilities.

What is even more commendable is that in addition to general human rights protection, disability specific initiatives have also been taken by African States. The first initiative of the OAU in relation to PWDs was the African Regional Conference on the International Year of the Disabled Person in 1980 and in the same year the African Rehabilitation Institute (ARI) was established as a specialised agency of the OAU to look after the agendas of persons with disabilities. In 1999, an OAU Ministerial Conference on Human Rights urged its members to pay special attention to the rights and needs of people with disabilities

---

[203] The AU had from its inception a much clearer human rights mandate. At its very first session it adopted the Continental Plan of Action for the African Decade of People with Disabilities (CPOA) with the aim of implementing equality and the empowerment of persons with disabilities.

[204] Established by Article 30of the African Charter, adopted 27 June, 1981.

[205] Established by Article 1of the Protocol to the African Charter on the establishment of an African Court on Human and Peoples' Rights, adopted 9 June 1998.

[206] Established by Article 32 of the African Children's Charter.

and soon after the conference the period 1999 to 2009 was declared the African Decade of Disabled Persons.

In 2003, in recognition of the importance of addressing disability rights, the Disability African Regional Consultative Conference was held in Johannesburg. At this conference the Secretariat of the African Decade of Persons with Disabilities (SAPDPD) was established. Subsequent instruments of the AU have made provisions for PWDs, such as the Protocol on the Rights of Women in Africa, the African Youth Charter, and the African Charter on Democracy, Elections and Governance. The second African Decade on the Rights of Disabled Persons was declared from 2010-2019.

It is deduced from the above that despite various shortcomings[207], significant improvements on the issue of disability rights have been made at the African Regional level. The clear shift from regarding disability as a welfare issue towards perceiving it as a social issue is one of the main reasons for this shift.

4.2.1 *African Charter on Human and People's Rights*

The most important African human rights instrument is the African Charter on Human and People's Rights 1981, which has been ratified by all AU member States. Nigeria ratified and transposed the Charter into its national law in 1983[208]. Various provisions of this Charter can be interpreted as conferring on States the duty to protect PWDs from discrimination[209]. Article 2 provides for a general duty of non-discrimination[210], while Article 28 of the Charter states that:

> Every individual shall have the duty to respect and consider his fellow beings without discrimination, and to maintain relations aimed at

---

[207] Which are discussed extensively in the ensuing parts of this book.

[208] African Charter on Human and Peoples' Rights (Enforcement and Ratification) Act, Cap 10, Laws of the Federation 2004.

[209] Perlin*Opcit*, n 15 above.

[210] Evans, M., and Murray, R., *The African Charter on Human and Peoples' Rights: The System in Practice 1986-2006* (2nd edition, Cambridge University Press, Cambridge 2008) 178.

promoting, safeguarding and reinforcing mutual respect and tolerance.[211]

This provision seems to confer on Signatory States a duty to take positive steps to safeguard the rights of PWDs and to promote the 'tolerance' of such persons within society. A right of non-discrimination can also be inferred from Article 3 of the Charter, which provides that "Every individual shall be equal before the law..." and that "Every individual shall be entitled to equal protection of the law...." This principle of equality is further defined in Article 19 of the Charter, and is very important for disability rights because it affirms that persons with disabilities are entitled to the same rights and protections under the law as their able-bodied counterparts[212]. These rights are broadly consistent with Section 17 of the Constitution of the Federal Republic of Nigeria 1999[213].

The Charter similarly provides for respect of the life, integrity, and dignity of every human being[214]. In addition to that, it abolishes all forms of exploitation and degradation (particularly cruel, inhuman or degrading treatment shall be prohibited)[215]. Whereas these provisions do not refer specifically to the rights of persons with disabilities, it is commonly acknowledged that the right to respect for dignity is one of the cornerstones of the protections available to PWDs under international law[216]. Other remarkable provisions of the Charter include the obligation for States to promote access to employment, healthcare services, and education for persons with disabilities[217]. While, again, these provisions do not specifically refer to the disabled, the provisions of the Pretoria Declaration on Economic, Social and Cultural Rights in Africa

---

[211] Article 28 of the African Charter on Human and People's Rights 1981.

[212] Cotter, A.M., This Ability: An International Legal Perspective of Disability Discrimination (Ashgate Publishing, Aldershot 2007) 127.

[213] Section 17 of the Constitution of the Federal Republic of Nigeria 1999; See also Equal Rights Trust, Letter to His Excellency, Mr.Goodluck Jonathan regarding the Nigeria Disability Bill (2011) <http://www.equalrightstrust.org/ertdocumentbank/GOODLUCK%20JONAT HAN%20SUBMISSION.pdf> accessed 11/05/2013.

[214] Article 4 of the African Charter on Human and People's Rights 1981.

[215] *Ibid*, Article 5.

[216] Riouxand, M.H., and Basser, L.A, Critical Perspectives on Human Rights and Disability Law (MartinusNijhoff Publishers, The Netherlands 2011) 30.

[217] Articles 15 to 18 of the African Charter on Human and People's Rights 1981.

2004[218]affirm that these interpretations are correct. However, such an approach does not enhance the visibility of people with disabilities or their right to equal treatment under the Charter.

The expert body that monitors States' compliance with the African Charter and the Protocol on the Rights of Women is the African Commission on Human and Peoples' Rights. Individuals and NGOs may submit complaints to the Commission alleging violations of the Charter. So far, the only communication of the Commission dealing with disability rights is *Purohit and Moore v The Gambia*[219]which was decided in 2003 and which has been cited by some legal scholars as one of the most important human rights cases on behalf of people with disabilities, decided by any regional human rights body[220]. In this case, two health care professionals from the UK who were visiting the Gambia, submitted the complaint on behalf of mental health patients detained under the Lunatics Detention Act (LDA) of The Gambia. They alleged that under the LDA, there was no definition of 'lunatic' or safeguards for patients under the Act, and that under the LDA there was no requirement to acquire consent for treatment or to review treatment. Legal aid was not available to the patients under the Act, and the patients were not allowed to vote. The Commission found that the people confined in the mental hospital have a right to participate in and enjoy life to the fullest, on an equal basis with people without disabilities. The Commission found therefore that their treatment constituted a violation of their right to human dignity, to have one's cause heard, and to vote, in violation of the African Charter.

The significance of the *Purohit* decision lies in the Commission's willingness to find the rights enumerated in the Charter as applicable to people with mental disabilities who had been confined against their will in a state run institution. A rights-based approach to disabilities recognizes people with disabilities as rights holders as opposed to the welfare approach, which does not. It is also significant that The

---

[218] Para. 6, 7 and 8 (respectively) of the Pretoria Declaration on Economic, Social and Cultural Rights in Africa 2004.

[219] Afr. Comm'n Hum. & Peoples' Rts., Comm. No. 241/2001, para 85 (2003).

[220] Kanter A.S., 'The Promise and Challenge of the United Nations on the Rights of the Persons with Disabilities' [2007] (34) *Syracuse Journal of International Law and Commerce*, p. 289.

Commission in the *Purohit* case recognized that people with disabilities are equal in every respect to people without disabilities and have a right to dignity, thereby upholding the rights-based approach to disability, even before the CRPD was adopted.

While there are a few provisions pertaining to the rights of people with disabilities in the African Charter, these provisions are not specific and do not comprehensively protect the rights of people with disabilities. Article 2 of the Charter lists 'other status' under its non-discrimination clause, which can be found to include disabilities. Article 18(4) of the African Charter specifically mentions persons with disabilities as needing special protection. However, this is the only explicit reference to persons with disabilities in the Charter, and it groups persons with disabilities with the elderly, thereby not recognizing persons with disabilities specific circumstances and rights.

4.2.2 *African Charter on the Rights and Welfare of the Child 1990*

The African Charter on the Rights and Welfare of the Child 1990 was ratified by Nigeria on 23rd July 2001. The Charter, not only mirrors the non-discrimination provisions of the African Charter on Human and People's Rights 1980 discussed above, but also provides a specific duty to introduce special safeguards to protect children who are physically or mentally disabled as:

> Every child who is mentally or physically disabled shall have the right to special measures of protection in keeping with his physical and moral needs and under conditions, which ensure his dignity, promote his self-reliance and active participation in the community.[221]

These positive duties extend to ensuring access to education, employment, recreation, social life and public highways and buildings. Thus, the Charter requires that:

> States Parties... shall ensure that the disabled child has effective access to training, preparation for employment and recreation opportunities in a manner conducive to the child achieving the fullest possible social integration [and] shall use their available resources with a view to achieving progressively the full convenience of the mentally and

---

[221] The African Charter on the Rights and Welfare of the Child 1990, Article 13(1).

physically disabled person to movement and access to public highway buildings and other places to which the disabled may legitimately want to have access to.[222]

The Pretoria Declaration on Economic, Social and Cultural Rights in Africa 2004, which necessitates States to respect and promote the equal enjoyment of all rights for all, including vulnerable persons such as the disabled, was also signed by Nigeria.

4.2.3 *The African Women's Protocol*

The Protocol to the African Charter on Human and Peoples' Rights on the Rights of Women in Africa, better known as the Maputo Protocol, was adopted by the African Union in July 2003 as a result of intensive advocacy by many organizations from all over Africa and entered into force on 25 November 2005. So far, 37 countries including Nigeria have ratified it[223].Since the UN Women's Convention (CEDAW) is limited to eradication of violence against women, the African Women's Protocol is the first treaty to provide specifically for a range of women's rights, including disabled women. It also seeks to eradicate harmful African Cultural practices such as early and forced marriage, female genital mutilation, gender stereotype, denial of inheritance and property rights, harmful widowhood practices, and denial of reproductive rights. While the Protocol was established to protect women as a vulnerable group, it recognizes that within this group, disabled women are more vulnerable. Article 23 gives Special Protection of Women with Disabilities. It provides that State Parties undertake to ensure the protection of women with disabilities and take specific measures commensurate with their physical, economic and social needs to facilitate their access to employment, professional and vocational training as well as their participationin decision-making; and to ensure the right of women with disabilities to freedom from violence, including sexual abuse, discrimination based on disability and the right to be treated with dignity.

The plight of women with disabilities in Nigeria clearly indicates that The African Women's Protocol has failed to impact on them. It is

---

[222]   *Ibid*, Article 13(2) and (3).
[223]   ratified by Nigeria on 16/12/2005.

submitted that potential success of this protocol depends on the knowledge and awareness of its contents and the possibilities of its use in advocacy, law reform and litigation. So far the general level of awareness and patronage of this Protocol in Nigeria is quite low, as many simply regard it as a document that is full of western ideals that are completely alien to Africa.

4.2.4 *The African Youth Charter 2006*

The latest important regional instrument is The African Youth Charter (AYC), which was adopted in Banjul, the Gambia on the 2nd of July 2006. Upon the attainment of 15 ratifications, The Charter entered into force on 8 August 2009. So far, 36 African States including Nigeria have ratified it[224]. Although its jurisdiction is restricted to Africa, The AYC is commended for being the first international treaty on youth development. In its definitions section, the age for 'youth or young people' is placed within the ages of 15 and 35 years.

The AYC contains 31 provisions and places significant emphasis on the rights contained in the African Charter on Human and Peoples' Rights (ACHPR). It goes a step further in providing for the right to gainful employment[225], right to rest and leisure[226] and the right of youths with disabilities. Article 24 specifically deals with disabled youths and guarantees their right to proper medical care, economic security, rehabilitation, training, education, and sports, as well as the right to live (life to its fullest) anywhere, whether in one's country or anywhere in Africa, either with one's own family or foster parents. A duty is also placed on States to eliminate obstacles towards the integration of youths with disabilities[227]. Article 25 is equally relevant to youth with disabilities as it condemns societal norms, customs, traditions and culture that have overtime acted as a hindrance to the development of the African youth. Obviously, youths with disabilities are particularly vulnerable to such traditions.

---

[224] Nigeria ratified the AYC on 21/4/09.
[225] African Youth Charter, Article 15.
[226] *Ibid*, Article 22.
[227] *Ibid*, Article 24.

4.3 International Legal Framework for the Protection of Persons with Disabilities

Being an active member of the United Nations since 7th October 1960, Nigeria has remained committed to ensuring the effective realization of the guiding principles, common standards and obligations contained in the Universal Declaration of Human Rights. The rights and freedoms contained therein have been articulated in subsequent international instruments[228], many of which have been ratified by Nigeria. Thus, the international instruments that are relevant to the protection of the rights of PWDs in Nigeria are discussed as follows:

4.3.1 *The International Covenant on Civil and Political Rights (ICCPR)*

The ICCPR[229] seeks to uphold the first generation rights and imposes obligations on the states that are signatory to the covenant to respect such rights as the right to life, liberty, equality before the courts, peaceful assembly, family life, freedom of association, conscience, thought and religion. This instrument does not explicitly mention the situation of PWDs; however, it does not operate to exclude them either. To hold otherwise would undermine the whole human rights mission. Article 26, which guarantees equality and non-discrimination, is very relevant to PWDs. Thus it states that all persons are equal before the law and are entitled without any discrimination to the equal protection of the law. In this respect, the law shall prohibit any discrimination and guarantee to all persons equal and effective protection against discrimination on any grounds such as race, colour, sex, religion, political or other opinion, national or social origin, property, birth, or other status. This provision clearly prohibits discrimination on any grounds except in situations where a reasonable justification is established by a State. Out of the

---

[228] The UNDHR together with the ICCPR and the ICESCR constitute the International Bill of Human Rights.

[229] adopted on 16 December 1966, entered into force on 23 March 1976 (UN Treaty Series, vol. 999, p. 171 and vol. 1057, p. 40. It was ratified by Nigeria on 29 July, 1993.

specific rights that the ICCPR sets out to protect, a number are of significance to PWDs. They can be summarized as follows[230]:

a. The right not to be subjected to torture or to cruel, inhuman or degrading treatment or punishment[231];
b. Not to be subjected without free consent to medical or scientific experimentation[232];
c. Not to be subjected to arbitrary and unnecessary arrest and any other kind of institutional abuse[233];
d. The right not to be subjected to arbitrary or unlawful interference with privacy, family, home or correspondence, or to unlawful attacks on one's honour and reputation[234].

Furthermore, States must recognize the right of men and women of marriageable age to marry and to found a family[235]. Article 25 further provides that states must recognize the right of everyone to participate in public affairs directly or through freely chosen representatives. This includes the right to vote and to access public services. Accordingly, the right for a person with disability to serve on a jury was upheld in *Donald Galloway v. the Superior Court of the District of Colombia*[236]. Notwithstanding the domestication of the ICCPR, evidence suggests that the vast majority of PWDs in Nigeria are subject to multiple or aggravated forms of discrimination on a basis of disability. They do not enjoy rights and fundamental freedoms on equal footing with others. Their dignity is rarely respected and accessing important public services and opportunities remains a constant challenge.[237]

---

[230] Queen, G., 'The International Covenant on Civil and Political Rights and Disability: A Conceptual Framework.' In T. Degener and Y. Koster-Dreese (1995) (eds) *Human Rights and Disabled Persons: Essays and Relevant Human Rights Instruments. International Studies in Human Rights, Volume 40* (Dordrecht: Martinus Nijhoff,1995).
[231] Article 7.
[232] Article 7.
[233] Article 9.
[234] Article 17.
[235] Article 23.
[236] 1993 U.S. Dist. LEXIS3314, March 16, 1993.
[237] Smith, N., The Face of Disability in Nigeria: A Disability Survey In Kogi and Niger States (2011) *The Journal of Disability, CBR and Inclusive Development*, Vol 22, No.1, 35-46, 35.

4.3.2 *International Covenant on Economic, Social, and Cultural Rights*

The ICESCR[238] is fixed towards second-generation rights. This essentially imposes direct obligations on states to implement strategies and policies that would lead to the full realization of economic, social, and cultural rights of all persons. Contracting states are obliged to take steps to the maximum of their available resources, progressively to achieve the full realization of the rights recognized in the Covenant[239]. These include such issues as medical services, employment, social security, family protection, education, and enjoyment of common cultural heritage. The covenant expresses the expectation that:

> All such rights will be exercised without discrimination of any kind as to race, colour, sex, language, religion, political or other opinion, national or social origin, property, birth or other status[240]

The provisions of the ICESCR which are of significance to PWDs include the right to just and favourable conditions of work ensuring a decent living[241]; the right to the enjoyment of the highest attainable standard of physical and mental health[242]; the right to equal access to higher education on the basis of capacity, by every appropriate means[243]; and the right of everyone to take part in cultural life.[244]

Although the Covenant does not explicitly refer to "persons with disabilities", its provisions apply to all members of society, including those with disabilities. Again, Article 3 requires that all contracting states must ensure the equal rights of both men and women to enjoy the economic, social and cultural rights set out in the covenant. Thus, if the disabled citizens of a contracting state are prohibited from enjoying such rights, that state stands in breach of the covenant.[245]

---

[238]   Adopted 16 December 1966, and ratified by Nigeria on 29 July, 1993.
[239]   ICESCR Article 2(1).
[240]   *Ibid.*
[241]   ICESCR Article 7.
[242]   *Ibid*, Article 12.
[243]   *Ibid*, Article 13.
[244]   *Ibid*, Article 15.
[245]   Both the ICCPR and ICESCR require contracting states to submit periodic reports regarding the   implementation of the provisions of the covenants to the UN. The

There is no doubting the fact that, Nigeria is clearly in breach of this provision because PWDs continue to be socially isolated. They also suffer economic exclusion and denials. Despite their right to be provided with gainful employment like others, what is obtainable is the reverse as their rights are being denied because of their condition. Even when PWDs have better qualifications on the capacity to work, there is indeed little or no support available to make that capacity marketable. Apparently, many employers of labour or interviewing panels often introduce new rules like fitness, or other requirements, which automatically disqualifies PWDs from being gainfully employed. While others introduce the process of categorization whereby certain jobs are reserved for the disabled. Indeed, the employment scope of PWDs is severely limited. Unfortunately, the economic, social and cultural rights of the Nigerian people embodied in Chapter II of the Constitution have been made non-justiciable, and the courts have repeatedly endorsed the non-justiciability of socio-economic rights.

It is important to note that prior to the adoption of ICCPR and ICESCR, a single instrument containing the whole cluster of rights was envisioned. However, the drafters were divided and this influenced the wording of the two instruments. As a result, Article 2(1) of the ICCPR and Article 2 (1) of the CESCR[246] (which both specify the general obligations of State Parties in relation to each of the substantive rights protected therein) are formulated differently, to reflect the drafters' perception regarding the implementation of these two sets of rights due to their different nature. This dichotomy was brought about by the perception that civil and political rights are capable of immediate implementation by any state regardless of its economic strength, since they cost the state nothing. All that is required of the state here is to

---

ICCPR, reports to Human Rights Committee of the UN, while the ICESCR reports to the Committee On Economic, Social And Cultural Rights. The committees are made up of human rights experts who study the reports, and give the relevant advice to the UN Secretary general. While the ICCPR has an Optional Protocol that gives competence to the human rights committee to receive and consider complaints from any individual who is subject to a signatory state. It will then forward its findings to the complainant and to the state in question. However, there is currently no equivalent Optional Protocol allowing groups and individuals to petition the Committee directly with regard to alleged violations of the ICESCR.

[246] Both Articles are contained in Part II of each of the covenants, which provides for the general obligations applicable to all the rights contained in Part III of each Covenant (Articles 6-27 ICCPR, and Articles 6-15 CESCR).

abstain from interfering in those rights, and also to enact legislation and adopt administrative measures to achieve such non-interference.[247] Social and economic rights on the other hand require economic resources for their enforcement-and by implication, gradual implementation. Thus, CESCR require for States not only positive action, but also financial backing, which could depend on available resources and competing interests for their fulfillment.

It is argued that the dichotomized view of the two sets of rights has led to the mistaken beliefthat rights can be severed and enforced differently because some deserve much more obligation from the state. Thus, Article 26, which is an autonomous right in itself, prohibits discrimination of any kind; and although the ICCPR does not provide for the right to own property, if a State decides to enact laws which discriminates in favour of some people being able to own property while denying others the same right on the basis of physical disability, this would violate Article 26 0f the ICCPR. It is thus observed that the underlying ethics of autonomy and equality drive and unite both the civil and political rights tradition and the economic and social rights tradition. The socio economic rights claims can therefore be seen in civil rights terms, and the civil rights perspective is important, giving rise to credible economic claims and fortifying the same. Both set of rights therefore go hand in hand, and due to the historical disadvantage of PWDs, any dichotomy will only serve to hinder them from enjoying even the most basic rights and freedoms considering their history of marginalization. Thus it has been argued, and rightfully so, that States have a duty to provide when individuals or groups are unable, for reasons beyond their control, to realise themselves by the means at their disposal[248]. Accordingly, it is the duty of the Nigerian State to provide for PWDs since most of them live in abject poverty.

---

[247] See ICCPR Committee General Comment No. 35(80) Nature of general obligation imposed on States Parties to the Covenant: 25/05/2005, para 14, where the Committee states that the requirement under Article 2(2) to take steps to give effect to rights under the Covenant is unqualified and of immediate effect. A failure to comply with this obligation cannot be justified by reference to political, social, cultural, or economic considerations within the state.

[248] WouterVandenhole, Non Discrimination and Equality in the View of the UN Human Rights Treaty Bodies (2005) 237, Quoted in Dube A.

4.3.3   *United Nations Convention Against Torture and other Cruel, Inhuman, or Degrading Treatment or Punishment*

Disability often arises as a result of torture and other forms of cruel, inhuman, and degrading treatment or punishment. Again, the very fact of being disabled as such makes the person concerned particularly vulnerable to inhuman or degrading treatment. Nowak and Suntinger[249] discern that certain prison conditions, interrogation techniques deportation measures and similar restrictions of human rights, which are ordinarily permissible under domestic or international human rights law may amount to inhuman and degrading treatment if applied to a person with disability[250]. They cited the case of *M.N. V. France*[251], where the European Commission of Human Rights decided that the expulsion of an Algerian Citizen who had lived since his childhood in France constituted a violation of his right to personal integrity and respect for his family life under Article 3 and 8 of the European Convention of Human Rights (ECHR)[252].

The Convention Against Torture and other Cruel, Inhuman, or Degrading Treatment or Punishment[253] may be utilized to ensure that appropriate state action is taken for those who have become disabled as a result of inhuman treatment as well as to promote prevention of torture. Article 2 of this Convention states, "Each State Party shall take effective legislative, administrative, judicial or other measures to prevent acts of torture under its jurisdiction." Article 16 further addresses prevention even beyond what is considered to be torture: "Each State Party shall undertake to prevent in any territory under its jurisdiction other cruel, inhuman or degrading treatment or punishment which do not amount to torture."

The Special Rapporteur on torture and other cruel, inhuman or degrading treatment or punishment has also issued a report that

---

[249] Manfred Nowak and Walter Suntinger, 'The Right of Disabled Persons Not to Be Subjected to Torture, Inhuman and Degrading Punishment' in T. Degener and Y. Koster- Dreese (eds), *Human Rights and Disabled Persons: Essays and Relevant Human Rights Instruments* (Kluwer Academic Publishers, 1995) pp. 117-130.

[250] *Ibid, p. 118.*

[251] Report of the European Commission of Human Rights of March 10 1994 in the case of *M.N. v France*, Appl. No. 19465/92.

[252] *Ibid.*

[253] Nigeria ratified on 28/6/2001.

addresses persons with mental disability in institutions where he condemned the seclusion and involuntary treatment of persons with psychosocial disabilities in institutions. Although it is commendable to criticize such inhuman treatment, the challenge of implementing this convention lies in the perception, by many societies especially in Africa, that disability is not only a physical or mental impairment, but in fact a spiritual sickness or curse that could either be healed by prayer or by confinement, and in some cases by physical violence[254]. Thus as a result of their condition, PWDs in Nigeria remain vulnerable to torture, and other forms of cruel and degrading treatment including sexual abuse by heartless individuals, which oftentimes involve care givers.

4.3.4 *United Nations Convention on the Rights of the Child (CRC)*

It is important to note that the CRC[255] is the first treaty before the adoption of the CRPD to explicitly give reference to persons with disabilities. It is the first binding global human rights instrument to expressly prohibit discrimination on the basis of disability. The Convention on the Rights of the Child specifically and generally addresses the rights of children with disabilities. Article 2 of the Convention states that:

> State Parties shall respect and ensure the rights set forth in this present Convention without discrimination of any kind irrespective of the child's or his or her parent's race, colour, sex, language, religion, political or either opinion, national, ethnic or social origin, property, disability, birth or status.

Article 23, which is very specific, further obligates that the Optional Protocol to the Convention on the Rights of the Child on the involvement of children in armed conflict and on the sale of children,

---

[254] Sophie Morgan, 'The country where disabled people are beaten and chained'<http://www.bbc.com/news/blogs-ouch-33523742> accessed 13 April 2016.

[255] Convention on the Rights of the Child, adopted on 20 November 1989, entered into force on 2 September 1990 (UN Treaty Series, vol. 1577).

child prostitution and child pornography[256] is also relevant to children with disabilities.

The Committee on the Rights of the Child monitors the implementation of the CRC. In 2006, the Committee issued General Comment No. 9 on the Rights of Children with Disabilities. The Committee thus detailed recommended actions for state parties to fully take measures, which ensure that children with disabilities realise their rights at an equal level with their non-disabled counterparts.

The main weakness of the CRC is that it follows the medical model of disability; and its use of derogatory terminology like 'mentally disabled' or physically disabled children does not conform with the rights-based approach to disability.

4.3.5 *United Nations Convention on the Elimination of All Forms of Discrimination Against Women (CEDAW)*[257]

Research has shown that the effects of disablement are especially severe for women[258]. Women with disabilities face discrimination on grounds of gender and disability, and often they have less access to essential services such as health care, education and vocational rehabilitation.[259] General Recommendation 18 by the Committee on the Elimination of All Forms of Discrimination against Women specifically deals with the issue of women with disabilities[260]. The Committee makes reference to women with disabilities in the following general recommendation:

Women with disabilities are more likely to be illiterate and generally

---

[256]   Adopted by General Assembly resolution 54/263 of 26 June 2000; and ratified by Nigeria on 19/4/1991.

[257]   The Convention on the Elimination of All Forms of Discrimination against Women, opened for signature Dec. 18, 1979, 1249 U.N.T.S. 13 and entered into force Sept. 3,1981.

[258]   Women and Girls with Disabilities, UNITED NATIONS ENABLE,< http://www.un.org/disabilities/default.asp?id=1514> accessed 5/5/16.

[259]   Information on the subject of women with disabilities, <http://www.worldenable.net/women/> accessed 5/516.

[260]   General Recommendation No.18, 10th Session (1991), Committee on the Elimination of Discrimination   against Women, < http://www.un.org/womenwatch/daw/cedaw/recommendations.htm>accesed 5/5/16.

have very low rates of school attendance. Among many other factors, this also means that they are very unlikely to have information on reproductive health. While biological differences between women and men may lead to differences in health status, there are societal factors that are determinative of the health status of women and men and can vary among women themselves. For that reason, special attention should be given to the health needs and rights of women belonging to vulnerable and disadvantaged groups, such as migrant women, refugee and internally displaced women, the girl child and older women, women in prostitution, indigenous women and women with physical or mental disabilities[261].

The Optional Protocol to the Convention on the Elimination of All Forms of Discrimination against Women[262], which was adopted by the General Assembly in 1999, may also provide an important venue to specifically address the issues concerning women with disabilities. Furthermore, the CEDAW states that parties are obligated to combat stereotypes by eliminating "prejudices and customary and all other practices."[263]

It is doubtful, however, that the CEDAW provides meaningful protection to women with disabilities going by the general nature of the provisions therein. This is because the plight of women with disabilities is not simply the computation of the barriers faced by persons with disabilities and the barriers faced by women; it goes beyond to utter neglect. Women with disabilities experience gross violations of their human rights as victims of rape, forced sterilization and multiple discrimination due to being a woman and a person with disabilities. Their parenting abilities are frequently questioned and their children taken from them against their will. Their right to marry and found a family is often limited to the point of complete denial[264]. High rates of violence both at the hands of family members and care–givers prevail among women with disabilities. The dependence on caregivers, personal assistants and family members makes it generally difficult for persons with disabilities to seek redress for such violations. Discrimination

---

[261] CEDAW, General Recommendation 24, Article 12 of the Convention (women and health), paras 11.

[262] Adopted by General Assembly resolution 54/4 of 15 October 1999.

[263] CEDAW *Supra*, at Art. 5(a).

[264] This denial also extends to men with disabilities.

against women in the labour market is widely prevalent, hitting women with disabilities even harder and frequently making it impossible for them to earn a living. According to UN statistics only 25% of women with disabilities are part of the workforce; they are twice as unlikely to find a job as men with disabilities. These challenges are hardly surprising given the lack of attention given to the exclusion of women with disabilities.

It is suggested that in order to effectively protect the rights of women and girls with disabilities, what is required is a law that would give it the attention it deserves by making provisions for certain rights which could be considered specific to them (such as rights against institutionalization and forced sterilization). This is in addition to other general safe guarding provisions such as non-discrimination, raising awareness, and protection from exploitation, violence and abuse. The law will also have to consider the special healthcare requirements of disabled women and girls.

4.3.6 *United Nations Convention on the Rights of Persons With Disabilities and its Optional Protocol (CRPD)*

Nigeria is signatory to the CRPD and its accompanying Optional Protocol, and as such is under the obligation to promote, protect and ensure the full and equal enjoyment of all human rights and fundamental freedoms by all persons with disabilities, and to promote respect for their inherent dignity.[265]

The CRPD is the first human rights Convention of the 21st century and the first legally binding instrument with comprehensive protection of the rights of persons with disabilities. While the Convention does not establish new human rights, it does set out with much greater clarity the obligations on States to promote, protect and ensure the rights of PWDs. Thus, the CRPD not only clarifies that States should not discriminate against them, it also sets out the many steps that States must take to create an enabling environment for them to enjoy real equality in society. For example, the Convention requires States to take measures to ensure accessibility of the physical environment and information and communications technology. Similarly, States have obligations in relation to raising awareness, promoting access to justice, ensuring personal mobility, and collecting disaggregated data relevant to the

---

[265] Article 1(1) of the UN Convention on the Rights of Persons with Disabilities 2008.

Convention. In this way, it goes into much greater depth than other human rights treaties in setting out the steps that States should take to prohibit discrimination and achieve equality for all.

The Convention specifically provides for a general duty of non-discrimination[266] (accompanied by a carefully crafted and highly detailed definition or test for discrimination[267]), the right of equal access to public services[268], the right to dignity and freedom from degrading treatment[269] and the duty to promote the social and economic integration ofPWDs in society[270]. The Convention also introduces a duty for signatory States to raise awareness of and, ultimately, respect for PWDs within society. It provides:

> States Parties undertake to adopt immediate, effective and appropriate measures: (a) To raise awareness throughout society, including at the family level, regarding persons with disabilities, and to foster respect for the rights and dignity of persons with disabilities; (b) To combat stereotypes, prejudices and harmful practices relating to persons with disabilities, including those based on sex and age, in all areas of life; [and] (c) To promote awareness of the capabilities and contributions of persons with disabilities.[271]

The Convention is intended as a human rights instrument with an explicit, social development dimension; thereby containing Civil and Political Rights, as well as Economic, Social and cultural Rights in one document. It adopts a broad categorization of persons with disabilities and reaffirms that all persons with all types of disabilities must enjoy all human rights and fundamental freedoms. It clarifies and qualifies how all categories of rights apply to persons with disabilities and identifies areas where adaptations have to be made for persons with disabilities to effectively exercise their rights and areas where their rights have been violated, and where protection of rights must be reinforced.

The problem with the CRPD is its failure to make adequate clarifications to tackle Africa's specificities and realities such as the need

---

[266] *Ibid*, Article 3(b).
[267] *Ibid*, Article 2.
[268] *Ibid*, Article 3(e) and (f).
[269] *Ibid*, Articles 15, 16 and 17.
[270] *Ibid*, Article 3(c) and (d).
[271] *Ibid*, Article 8.

to protect parents, guardians and caregivers from discrimination on the basis of their relationship with PWDs; the need to protect PWDs from harmful practices; and the need for provisions against any presumption that PWDs cannot be trained or educated.Fortunatelythe UN Convention on the Rights of Persons with Disabilities was recently domesticated in Nigeria through a federal law[272] i.e, Discrimination Against Persons with Disabilities (Prohibition) Act, 2018. However, the provisions of the law have not been put to test as government is yet to advance any administrative infrastructure for its implementation.

4.3.7 *Other International Standards on Disabilities*

Having discussed the key international legal instruments, which are binding on signatory States, it is pertinent to discuss important non-binding normative pronouncements with regards to the protection of the rights of persons with disabilities and which serve as guidelines to states. They include The Declaration on Social Progress and Development, The World Programme of Action Concerning Disabled Persons[273], the Tallinn Guidelines for Action on Human Resources Development in the Field of Disability,[274] and The Standard Rules on the Equalization of Opportunities for Persons with Disabilities[275].

---

[272] Section 12 (1) of the 1999 Constitution provides that no treaty between the Federation and any other country shall have the force of law except to the extent to which any such treaty has been enacted into law by the National Assembly.

[273] Adopted by the General Assembly on 3 December 1982, by its resolution 37/52. The World Programme of Action (WPA) is a global strategy to enhance disability prevention, rehabilitation and equalization of opportunities, which pertains to full participation of persons with disabilities in social life and national development. The WPA also emphasizes the need to approach disability from a human rights perspective.

[274] Adopted by General Assembly resolution 44/70 of 15 March 1990. The Tallinn Guidelines prioritizes the development of the human resources ofPWDs, with specific reference to education, training, employment, science, and technology.

[275] Adopted by the United Nations General Assembly, forty-eighth session, resolution 48/96, of 20 December 1993. The Standard Rules represent a strong moral and political commitment of Governments to take action to attain equalization of opportunities for persons with disabilities. The rules serve as an instrument for policy-making and as a basis for technical and economic cooperation.

a. The Declaration on Social Progress and Development

Before 1970 the UN's approach to disability issues was mainly from a social welfare perspective. Little attention was paid to obstacles created by social institutions and society in general. The late 1960s became a time for re-evaluation. On December 11, 1969, the General Assembly adopted the Declaration on Social Progress and Development. This declaration proclaims in Article 11(C) the necessity of protecting the rights and assuring the welfare of children, the aged and the disabled, and the protection of the physically and mentally disadvantaged. Article 19 specifically advocates the provision of free health services and the institution of measures to provide social security and social welfare services for all persons. Those services include measures to rehabilitate the mentally and physically disabled to facilitate their integration into society. Provisions for education, job training and placement, and vocational and social guidance are also included.

b. World Programme of Action Concerning Disabled Persons (WPA)

In 1982, the United Nations adopted the World Programme of Action Concerning Disabled Persons[276]. The main aims of the WPA were to prevent exclusion and marginalisation of persons with disabilities. One of the goals of the WPA was the equalisation of opportunities for persons with disabilities. The WPA defined equalisation of opportunities as, '…the process through which the general system of society, such as the physical and cultural environment, housing and transportation, social and health services, educational and work opportunities, cultural and social life, including sports and recreational facilities, are made accessible to all.'[277]

This at least marked the beginning of a significant shift from a medical approach to disability to a focus on human rights and equality in general. As a follow-up to the WPA, the UN launched the Decade of Disabled Persons and it was set from 1983 to 1992. Thus the disability

---

[276] World Programme of Action Concerning Persons with Disabilities, adopted by UN General Assembly Resolution 37/52 on 3 December 1982 (UN Doc A/RES/37/52).

[277] ibid

agenda was eventually getting some momentum at least from the perspective of the United Nations.

c. Standard Rules on the Equalization of Opportunities for Persons with Disabilities (Standard Rules)

In 1993, the UN adopted the Standard Rules on the Equalization of Opportunities for Persons with Disabilities[278]. The Standard Rules were firmly built on the above-discussed WPA and clearly emphasised equality of opportunities for persons with disabilities. The main aim of the Standard Rules was therefore to achieve full and effective inclusion of persons with disabilities in all aspects of the society. Furthermore, the Standard Rules sought to ensure that persons with disabilities exercise that same rights and bear same obligations as their non-disabled counterparts[279].

The Standard Rules developed the work of the WPA in situating impairment as an incident of human diversity. Accordingly, states were urged to incorporate disability into policy and planning. Unlike the above-discussed Declarations, the Standard Rules made clear statements about the rights of persons with disabilities and the promotion of accessible environments. To that extent, the Standard Rules embraced a rights-based approach to disability.

Although international monitoring of disability rights was limited, the Standard Rules made provision for the appointment of the Special Rapporteur on Disabilities. The Special Rapporteur performs duties under the auspices of the UN Commission on Social Development (CSD). The Special Rapporteur may initiate surveys, report to the CSD, render advisory services to states on implementation and monitoring of the Standard Rules and assistance in preparation of replies to surveys, and to initiate direct dialogue with states and local non-governmental organisations in sharing their views for purposes of compilingreports to the CSD.

---

[278] Standard Rules on the Equalization of Opportunities for Persons with Disabilities, adopted by UN General Assembly Resolution 48/96 on 18 December 1992 (UN Doc A/RES/48/96).

[279] The rules are indicated as follows: *Rule 5. Accessibility; Rule 6. Education; Rule 7. Employment; Rule 8. Income maintenance and social security; Rule 9. Family life and personal integrity; Rule 10. Culture;Rule 11. Recreation and sports; and Rule 12. Religion.*

d. Millennium Development Goals (MDGs) and Sustainable Development Goals (SDGs)

The UN formulated the Millennium Development Goals in 2000, with the primary aim of halving global extreme poverty by 2015. It is well known that persons with disabilities have been classified to be among the 'poorest of the poor' especially in developing countries. As such, the MDGs are of importance in the present discussion[280]. It should be noted that persons with disabilities were not identified as a specific target group for action in the MDGs, however, this lapse was addressed under the Sustainable Development Goals (SDGs), which was developed to replace the MDGs at the conclusion of its achievement period in 2015. The SDGs are to address all three dimensions of sustainable development (environmental, economic and social) and be keyed into the United Nations global development agenda beyond 2015. The SDGs have a time horizon of 2015 to 2030.

Disability is referenced in various parts of the SDGs, particularly in parts related to education, growth and employment, inequality, accessibility of human settlements, as well as data collection and monitoring of the SDGs. For instance, Goal 4 on inclusive and equitable quality education and promotion of life-long learning opportunities for all; focuses on eliminating disparities in education and ensuring equal access to all levels of education and vocational training for the vulnerable, including persons with disabilities. In addition, the proposal calls for building and upgrading education facilities that are child, disability and gender sensitive and also provide safe, non-violent, inclusive and effective learning environments for all.

Goal 8 seeks to promote sustained, inclusive and sustainable economic growth, full and productive employment and decent work for all including persons with disabilities, and equal pay for work of equal value.Closely linked is Goal 10, which strives to reduce inequality within and among countries by empowering and promoting the social, economic and political inclusion of all, including persons with disabilities.

---

[280]The eight millennium development goals for eradicating poverty globally are: to eradicate extreme hunger and poverty, to improve maternal health, to combat HIV/AIDS, malaria and other diseases, to ensure envioronmental sustainability, and to develop a global partnership for development.

Goal 11 seeks to make cities and human settlements inclusive, safe and sustainable. To realize this goal, countries are expected to provide access to safe, affordable, accessible and sustainable transport systems for all by expanding public transport, with special attention to the needs of those in vulnerable situations, such as persons with disabilities.

Goal 17 stresses that in order to strengthen the means of implementation and revitalize the global partnership for sustainable development, the collection of data and monitoring and accountability of the SDGs are crucial. Therefore, States are expected to adapt measures that will significantly increase the availability of high-quality, timely and reliable data that is also disaggregated by disability.

4.4 Level of Compliance with the Laws Protecting Persons with Disabilities in Nigeria

Nigeria's legal obligations with respect to its disabled citizens can be summarised as follows: The duty to prevent discrimination and promote equal treatment; the duty to promote respect for the dignity of PWDs and raise awareness of their plight and their needs; the duty to protect them from cruel or degrading treatment or punishment; the duty to promote access to healthcare; the duty to promote access to education; the duty to promote access to employment opportunities, the duty to promote access to housing; the duty to promote access to transportation; the duty to promote access to social services; the duty to promote social integration including access to sport and recreation; the duty to promote access to telecommunications; the duty to promote access to voting and political processes; and, the duty to promote access to legal services for PWDs. This taxonomy has been derived from the various legal instruments already discussed in this book.

Yet despite Nigeria's commitment to International and domestic instruments as discussed, evidence suggests that the perception of disability continues to be highly problematic in the country. This is because within contemporary Nigerian society, there is little appreciation that disability is fundamentally an issue evidently linked to and rooted in human rights. The common perception, held by policy-makers and the public at large, is that disabled people and disability issues are viewed in terms of charity and welfare. As a matter of fact, many existing government policies and programmes are paternalistic and seem to legitimise segregation of persons with disabilities through specialised services and institutions. Thus, this viewpoint is a significant, entrenched factor that seriously militates against the social inclusion of disabled people within the country. This is manifested in a number of ways.

Firstly, despite many years of agitation, Nigeria never had a disability specific federal legislation until the 2018 Act was signed; and because this legislation is still new,the provisions are yet to be tested. Moreover, the few states that have passed disability laws have not put in place the necessary administrative mechanisms and funding for the smooth operation of the laws. Secondly, there is no form of social protection for PWDs in Nigeria, which exacerbates the level of poverty that they encounter. Thirdly, the Ministry of Women Affairs and Social Development (which is arguably the most underfunded in the country) has been the lead government department for disability issues in Nigeria. The ministry only provides services that are based on a charity/welfare approach to disability issues, with demand for such services far outstripping supply. Although there are some international NGOs that supply services to disabled people, their geographical coverage is very limited[281].

Consequently the vast majority of PWDs in Nigeria continue to live in poverty and are unable to access important public services and opportunities including education, healthcare and employment[282]. There is evidence that many of them remain socially and economically ostracized, due to the prevailing perception that PWDs require charity and welfare rather than human rights protection, *per se*[283]; there is also evidence that the Nigerian justice system routinely ignores their needs and has failed to respect the rights of mentally ill detainees to dignity and freedom from degrading treatment or punishment[284]; and there is also evidence that, contrary to the ethos of the African Charter on the Rights and Welfare of the Child 1990, disabled women and children continue to be abused at substantially higher rates than their non-disabled

---

[281] Lang and Upah, *Supra.*

[282] Smith, *Supra.*

[283] *Ibid.*

[284] Equal Rights Trust, Developing Resources and Civil Society Capacities for Preventing Torture and Cruel, Inhuman and Degrading Treatment of Persons with Disabilities (September 2012)<http://www.equalrightstrust.org/torture_indianigeri a/index.htm>accessed 11/05/2013.

counterparts[285].

Globally, the growing theme is that adequate legal protection must be given to persons with disabilities.[286] However, the present state of affairs shows that Nigeria is still far from achieving a decent level of protection of rights and living condition of PWDs in the country. This underperformance, however, does not amount to the complete absence of a legal framework, because we have seen that even before the 2018 Act, there were other subsisting domestic, regional, and international legislation and policies, which focus on the interests and rights of PWDs in Nigeria (although there seems to be no synchronization as many provisions of these legislations are clearly duplicated). The problem, however, rests on the fact that these subsisting laws are not being implemented and are therefore rendered ineffective. Consequently, the disabled continue to be marginalized, silenced, and invisible. They remain the least cared for in society, and are subjected to widespread discrimination and abuse.

Though the present Discrimination Against Persons with Disabilities (Prohibition) Act, 2018 is a commendable legislation that seems to offer comprehensive protection from discrimination, and project their rights, being a disability specific enactment, its potentials remain untested so far because its provisions are yet to be implemented. While it is generally believed that the Act will herald a fundamental change in the treatment of PWDs in Nigeria in line with the principles of CRPD, the body which is charged with the coordination of the Act (National Commission for Persons with Disabilities) is yet to be established at the time of publishing this book.

Going beyond laws, it is detected that the main obstacle in Nigeria for the effective protection of the rights of PWDs is the social psyche

---

285   *Ibid.*

286   The absence of an explicit, disability-related provision in earlier human rights instruments can be attributed to the lack of awareness of the importance of addressing this issue explicitly, rather than only by implication, at the time of the drafting of the Covenant over a quarter of a century ago. More recent international human rights instruments have, however, addressed the issue specifically. They include the Convention on the Rights of the Child (art. 23); the African Charter on Human and Peoples' Rights (art. 18 (4)); and the Additional Protocol to the American Convention on Human Rights in the Area of Economic, Social and Cultural Rights (art. 18). Thus it is now very widely accepted that the human rights of persons with disabilities must be protected and promoted through general, as well as specially designed, laws, policies and programmes.

that is present; therefore, any meaningful legislative protection must include safeguards that promote change in social attitudes, and thankfully, the 2018 Act has aptly captured this vital requirement.

CHAPTER FIVE

Institutional Framework for the Protection of Persons with Disabilities in Nigeria

Many countries have certain legal mechanisms within which disability policies are set and implemented. To realize this, institutional mechanisms are put in place to supervise the implementation of such laws. While it is the relevant state that creates and gives powers to these institutions, the establishment of the World Programme of Action concerning Disabled Persons (1982) and the subsequent adoption by the United Nations General Assembly of the Standard Rules (1993) are significant events that have shaped the development of disability policies and improved the human rights of Persons with Disabilities globally. Specifically, these two events set the outline for establishing national institutions. While in certain countries national disability institutions or mechanisms were established directly in relation to the adoption of the Standard Rules, in other countries that have no national disability mechanisms, legislative frameworks have played more significant roles for the institutional agendas. Nigeria belongs to the second group.

Again, a UN report has indicated that based on information from the twenty-six Member States reported under the World Programme of Action, the overall responsibility for national disability policies (including rights-based policies) mostly falls on government departments that deal with health, education, social affairs, welfare or related matters.[287] Thus the institutional framework for disability rights represents a complex system of coordination and implementation-agencies, and independent and semi-independent monitoring institutions.

Having established in the preceding part of this book that the absence of disability specific legislation does not mean that the rights and interest of PWDs are completely ignored under Nigerian laws, this

---

[287] "Implementation of the World Programme of Action concerning Disabled Persons: towards a society for all in the twenty-first century, Report of the Secretary-General," A/60/290.

chapter considers the institutional framework within which rights of persons with disabilities are addressed in Nigeria. It identifies the core institutions concerned with disability rights and discusses their establishment, mandate, and organizational structures. It further examines the activities of these institutions, and assesses the extent of their impact on the lives of PWDs in Nigeria. The role of Disabled Peoples Organizations is also considered.

5.1 The National Human Rights Commission

The National Human Rights Commission (NHRC) was established in September 1995[288] with the aim of promoting and protecting human rights, and also upholding Nigeria's human rights obligations[289]. Accordingly, the NHRC deals with all matters relating to the protection of human rights as guaranteed by the Nigerian Constitution, the African Charter on Human and Peoples Rights, United Nations Charter, the Universal Declaration of Human Rights and other International treaties on human rights to which Nigeria is a signatory.

Section 5 of the National Human Rights Commission (Amendment) Act 2010[290] expresses the mandate of the NHRC. Thus, the Commission is empowered to, inter alia, "deal with all matters" relating to the promotion and protection of human rights in Nigeria; "monitor and investigate all alleged cases of human rights violation" in Nigeria; "assist victims of human rights violations and seek appropriate redress and remedies on their behalf"; and "undertake studies on all matters pertaining to human rights and assist the Federal, State and Local Governments...in the formulation of appropriate policies on the guarantee of human rights." The Commission is further empowered to "receive and investigate complaints concerning violations of human rights and make appropriate determination as may be deemed necessary in each circumstance"; "examine any existing legislation, administrative provisions and proposed bills or bye-laws for the purpose of ascertaining whether such enactments or proposed bills or bye-laws are consistent

---

[288] by the NHRC Act Cap. N46 Vol.11 Laws of the Federation of Nigeria 2004.
[289] In line with the UN General Assembly which enjoins all member states to establish national human rights institutions for the promotion and protection of human rights.
[290] The 2010 amended Act enhances the status, independence, and mandate of the NHRC.

with human rights norms"; and, with leave of court, "intervene in any proceeding that involves human rights issue[s]." In a radical departure from the limited status and mandate of the Commission at its inception, the 2010 amendment introduces a new Section 22 pursuant to which"an award or recommendation made by the Commission shall be recognized as binding and... shall, upon application in writing to... [a High Court], be enforced by the Court." Thus, the Commission serves as an extra-judicial mechanism for the enhancement of the enjoyment of human rights. For instance, the Commission awarded N10 million against Federal Government as compensation to each family of the eight victims of September 20, 2013 killing in Apo, Abuja[291].

From the foregoing, it is clear that the mandate of the NHRC extends to the protection of the rights of every Nigerian, including those with disabilities. Thus, in line with the Commission's mandate to assist all victims of human rights violation, offices were assigned within the Commission for a special rapporteur as well as a program officer on persons with disabilities in order to integrate disability issues into the National Human Rights Commission's work and to have a desk responsible for disability concerns. Through this desk, complaints brought to the Commission on infringement on the rights of a PWD are admitted, investigated, and necessary actions are taken by the Commission to tackle and redress the said violations.

Also, the Commission has addressed issues relating to the rights of persons with disabilities in Nigeria in several ways. For example, the Commission recently conducted a survey of support facilities in tertiary institutions aimed at assisting persons with disabilities to enjoy inclusive education. From the survey, it was found that few tertiary institutions in Nigeria have basic facilities like ramps, lifts with sound and brailed floor numbering to assist persons with disabilities. The Commission also organizes regular workshops and advocacy visits with the aim of getting institutions to improve access to persons with disabilities. Other activities that promote the rights and welfare of PWDs include training of PWDs on human rights issues, general advocacy on the rights of PWDs, and advising the government on disability issues. Hence the NHRC played a prominent role in pushing for the signing and ratification of the

---

[291] P.M News <http://www.pmnewsnigeria.com/2014/04/07/federal-government-to-pay-families-of-apo-killing-n10m-each>accessed 4/1/17.

Convention on the Rights of Persons with Disabilities, and its recent domestication in Nigeria which gave rise to the 2018 Act.

Despite the modest achievements highlighted above, it is our view that the NHRC has not fully lived up to expectations in the promotion and protection of the rights of PWDs due to a number of significant problems and challenges, including poor funding, and accessibility[292]. For instance, there is no effective mechanism within the commission to assess the impact of their interventions in the area of disability[293]. Furthermore, it has been reported that the state offices are not in good shape both in terms of infrastructure and funding[294], with the state offices receiving about N100,000 per month to fund electricity, water, Internet, research, monitoring and investigation of complaints among others[295]. Thus, the Commission as it presently stands cannot effectively carry out its mandate to the extent of protecting the rights of PWDs because this would involve additional costs in terms of making the offices of the Commission structurally accessible to PWDs and providing information on the activities of the Commission and documentation of complaints in an accessible form for PWDs such as Braille and sign language. It would also require engaging the services of professionals such as psychiatrists, sign language interpreters, etc.

It is therefore recommended that to enable the Commission to effectively discharge its enhanced mandate,[296] it must be adequately funded to ensure that the State Offices which are closest to the rural areas are well positioned to meet the needs of PWDs as much as possible. Furthermore, the Commission will be more effective in promoting the rights of PWDs if it recruits more professionals that are

---

[292] David Aduge-Ani, 'Human Rights: Before PMB Considers Stakeholders; Position on NHRC, Others' Leadership Newspaper of April 16, 2016 <Leadership.ng> accessed 4/1/17.
[293] Lang and Upah, *Supra.*
[294] *Ibid.*
[295] *Ibid.*
[296] The National Human Rights Commission (NHRC) Amendment Act 2010 amongst other things empowers the commission to compel to investigate human rights violations, register her decisions with the high court as equivalent to decisions of the high court and enforceable as such, get her finances as a first line charge on government finances, independent in its operations and not subject to the directives of any authority or person, secured tenure of members who cannot be removed before the end of their tenure without an act of misconduct which removal shall be concurred by the senate.

trained in the areas of disability-related disciplines. Inaddition to that, the Commission should also make it a policy to employqualified PWDs into its workforce both at junior and senior levels, as the social model of disability encourages the involvement of PWDs in the development and implementation of disability policies and practice. Thus the clarion call for the disability movement globally remains, "Nothing about us without us."[297]

5.2 The Public Complaints Commission

The Public Complaints Commission of Nigeria (PCC), which is also the Nigerian Ombudsman, was established[298] to redress administrative injustices for the purpose of improving good governance.

The PCC is established on values of human dignity and justice, and is dedicated to the fair and equitable treatment of every individual in society. It equalizes the balance of power between the government and citizens, by offering an avenue to lay complaints, and hopefully rectify a failure on the part of the government to fulfil their obligations. Hence it provides an opportunity for Nigerians, particularly the less privileged, to seek and obtain redress for their grievances at no cost and with minimum delay. In situations of administrative lapses, the Ombudsman is seen as a watchdog against injustice by ensuring that bureaucrats treat employees fairly, respectfully and promptly. For this purpose, the Commission is given authority to question government officials and other persons and to inspect documents.

Accordingly, the powers and duties of the commission are set out under Section 5to cover all types of administrative lapses, whether by government or private institutions or their agents. Thus it provides that:

---

[297] James Charlton, Nothing About Us Without Us: Disability Empowerment and Oppression (University of California Press, 2000)- This statement, *Nothing About Us Without Us* expresses the conviction of people with disabilities that they know what is best for them. It comes originally from the Disability Rights Movement. Founded by people and communities who were defined by the medical establishment as physically and/or mentally 'handicapped,' this movement rejects the idea that there are normal kinds of bodies, and that all others fall into the category 'handicapped.'

[298] Under Decree No. 31 of 1975, now Cap. 377 Laws of the Federal Republic of Nigeria 1990

A Commissioner shall have power to investigate either on his own initiative or following complaints lodged before him by any other person, any administrative action taken by-

a. any Department or Ministry of the Federal or any State Government;
b. any Department of any local government authority (howsoever designated) set up in any State in the Federation;
c. any statutory corporation or public institution set up by any Government in Nigeria;
d. any company incorporated under or pursuant to the Companies and Allied Matters Act whether owned by any Government aforesaid or by private individuals in Nigeria or otherwise howsoever; or
e. any officer or servant of any of the aforementioned bodies.

Section 5 (7) of the Public Complaints Commission Act requires that when any letter is written to any respondent, the respondent has 30 days to respond. Furthermore, Section 8(2) of the Act criminalizes failure to respond, and makes it punishable with either a fine of N500 or imprisonment, or both[299].

If there is evidence of what might broadly be called maladministration the Commission will make recommendations for remedial action. If its recommendations are not accepted, or other appropriate remedial action not taken, the Commission can inform the Head of State through appropriate report[300].

Although the PCC does not specifically mention persons with disabilities, its mandate is wide enough to cover and address the complaints of any citizen concerning any injustice stemming from administrative lapses. Hence, the PCC provides an avenue for complaints to be made by and on behalf of PWDs on any matter of discrimination or denial by public authorities (such as hospitals, schools, police, civil service, etc.) in matters of service delivery, recruitment, promotion, benefits, that PWDs are entitled to. The PCC, in turn, can recommend appropriate action to be taken by the offending body in line with Section 5 of the Public Complaints Act.

Despite the provisions of the Act, it is observed from the foregoing that a major drawback to the effective functioning of the PCC is that it

---

[299] Johnson Agbakworu, 'Public Complaints Act Breach: Two Heads of Government Agencies, Three Others for Prosecution', *The Vanguard* of 10/11/13 < vanguardngr.com>accessed 10/11/16.
[300] *Ibid.*

lacks statutory powers to sanction any respondent who refuses to accept their recommendations. In such situation, the PCC can only inform the Head of State through a report- one can only wonder:what if the Head of State, or his direct agents are the respondents? Another challenge is that the PCC is grossly underfunded, and this has led to a dearth of supplies and manpower to adequately cope with the task of the Commission[301]. For instance, it was revealed by the Joint Workers Union of the Public Complaints Commission, which recently embarked on a protest against the 50% slash in their salaries since January 2016, that only N2 billion was approved for PCC in the 2016 budget and this represents 50 per cent of what is needed to run the commission[302].

We have also noted that the PCC is by no means living up to its mandate of promoting social justice for citizens as disability has not been mainstreamed into the activities of the PCC. For instance, there is poor publicity network of the activities of the Commission in rural areas, which is where a majority of PWDs live[303]. Again, most offices of the Commission are structurally inaccessible to PWDs while the information on the activities of the Commission and documentation of complaints are also not accessible for PWDs. There are also no professionals such as psychiatrists or sign language interpreters that will attend to the needs of disabled complainants.

Furthermore, there seems to be an issue of duplicity of functions with the Human Rights Commission; hence, even the enlightened PWDs often get confused as to whether to lodge a complaint before the Human Rights Commission or the Public Complaints Commission. This is not surprising as the White Paper Committee set up by the Federal Government on the restructuring of its Parastatals, Commissions and Agencies directed that the PCC be merged with the Human Rights Commission, which they reasoned has the capacity to perform the functions of the PCC[304]. Thankfully, this White Paper was never implemented. Although a traditional way of distinguishing between the ombudsman and the Human Rights Commission has been to point out

---

[301] See *Punch News* of 11/10/16, 'Public Complaints Commission Workers Protest Slash in Salaries':<pnchng.com>accessed 10/11/16.

[302] *Ibid.*

[303] *Ibid.*

[304] Wale Oloye, 'Wages Commission, Others to be merged, scrapped', *Eagle Newspaper* of 1/7/13, <theeagleonline.com.ng>accessed 1/6/17.

that, in most cases, the primary function of the Ombudsman is to ensure fairness and legality in public administration. Human Rights Commissions are, or have been, more specifically concerned with all forms of human rights abuses or infringements and in this respect will often address the actions of private bodies and individuals as well as the Government. With due respect, we are of the view that such a simplistic approach in distinction would grossly undermine the interest of PWDs. This is because oftentimes, the denial or violation of the rights of PWDs in Nigeria is a result of the failure of public institutions or personnel to recognize and accommodate them on equal basis with others. For example, even the most basic public institutions such as buildings, markets, hospitals, schools, and courts are physically inaccessible to them. Hence, in order to effectively protect the rights of PWDs, it is best to combine the traditional function of the PCC as defender of citizens against administrative abuses with the role of human rights monitoring, creating a kind of hybrid model.[305] Thus, instead of calling for a merger between the PCC and HRC, more budgetary allocations should be given to both institutions in order enable them to carry out their mandates effectively.

The PCC also has the role of improving public administration in general and should therefore do more in the area of pointing out weaknesses observed in procedures, practices, rules and regulations and standard behaviour of officials especially as it relates to attitudinal barriers against PWDs within the public service whether as applicants, employees or clients.

5.3 The Legal Aid Council of Nigeria

The Legal Aid Council of Nigeria was established pursuant to the promulgation of the Legal Aid Decree No. 56 of 1976 to render legal aid and access to justice to indigent persons as widely as possible within its financial resources. The decree was amended by Cap 205, 1990 Laws of the Federation which later became the Legal Aid Act Cap. L 9 Laws of the Federation of Nigeria, 2004. All the above-mentioned laws have been repealed by the 2011 Legal Aid Act[306], which is designed to provide a

---

[305] Sanstitevan, J, *'The Ombudsman Institutions and Accountability in Societies of Transitions'*,The Helen Kellog Institute for International Studies, Notre Dame University, 2003.

[306] Act 17 of 2011.

good welfare system for poor people to be able to access justice through the Legal Aid Council. For instance, it provides for the establishment of a legal aid and access to justice fund. Through the fund, financial assistance is made available to the Legal Aid Council on behalf of indigent citizens for the prosecution of claims in accordance with the Constitution. The Act empowers the Legal Aid Council with responsibility for the operation of a scheme for the grant of legal aid and access to justice in certain matters or proceedings to persons with inadequate resources. Thus, Section 8 (1) of the Legal Aid Act, 2011 mandates that, "The grant of legal aid, advice and access to justice shall be provided by the Council in three broad areas, namely Criminal Defence Services, Advice and Assistance in Civil Matters including legal representation in court and Community Legal Services subject to merits and indigence testsfor the parties."

Presently operating as an agency under the Federal Ministry of Justice, The Legal Aid Council provides free legal aid services to disadvantaged Nigerians, whose income does not exceed the minimum wage or those who cannot afford the services of private legal practitioners. The Council offers free legal advice and representation through its in-house counsels and also coordinates the activities of other lawyers who provide *pro bono* services in all criminal cases, as well as civil claims in respect of accident cases and claims for damages for breach of human rights. As part of its mandate, officials of the Council also visit prisons to monitor the condition of detainees.

The beneficiaries of legal aid include PWDs because they are the poorest, most marginalized, and socially excluded group in society[307]. They are more likely to be unemployed, illiterate, to have less formal education, and to have less access to developed support networks and social capital than others[308].

There is no doubt that there are concerted efforts by the Legal Aid Council to live up to its mandate of providing legal advice and representation for the poor. However, these efforts are not yielding enough benefits for PWDs. A few years ago, in a detailed and scathing 50-page report, Amnesty International revealed how at least 65 percent

---

[307] DFID Report, 2005; Disability and Inclusive Development, Barron &Amerena ed., (London: Leonard Cheshire International, 2007).
[308] *Ibid.*

of Nigeria's inmates have never been convicted of any crime, with some awaiting trial for up to ten years; how most in Nigerian prisons are too poor to afford a lawyer, with only one in seven awaiting trial having access to private legal representation -with only 91 legal aid lawyers working in the country; and how appalling prison conditions, including severe overcrowding, are seriously damaging the mental and physical health of thousands. Amnesty International also revealed how, all too often, people not suspected of committing any crime are imprisoned along with convicted criminals. Of particular interest is the case of those suffering from mental illness that are brought to prison by families unable or unwilling to take care of them. Most have no lawyer to advocate on their behalf[309].

In one such case, Bassy, a 35-year-old woman with mental illness, was brought to prison by her brother, who said the family could no longer cope with her. Prison authorities classified Bassy as a "civil lunatic." Accused of no crime and never brought before a judge, Bassy spent almost three years in prison, sleeping on the floor in a cell with 11 women. After the intervention of PRAWA, a Nigerian non-governmental organization dealing with the incarceration of mentally ill prisoners, Bassy was finally transferred to a hospital, where she received treatment[310].

The major problem with legal aid in Nigeria is lack of proper funding[311]. Hence, its inability to retain the services of dedicated legal personnel, and other professionals such as interpreters and psychiatrists that can cater for the needs of PWDs in particular. So, for most indigent and vulnerable Nigerians, especially those with disabilities, access to justice remains a myth rather than a reality.

Thus, there has rightfully been a call for review of the 2011 Act to address these challenges[312]. Furthermore, we propose that the Nigerian Bar Association should do more to encourage the culture of legal aid among its members, and also mainstream disability intoits agenda and activities.

---

[309] Nigeria: Prisoners' Rights Systematically Flouted, AFR 44/001/2008 Amnesty International February
2008<amnesty international.org> accessed 5/1/17.
[310] *Ibid.*
[311] Dele Alabi, 'Legal Aid Council Grapples With Challenges of Logistics, Poor Funding' <legalaidcouncil.gov.ng>accessed 15/11/16.
[312] *Ibid.*

5.4 The Legislature

The legislature is the representative of the people elected by the people from all areas of the country. Section 4(1) of the Constitution provides that the primary function of the legislation is to make laws for the peace, order and good government of the country. However, in doing this, the security and welfare of the people shall be the primary focus[313].

In addition to law making, the legislative arm of government has oversight functions over public institutions[314]. The purpose of oversight functions is to ensure that acts of the national assembly are well implemented. This is due to the fact that Constitution recognizes the legislature as the custodians of the revenue of the federation, which is tied to the responsibility to approve the budget of the federation[315]. Therefore, as custodians of revenue, it is inherent on them to ensure that the all budgetary allocations are properly utilized. Another example of oversight of the executive by the legislature is the confirmation of the appointment of ministers and other officials of the federation. This is contained under S.147(2) CFRN 1999.

The legislative initiatives that concern the rights and welfare of PWDs are concomitant to the activities of the Senate and House of Representatives (at the Federal level); and the various state houses of assembly committees on human rights, judiciary and legal matters. These committees are conferred with the oversight function of all legal and judicial institutions and their supervisory ministries in order to safeguard the effective promotion and protection of human rights in the country[316]. Thus, this oversight function covers the activities of the police, courts, prisons, ministry of justice, legal aid council, human rights commission,

---

[313] S.14(2)(b) CFRN 1999.

[314] *Ibid*, S.62.

[315] *Ibid*, S. 80 -8.

[316] Some of the legislations passed, or are in the process of being passed by the Assembly include: (a) National Action Plan on Human Rights, (b) Domestication of the International Convention on the Rights of the Child into the Child Rights Act, (c) The Freedom of Information Bill, (d) Anti-discrimination Bill, (e) Prison Reform Bill, (f) Administration of Justice Reform Bill, and (g) Debate on the Death Penalty.

public complaints commission, etc.[317] The Committee promotes human rights legislations by conducting public hearing on issues that pertain to human rights, and adopting appropriate legislation for the promotion and protection of human rights in Nigeria. Accordingly, some of its engagements include: parliamentary working group on justice sector reform, protecting the right of women and children, monitoring Nigeria's ratification of international human rights instruments, monitoring economic and social rights, and quarterly publication on the activities of the work of the committee/parliamentary report on the state of human rights in Nigeria.

Presently, several states in Nigeria have enacted laws on disability[318]. Also, at the federal level, legislators having acknowledged that the plight of PWDs in Nigeria is further aggravated by the lack of comprehensive legislation to ensure their full social integration into society,have enacted the Disabilities Against Persons (Prohibition) Act, 2018 which seems to provide comprehensive care for PWDs in the country. The initial attempt was made by the Assembly during the administration of the Former President OlusegunObasanjo to this effect.[319] Unfortunately, the bill never received the assent of the former president required to make it a law. Again, the 6th and 7th National Assembly passed the Bill and sent it for mandatory assent; however, former President Goodluck Jonathan also failed to sign it into law. However, in its efforts to ensure that the rights of PWDs are protected and also recognized and enjoyed, the 8th Senate reintroduced and once again passed the Disability Bill in June 2016, which was finally assented to by President Muhammadu Buhari in 2018.

The Act provides for the social protection of persons with disabilities against any discrimination that they may suffer from and also to establish a national commission for persons with disabilities, that will be responsible for their education, healthcare, social, economic, and civil rights as both under the directive principles of State Policy and

---

[317] Affiliations of the Committee on Human Rights include the national working group on prison decongestion; parliamentary working group on justice sector reform; commonwealth human rights forum, etc.

[318] Examples are Lagos, Plateau, Ogun, and Bauchi States.

[319] That bill was titled: "A Bill to Ensure Full Integration of Persons with Disabilities into the Society and to Establish a National Commission for Persons with Disabilities and Vest it with the Responsibilities for their Education, Healthcare, Social, Economic and Civil Rights (Establishment, etc)"

Fundamental Rights in the Constitution.[320]

Another commendable initiative by the Nigerian legislature, both at the federal and state levels to address the plight of PWDs, is that they have mainstreamed the issue of disability and have passed progressive legislation which, though not disability specific, recognizes and holds out many prospects for the protection of PWDs. Examples of such legislation include The Child's Right Act (2003), the UBE Act (2004), and the Employees Compensations (all of which have been exhaustively discussed in preceding chapters of this book).

Unfortunately, it is very evident that these subsisting laws are not being properly implemented and are therefore ineffective. As a result of this, the disabled continue to be marginalized, silenced, and invisible. Thus, although the Constitution provides that the security and welfare of the people shall be the primary purpose of government[321], PWDs remain the least cared for in society, and are subjected to widespread discrimination from their families and the Nigerian society in general, elicited by the prevailing perception that they require charity and welfare rather than human rights protection *per se*[322].

Hitherto disability is seen by policymakers as a specialist field that requires significant public expenditure, which is hard to justify in the light of other competing social and economic development challenges[323]. Thus, even in the states that have successfully enacted legislation on disability, there are insufficient financial resources to ensure its effective implementation[324]. There is also the underlying assumption held by government that disability is a "charity issue" and not an issue of human rights. This assumption is a major obstacle in promoting the Human Rights-based agenda in promoting disability issues in Nigeria.

Regardless ofthe challenges noted above, it is our view that as

---

[320] Sani Onogu, 'Disability Bill: A legislation as a phoenix', *Vanguard News* of 16/8/16, <http://www.vanguardngr.com/2016/08/disability-bill-legislation> accessed 5/1/17.

[321] Section 14(2)(b) CFRN 1999.

[322] Lang and Upah*Supra*, p.6.

[323] Raymond Lang, 'The Challenges of Implementing the UN Convention o the Rights of Persons With Disabilities in Developing Countries', Manchester Metropolitan University Annual Conference, 7th July 2011.

[324] Examples are Plateau, Lagos, Bauchi and Ogun States: Statistics gathered from questionnaire for the preparation on the analytical study on violence against women and girls with disabilities (A/HRC/RES/17/11).

---

representatives of the people including PWDs, it is the legislature that should be at the forefront of raising the political profile of disability issues in Nigeria; andhaving successfully enacted a federal disability law, the legislature should also ensure its full implementation by the executive. We therefore suggest that a starting point would be for the legislature to utilize its oversight powers by ensuring that adequate budgetary allocation is given to all the institutions involved in social services to enable them carry out their respective mandates to the maximum level in order to positively impact on the lives ofPWDsand other vulnerable persons in Nigeria. The legislature can also use its oversight powers to guarantee that only well qualified professionals are recommended to head these institutions. Furthermore, there should be a legal provision that mandates representatives of persons with disabilities to participate in policy making and to work with government institutions at every level.

Finally, The Nigerian Constitution needs to be amended to include disability rights specifically, and these rights should be made justiciable.

5.5 The Judiciary

Section 6 of the Nigerian Constitution 1999 provides that the judicial powers of the Federation shall be vested in the courts to which this section relates, being courts established for the Federation[325]. As a consequence of Section 6, it has been held that judicial power is the power of a court to decide and pronounce judgement and carry it into effect between persons before it. The responsibilities captured here are enormous as it involves the resolution of disputes embracing social and moral questions of profound importance to society.

The role of the judiciary is to interpret laws made by the legislature, although sometimes in exercising their powers, the courts can expand the

---

[325] These courts are: The Supreme Court of Nigeria, The Court of Appeal, The Federal High Court, The National Industrial Court, The High Court of the FCT Abuja, The High Court of the States, The Customary Court of Appeal of the FCT, The Shariah Court of Appeal of the FCT, The Customary Court of Appeal of the States, The Shariah Court of Appeal of the States; such other courts as may be authorised by law to exercise jurisdiction on matters with respect to which the National Assembly may make laws; and such other courts as may be authorised by law to exercise jurisdiction at first instance or on appeal on matters with respect to which a House of Assembly may make laws.

scope and applicability of laws and such pronouncements particularly of the superior courts are considered as binding. Thus, considering that there is no comprehensive legislation on disability, the courts have a very important role to play in developing disability rights in Nigeria by expanding the provisions of existing legislation to accommodate the rights of PWDs. It is observed however that not much litigation is going on to challenge violations of the rights of PWDs and the few cases are mainly cases that have to do with termination of employment. The following cases are illustrative:

> In *Obere v. The Board of Management Eku Baptist Hospital*[326], the plaintiff was employed as a boiler and steam operator of the defendant company. In that capacity, he was obliged to operate a defective machine which the defendant failed to repair despite several complaints by the plaintiff. The said defective machine eventually chopped off the plaintiff's right thumb, thereby causing substantial and long term damage. For three years, after the injury, the plaintiff continued in the employ of the defendant. He brought this action when his employment was terminated claiming special damages for the disability suffered. The learned trial judge awarded only nominal damages holding that the plaintiff had waived any rights to special damages as he brought the claim only because he had lost his job. The court failed to take into consideration his diminished capacity to work as well as his inability to get another job as he would be considered partially disabled by prospective employers. The Supreme Court, based on these facts, increased the amount of damages awarded to the plaintiff.

Again, in *R. Iyere v. Bendel Feed and Flour Mill Limited*[327], the appellant, the plaintiff in the High Court, was employed by the respondent's mill at Ewu. The servant of the respondent sent the plaintiff to clear the blockings in the plant and, without notifying the appellant he sent to clear the fault, the servant switched on the plant. The appellant was injured in the process and his right hand was fractured and twisted. His permanent disability was assessed at 60%. He sued, claiming the sum of five million naira for special and general damages. The learned trial judge dismissed the claim mainly on the grounds that the appellant did not join the duty operator, an employee of the company, who was responsible for

---

[326] (1978) 6-7 SC REPRINT 12.
[327] (2008) 7-12 S.C. 151.

the injury. The Court of Appeal affirmed the decision. On further appeal to the Supreme Court, it was held that failure of the appellant to join the operator as a defendant in the action against his master was not fatal to the claim. The court was in favour of granting a fair compensation to the appellant to reduce the rigor of life for him and in order not to render him destitute.

It is observed that the court's demonstration of sympathy and its final awards to the plaintiffs in both cases above indicates a charity or welfare approach to disability, and in the absence of a clear law to specifically uphold their rights, plaintiffs in both cases were left only to claim for damages. We are therefore in no doubt that a disability specific legislature would have best protected them, as the issue would then not be left at the sole discretion of the court, but the disability legislation would mandatorily prescribe what plaintiffs in these kind of cases would be entitled to.

In a contrasting development, one Jane Ottah, a 28-year-old disabled student, sued the management of the Rivers State University of Science and Technology for damages along with other benefits such as provision of necessary support facilities to aid her learning process, and a perpetual injunction restraining the university or their agents from discriminating against her in any way[328]. She had been admitted on merit into the University in 2015, however, due to her challenge with speech and hearing she was deregistered and handed a letter to the effect that the school was not equipped to train her.The case was eventually settled out of court in her favour.[329]This case is being celebrated as a channel that has set a standard of best-practices for addressing the equal access needs of disabled graduate students in Nigerian universities. However, only a disability specific legislation would produce the best outcome for the plaintiff in this case.

Correspondingly, the Federal High Court Lagos Division reaffirmed the fundamental rights of persons with disabilities on 29 March 2018, in the momentous case of Daniel *v. President Federal Republic of Nigeria and National Assembly*[330]. The applicant Mr. Daniel Onwe, who is also

---

[328] *Jane Ihuoma Ottah v. Rivers State University of Science and Technology and The Vice Chancellor, Rivers State University of Science and Technology* (Suit No: PHC/1746/2015).

[329]Disabled student wins court case against Rivers state university Read more: <www.legit.ng>accessed 27/5/2020.

[330] Suit No: FHC/L/CS/188/17.

President of the Association of Lawyers With Disabilities, brought an application for the enforcement of his fundamental rights pursuant to provisions of the Nigerian Constitution; Fundamental Human Rights (Enforcement Procedure Rules) 2009; and the African Charter on Human and Peoples Rights. The court found in favor of the applicant, and declared that the absence of a federal law for protection of PWDs was a violation of their fundamental human rights. The court further declared that inaccessibility of public buildings and non-use of sign language and braille in government public functions violated the rights to freedom of expression and right to dignity of PWDs.

In another case pending before the Rivers State High Court[331], Mr. Gaius Ogan, a disabled lawyer, sued the Rivers State government over the inaccessibility of court rooms in the state for lawyers with disabilities. Relying on the provisions of the Constitution and the African Charter on Human and Peoples' Rights (Ratification and Enforcement) Act, he argued that court rooms were public buildings and their inaccessibility to disabled lawyers posed a threat to their livelihood and that their freedom of movement and right to be treated with dignity, right to equal access to public properties and services, amongst others, had all been infringed. He is therefore seeking an order from the court that the respondents, jointly and severally, pay him N70 million as general damages for loss of income and opportunities, and negligence to the plight of persons living with disabilities. He is also seeking an order of court for an additional N5 million as exemplary damages from the respondents. In addition, he is also seeking, "An order directing the respondents to install, where necessary, functional lifts in all courts in the states and to ensure that the state courts have no architectural barriers to inhibit the applicant's right of ingress and egress in these courts to earn his livelihood or do anything in pursuance of his social and economic development," and "An order that the respondents place the applicant on an employment that is sedentary while they remove the architectural barriers complained of." In addition to adopting the reliefs, theplaintiff prayed the court to, if the respondents are unable to offer him employment, award him N10 million to enable him establish a medium scale business as an alternative source of livelihood.

Although this stimulating case is still pending before the court, it will

---

[331]*Gaius Ogan v. Government of Rivers State and 7 Ors* (Suit No: PHC/361/2016).

be interesting to see if and to what extent the court will grant Mr.Ogan's prayers now that a disability specific legislation is in place in Nigeria, notwithstanding that processes andprocedures are also not available in versions such as Braille, which PWDs can access. Furthermore, the courts do not employ professionals such as psychiatrists or sign language interpreters that attend to the needs of disabled complainants.

It is observed that there is a dearth of litigation in the area of challenging violations of the rights of PWDs in Nigeria. However, it is also noted from the few cases discussed abovethat the courts, based on prevailing attitudes and orientation,[332] have demonstrated their willingness to strike down practices that undermine the full enjoyment of human rights, even in the absence ofa federal disability legislation. Now that such legislation is in place, the coast appears clear.A proactive judge can utilize relevant provisions in the Disabilities legislation, Nigerian Constitution, the African Charter, and other laws where possible to safeguard the rights of PWDs.

We therefore recommend that disability should be mainstreamed into the policy and activities of the judiciary and steps should be taken to enable PWDs access the justice system by removing all communication and physical barriers. Courts should also include, in their workforce, sign language interpreters and other professionals that are trained to cater for the needs of PWD. Furthermore, the judiciary should organize sensitization programmes in the area of disability for Judges and their support staff.

5.6 Law Enforcement Agencies

Nigeria as a nation is founded on ideals of freedom, equality, and justice[333]. In furtherance to these ideals, every citizen is to have equality of rights, obligations, and opportunities before the law. The rule of law

---

[332] A study of judicial decisions relating to constitutionally guaranteed rights in Nigeria since independence in 1960 shows that the Nigerian judiciary has adopted different attitudes at different times. Thus, judicial attitude to the legal protection of human rights has transferal from a traditionalist or passivist to a liberal, radical or activist posture. There has also been a clear change from a declaratory, mechanistic to a purposive, bold and imaginative approach. Thus the period 1960-66, is the evolutionary epoch; the era, 1966-67, is the challenge era and the year 1979 till date, as the radical, activist and revolutionary years.
[333] S. 17(1) CFRN 1999.

presupposes that no one is punished, or can lawfully be made to suffer personally or materially, except for a distinct breach of the law[334], the proof of which is established by due process in the ordinary courts of the land. The obligation to promote and protect human rights by the Police, the Prisons service and the Immigration Service as well as special agencies like the EFCC, ICPC and NDLEA is contained in Chapter 4 of the Constitution. All the Acts and other legislations or enabling laws that empower these agencies as well as in the various provisions of the International Bill of Human Rights and relevant international and regional human rights treaties to which Nigeria is a signatory are not implemented especially regarding people living with disabilities..

The Nigerian legal system provides the opportunity for citizens to tackle critical issues that affect their lives. It offers a forum to seek justice when their rights have been violated and conceivably redress such violations. However, the system is very complex and can be difficult to navigate without the assistance of a trained lawyer. For underprivileged and mostly illiterate Nigerians, (including PWDs) who represent 61% of the population[335],it can also be difficult to find and understand information on simple procedural issues, like what rights you have before the law enforcement agencies[336]. In pursuance of this, all law enforcement outfits have established human rights desks for the purpose of human rights training, as well as monitoring activities of the law enforcement agents to ensure that they comply with acceptable human rights standards.

Unfortunately, these agencies are ill equipped to cater for the needs of PWDs, who must overcome the obstacles of discrimination, communication, and physical access. Generally, any situation involving a law enforcement officer is a stressful experience for anyone, and is bound to be even more stressful where a person with disability is involved. This is because the officer may not understand how to work with people with disabilities and the person with a disability may be struggling to communicate with the officer. Also in Nigeria today, many police stations and other law enforcement agencies have no access ramps

---

[334] *Ibid*, S.17 (2); Article 3 of the African Charter.

[335] The World Bank estimates that 70 per cent of 160 million Nigerians live on less than US$1.25 a day. <http://databank.worldbank.org> accessed 13/8/16.

[336] Persons with disabilities face additional hurdles, as they will also have to contend with structural and language barriers to access the legal system.

for wheel chair users, no instructions in Braille, no sign language interpreters, and the officers cannot use sign language. These factors constitute a major challenge among other difficulties which PWDs encounter before law enforcement agencies whether as a complainant, witness, victim, or even offender. Sadly, people with disabilities and their family members do not always receive the help they expect to. In fact, they may receive something that is quite the opposite.

In view of the foregoing, there is a need to enhance capacity of the law enforcement agencies towards understanding issues of disabilities and also mainstreaming disability into their line of work.

5.7 Disabled Persons Organizations (DPOs)

In Nigeria and many other countries, civil society organisations have been prominent in the struggle for human rights protection and promotion, and disabled persons organisations[337], which are usually managed by disabled people, have become increasingly instrumental in working with national governments, as well as other institutions, in developing policies and operational modalities for the effective social inclusion of disabled people in the societies in which the live. The Government gives financial and organizational/logistic support to existing or new organisations to person with disabilities. The organisations have the role to advocate rights and improved services; mobilize persons with disabilities; identify their needs and priorities; participate in the planning, implementation, and evaluation of service and measures concerning the lives of persons with disabilities; contribute to public awareness; provide services; and promote/organize income generating activities.

Within Nigeria there are two national umbrella DPOs, namely, the Joint National Association of Persons with Disabilities (JONAWPD) and the Association for the Comprehensive Empowerment of Nigerians with Disabilities (ASCEND).

JONAPWD was created in 1992 at the first Conference of disabled people in Nigeria at the University of Jos. The aim of the conference was to unite one umbrella, which however at this time was not a recognised

---

[337] Globally, the past 40 years have witnessed the emergence of the international disability movement, and DPOs now constitute a critical and essential component of civil society.

entity by the Federal Government. In the course of time, as Nigeria had no umbrella body to represent the growing population of persons with disabilities, JONAPWD was given recognition as the umbrella body of disabled people in Nigeria that would represent Nigeria at the international level, with its Executive Council acting as an emissary between the Government and disabled people, to promote their rights[338]. ASCEND on the other hand started as the Movement for the Empowerment of Nigerians with Disabilities (MEND) in 2002. The formation of the group was to create a platform for all Nigerians with disabilities to join forces and speak with one voice.[339] Today ASCEND has become anational socio-political organisation, and its goal is to mainstream PWDs through active participation in every sphere of life, particularly politics.

Besides these two national DPOs, there is a multiplicity of other DPOs working at the national, state and local levels. Examples include the Spinal Cord Injury Association of Nigeria (SCIAN), the Centre for Citizens with Disabilities (CDD),The Association of Lawyers with Disability in Nigeria (ALDIN), the Accidents Victim Support Association, Deaf Women in Nigeria (DWIN), the Nigerian National Association of the Deaf (NNAD), and the Resource Centre for Advocacy on Disability. Similarly, international organisations such as Christian Blind Mission (CBM), Ford Foundations West Africa, Open Society Initiative for West Africa, USAID Nigeria, and DFID Nigeria have also made immense contributions to the disability rights campaign in Nigeria.

Generally, it is conceived that the DPOs in Nigeria have done very well and must be commended for being in the forefront of the struggle for better living conditions for PWDs, and they have recorded some successes. For example, they actively lobbied for the ratification and domestication of the CRPWD; and they also lobbied the Independent National Electoral Commission (INEC) to amend Section 57 of the 2004

---

[338] In 2004, JONAPWD received a grant from the Federal Government to conduct election of its National Executive Council; following which a National Executive Council was constituted at a Convention of disabled people held in Minna.

[339] However, before MEND could be launched as an organisation, another organisation, Movement for the Emancipation of Niger Deltans came into existence with the same acronym (MEND). Coupled with other exigencies, it decided to change the name to ASCEND, which was finally launched in 2006.

Electoral Act, so as to ensure that all Nigerians with disabilities vote in elections. The DPOs have also been proactive in establishing strategic partnerships with other mainstream human-rights-based organisations, with the objective of broadening the support for lobbying for a rights-based approach to disability to be adopted.

It is noted, however, that the DPOs have a myriad of problems that continue to undercut their efforts. First of all, there seems to be insufficient organisational capacity for effective rights-based advocacy, demonstrated by questionable democratic credentials; the absence of a strategic plan; and a palpable lack of transparency in terms of governance and decision-making[340]. Secondly, the DPOs are largelypopulated by "disability elites", with a middle-class and urban-based leadership, while an overwhelming majority of disabled people in Nigeria, who ought to be represented by DPOs, live in rural areas. Thirdly, in common with many other developing countries, many DPOs cater for the needs of single impairment groups, and this encourages acrimony and bickering that ultimately weakens the disability movement at State and Local Government levels[341]. Furthermore, DPOs have themselves been heavily influenced by the charity/welfare model approach to disability issues; thus, many DPOs in Nigeria have no clear understanding of the social model of disability which in turn results in the adoption of inappropriate advocacy and campaigning strategies. Fourthly, the advocacy of many DPOs is centred on overcoming environmental barriers rather than dealing with more deep-seated institutional and attitudinal barriers; hence, to date the disability movement is still battling significant progress in taking forward a rights-based approach to disability.

While the disability movement in Nigeria can be said to be robust, the challenges observed above have undermined the overall impact of the activities of the DPOs.Furthermore, the two national umbrella DPOs, the Joint National Association of Persons with Disabilities (JONAWPD) and the Association for the Comprehensive Empowerment of Nigerians with Disabilities (ASCEND), maintain a constant rivalry with both groups claiming to speak on behalf of all Nigerians with disabilities, thereby impeding their ability to lobby the government. It is therefore suggested that the government and other

---

[340] Lang and Upah, *Supra.*
[341] Shakespeare, T., The Social Model of Disability (New York: Routledge, 2006) p. 197.

stakeholders should broker peace among the DPOs, and encourage them to work together in the overall interest of their members. There is also the need for DPOs to embark on capacity building for members, to understand the social or rights-based model of disability and the provisions of the 2018 Disability Act, so as to channel their programmes and policies and activities towards this model.

5.8 Government Agencies Involved In the Promotion and Protection of the Rights and Welfare of PWDs

5.8.1 *Federal Ministry of Women Affairs and Social Development*

The lead government department with regard to disability is the Federal Ministry of Women Affairs and Social Development. In line with Government's repositioning and reform agenda for better service delivery in the Country, the Ministry maintains the vision to help build a Nigerian Society that guarantees equal access to social, economic and wealth creation opportunities to all. The ministry places priority on protection of women, children, the aged and persons with disabilities and directs the attention of key operators in both private and public sectors on mainstreaming the concerns of these groups of people in national development process. Following Nigeria's ratification of the CRPWD on 30 March 2007 and its Optional Protocol on 24 September 2010, the Ministry of Women Affairs and Social Development is charged with submitting reports on progress[342].
The broad mandate of the Ministry is:

> to advise government on gender and Children issues. Issues affecting Persons with Disabilities and the Aged; initiate policy guidelines and lead the process of gender equality and mainstreaming at both the national and international levels.

The Department of Rehabilitation has the mandate to care for the neglected and less privileged members of society with particular emphasis on the rehabilitation of PWDs. This includes those who have long-term physical, mental, intellectual or sensory impairments which in

---

[342] Umeh, C., and Romola, A., 'Nigeria' *African Disability Rights Yearbook* , 2016.

interaction with various barriers may hinder their full and effective participation in society on an equal basis with others. The Department also plans programmes, policies and actions in line with accepted United Nations Convention on the welfare and Development of PWDS.

A very critical project on disability carried out by the Ministry is the National Baseline Survey on Persons With Disabilities in Nigeria (hereinafter "the Survey")[343]. The Survey was planned and executed with the aim of generating National Baseline Data on PWDs in Nigeria, which would form the foundation of interventions by Governments, Non-Governmental Organizations (NGOs) and other service providers. This is in line with the World Programme of Action launched in 1980, which laid emphasis on the need to isolate indicators on disability for effective formulation and implementation of policies aimed at ameliorating the living conditions of PWDs. This is also in consonance with Article 31 of the United Nations Convention on the Rights of Persons with Disabilities, which Nigeria became a signatory to on the 28th day of May, 2007. The Survey, therefore, represents a bold attempt to collect comprehensive information on PWDs in Nigeria. While the National Population Census exercise isolates only few characteristics, in this Survey, a more in-depth study of PWDs was undertaken. It gives insight into the economic, social, demographic and geographic characteristics of PWDs. Furthermore, it studied the accessibility of PWDs to means of equalization of opportunities, and analysed areas of perceived needs of PWDs. The aim of the Ministry is that this Report will serve as a reliable source of data and information for stakeholders in appreciating the plight of PWDs in the Country, and in addition, serve as a stepping stone for future research by Government. Unfortunately, apart from International Donor Agencies like DFID and the DPOs, we found little evidence showing that the Government and its agencies have utilized the findings of this Survey in planning their activities.

In spite of the impressive mandate above, it is observed that the Ministry of Women Affairs and Social Development inappropriatelydoes not have sufficient political leverage within the Nigerian Government to effectively take forward disability issues in a competent and effective manner[344]. Thus, it has not done enough to mitigate the level of hardship

---

[343] National Baseline Survey on Persons With Disabilities in Nigeria (2010), Document of the Federal Ministry of Women Affairs ad Social Development, <womenaffairs.gov.ng> accessed 9/1/17.

[344] Lang and Upah, *Supra.*

that PWDs encounter on a daily basis. This is mainly because the services they provide are based on welfare/charity model with demand far outstripping supply[345]; and this, in our view, is counterproductive. The best alternative is to adopt the social model or rights-based model that will empower PWDs and give them respect, dignity, equal opportunity and accessibility that will bring them into mainstream society on an equal basis with others.

Furthermore, it is well documented that in recent years, the Ministry has been grossly under-funded. Thus, a breakdown of the Ministry's budget by the Federal Budget Office revealed that within a period of six years (2011 to 2018) there has been a steady increase with each yearly allocation[346]. Within this period, the highest budgetary allocation awarded to the Ministry was 6.23 billion allocated in 2018 (a slight increase from 5,467,266,200 allocated in 2017); and the least is 2,938,380,649 allocated in 2011. The analysis also indicates a substantial increase in Capital Expenditure starting from 30% of the Ministry's budget in 2011, and steadily rising to 73% of the Ministry's budget in 2017[347]. Nevertheless, despite the yearly increase in allocation, the Ministry of Women Affairs consistently gets the lowest allocation, which barely covers the Ministry's needs and programmes. Consequently there is scarcity of publicly-funded affordable and appropriate services that are available to disabled people, especially at state and local levels, where over 50% of public expenditure is spent[348]. It is on record that in 2017, the poor allocation to the Ministry generated a heated debate before the Senate, where Senator RemiTinubu pointed out that the N1 billion earmarked for recurrent expenditure will hardly cater for the empowerment programmes under the ministry. These programmes include: human resources and capacity building; promotion of education; development of women in the civil, political, socio-cultural, and economic sectors;promoting women's health; and not only that, they are supposed to fund six zonal political empowerment offices,Subventions and grants to NGOs, Nigerian

---

[345] *Ibid.*

[346] Federal Ministry of Women Affairs and Social Development Budgets (2011-2017), Budget Office of the Federation < http://budgetoffice.gov.ng>accessed 23/2/18.

[347] *Ibid*

[348] '2016 Budget: N4bn allocation to women affairs ministry inadequate – Tinubu' *Vanguard Newspaper* of 16/1/16<http://www.vanguardngr.com/2016/01/2016> - accessed 6/3/ 17.

women trust fund, management of shelter for female victims of violence, 100 women lobby groups, welfare support for indigent women, etc. She then called on the Senate Committee on Appropriation to increase the allocation considerably to enable the ministry meet its obligations to Nigerian women.[349]

Presently, the Rehabilitation Department of the Ministry provides prosthetics and orthotics through its regional offices, however, such appliances are too expensive for the vast majority of disabled people to ever really benefit from such provision. Also, demand far outstrips supply for such appliances, which means that, even if they were affordable, only a very tiny proportion of disabled people would be able to benefit. Besides, no monitoring and evaluation framework have been developed for assessing the impact of the activities undertaken by the rehabilitation department.

It is observed that there remains a wide gap between the mandate that is vested in the Federal Ministry of Women Affairs and the funds allocated to it by the government. Thus, as it stands, the Ministry cannot address the issues of women, children, the aged, and physicallychallenged persons under its present bare condition.It is also observed that although the Ministry provides free training in the fields of farming, poultry, carpentry; and also written materials in Braille, it isquestionable whether these training and resources have actually changedthe lives of the beneficiaries for the better as there is no robust method to access the impact of these programmes. Thus, solid monitoring and evaluation techniques must be put in place to address this lapse.

Finally, the Ministry should lead other stakeholders to lobby the government to implement the provisions of the 2018 Disability Act; and also educate the general public on the laudable provisions of the Act.

5.8.2 *Other Relevant Ministries, Departments, and Agencies*

At both Federal and State levels, there are some Ministries which collaborate with the Federal Ministry of Women Affairs and Social Development towards mainstreaming the needs of PWDs in national planning and policy making. These line Ministries and Agencies have

---

[349]   *Ibid.*

been identified by the National Policy of Rehabilitation of Persons With Disabilities in Nigeria, to include the following:

a. The Ministry of Education

In line with the National Policy on Education, the Ministry of Education supervises the implementation of policies for the Provision of Basic Education for all children of school age including children with Special needs[350]. Thus, in 2016, the Federal Ministry of Education finalized the *National Policy on Inclusive Education* which was developed in close cooperation with the Universal Basic Education Commission, National Education Research and Development Council, National Commission for Colleges of Education, National Commission for Mass Literacy, CSOs, and DPOs after consultations at state and national levels[351].

There is also a *National Policy on Albinism* which intends to improve the status of persons with albinism by guaranteeing their equal access to education, health, social, political, and economic opportunities[352].

b. Ministry of Health

In many developing countries including Nigeria, a majority of the population have difficulties accessing social services and PWDs suffer more as they are often deprived of opportunities in all aspects of life including access to social services such as health[353].

The National Health Act of 2014 and the National Health Policy of 2016 established a framework for the regulation, development and management of a national health systems and set standards for delivery of services. This framework mandated the revamping and construction of primary health centers in each of 10,000 wards to provide 100 million Nigerians with access to basic and affordable health care services. The Act made provisions for persons with disabilities to access free

---

[350] Federal Ministry of Education Website <Education.gov.ng> accessed 5/12/16.
[351] *Ibid.*
[352] Federal Ministry of Education. National Policy on Albinism, 2012< http://albinofoundation.org/wp- content/uploads/2017/04/National-Policy-on-Albinism.pdf>accessed 7/6/20.
[353] WHO/UNPF Guidance Note, *Promoting Sexual and Reproductive Health for Persons With Disabilities*, <who.int>accessed 9/1/17.

healthcare services.Thus the Ministry of Health in line with the health policy provides health services for the disabled and undertakes activities for disability prevention and rehabilitation[354]. These activities include:

1.   Ensuring improvements in primary health care, immunizations activities, Hygiene, nutrition and occupational health and safety.
2.   Improving the educational, economic and social status of the poor.
3.   Identifying impairment and developing appropriate intervention.
4.   Designing appropriate, accessible and affordable health services at primary, secondary and tertiary levels for persons with disabilities.
5.   Including general medical and nursing assistance on an in-patient, out-patient or community home care bases and specialized health professional assistance.
6.   Developing measures to identify and reduce discrimination on the basis of disability in thehealth sector. Particularattention should be given to the elimination of discriminations against Persons With Disabilities.
7.   Ensuring comprehensive free health care for all children with disabilities under twelve years including free accesto assistive devices and rehabilitation services.
8.   Carryout and encouraging research on diseases that cause disabilities.

c.Ministry of Communication

Communication and information are important aspects of access to public services. Access to communication and information therefore forms an integral part of the equalization opportunities for people with disabilities, such as the Deaf, people with speech disabilities and people with visual disabilities. The role of the Ministry of Communications in the rehabilitation agenda for PWDs includes:

1.   Developing strategies to make information and communication service and documentation accessible to all Persons With Disabilities.
2.   Making information available in formats that can be used and understood by people with hearing, visual and other communication needs.

---

[354]   Federal Ministry of Health Website<health.gov.ng> accessed 4/12/16.

3. Promoting the development and implementation of standards and best practices to make information and communication accessible to persons with disabilities.

4. Ensuring that television stations provide sign language inset or subtitles in at least one major newscast programme each day and in all special programmes of national significance.

5. Ensuring that telephone and telecommunication companies provide at reasonable price special telephone and telecommunication devices for the hearing impaired.

6. Ensuring that postal agencies provide for persons with disabilities free postal services for all materials to aid the learning or improvement of persons with disabilities.

d. Ministry of Information and National Orientation

One of the greatest hurdlespersons with disabilities face when trying to access mainstream programmes[355] is a negative attitude. It is these attitudes that lead to the social exclusion and marginalisation of people with disabilities. The attitudinal change is not something that happens spontaneously. It is a complex process which involves moving in a series of stages from one set of attitude to another[356]. Thus, raising awareness is central to the changing of attitudes, and the role of the National orientation Agency in the Disability Rehabilitation agenda includes:

1. Raisingawareness of disability as a Human Rights and Development issue targeting every component of government and society at large.
2. Reducingdiscrimination against persons with disabilities based on archaic beliefs and customs.
3. Givingadequate publicity on issues affecting persons with disabilities.

---

[355]Federal Ministry of Information and National Orientation Website at < https://fmic.gov.ng>assessed 6/3/18.
[356]Lang and Upah, *Supra.*

e. Ministry of Power, Works and Housing; and Ministry of Transportation[357]

The way in which the environment is developed and organized in Nigeria contributes to a large extent to the level of equality that people with disabilities enjoy. There are a number of barriers in the environment, which prevent persons with disabilities from enjoying equal opportunities with non-disabled people. Examples arestructural barriers in the built environment, inaccessible service point, inaccessibleentrances due to security system, poor town planning and poor interior design. There should be a national requirement for an accessible built environment because this is an important development in the equalization of opportunities for persons with disabilities. Development agencies do not have clear policies on environmental access. The result is that hundreds of schools, Clinics and other public buildings are presently being built with no regard for barrier-free requirements. Thus, the two Ministry's activities towards rehabilitation and inclusion of PWDs are:

1. To introduce programmes of action to make physical environment accessible to all persons with disabilities.
2. To develop standards and guidelines and to consider a lasting legislation to ensure accessibility to housing, buildings, public transport services and other means of transportation, streets and other outdoor environment.
3. To ensure that architects, construction engineers and others who are professionally involved in the design and construction of the physical environment have access to the disability policy and the requirements for making places accessible to People With Disabilities.
4. To develop standards and guidelines for accessibility to all public buildings and facilities, for example, transport, telecommunications, sports and recreation facilities.
5. To enact legislation to ensure compliance.
6. To ensure that professionals who are involved in the design and construction of the physical environment have access to adequate information on disability policy and measures to achieve accessibility.

---

[357] Federal Ministry of Power, Works and Housing Website at <
https://www.pwh.gov.ng>assessed 6/3/18.

Other Ministries identified as line ministries in the Rehabilitation Policy Document includethe Ministry of Labour and Productivity, which provides for vocational training and skills acquisition for the disabled, and also provides employment opportunities for the disabled; Ministry of Justice, which provides legal aid services for the poor including the disabled; National Planning Commission; National Poverty Eradication Programme (NAPEP); National Directorate of Employment (NDE), etc.[358].

Although it is quite commendable that almost all ministries in Nigeria have various plans and programmes for PWDs, their policies and the services they provide are driven largely by affecting appeals of the charity model, which considers PWDs as helpless victims needing 'care' and 'protection' (rather than justice and equality)[359]. This ultimately creates an army of powerless individuals dependent on state sponsored mechanisms of social support like special schools and protection homes for PWDs.

The primary duty of protecting persons with disabilities lies with states through institutions. In Nigeria, efforts have been made to mainstream disability issues into the various key ministries and agencies as an integral part of relevant strategies of sustainable development. Disabled Peoples Organisations, and other Non-Governmental Organizations are also involved in safeguarding the welfare, and promoting the social inclusion of PWDs.

An assessment of the mandate and activities of the institutions discussed in this chapter indicates a duplication of roles, and lack of proper coordination between the agencies involved. Disability is perceived more as a "charity issue", and there is also the general problem of insufficient funding to carry out disability programmes in most of the institutions. Presently, the Federal Ministry of Women Affairs and Social Development which is the parent ministry for disability issues in the country, is grossly underfunded, and thus cannot handle the daily challenges encountered by PWDs. Also, the Ministry does not have the technical and financial resources to embark on massive public awareness campaigns aimed at promoting awareness on disability issues. Besides,

---

[358] See National Rehabilitation Policy Document at<womenaffairs.gov.ng> accessed 6/3/18.
[359] *Ibid.*

there are no reliable statistics on disability in Nigeria, which compounds the problem of planning, monitoring and evaluating any services provided by the institutions.

In view of the annotations made above, it is submitted that the institutional mechanisms for the protection of PWDs in Nigeria have been weak and ineffective.Thankfully, the Persons with Disabilities Act, 2018 (the long awaited legislation)specifically provides for the establishment of a National Commission for Persons with Disabilities which will cater for the needs of disabled Nigerians and fully integrate them into mainstream society. It is hoped that when the Commission is finally created, it will be properly funded and given all the necessary support to enable it achieve its mandate.

CHAPTER SIX

Human Rights through the Lens of Disability

H uman rights are the rights held by all persons by virtue of their common humanity to live a life of freedom and dignity. These rights are universal and everyone regardless of sex, race, nationality, and economic background shares them equally. They are inalienable (they can neither be taken away nor given up) and they are indivisible (no right can be suppressed in order to promote another right).[360] Human rights define and affirm humanity; they exist to ensure that human life remains sacred and guarantee that inhumanity and injustice are prevented or redressed.[361] Accordingly, the United Nations Charter affirms that, "Universal respect for, and observance of, human rights and fundamental freedoms for all without distinction"[362] is essential.

In spite of the explicit significance of human rights, in reality human rights continue to elude the vast majority of persons with disabilities (PWDs) in many parts of the world including Nigeria. The questions that readily come to mind at this juncture are: whether persons with disabilities are entitled to human rights, and whether such rights protect them in reality. It is in this context that this chapter examines specific rights of PWDs, and attempts an exegesis of the challenges of protection, enforcement and monitoring violations of such rights in Nigeria. The chapter also examines the unique vulnerability of women, children, and elderly persons with disabilities and the need to give them special protection. The importance of disability in national planning is also considered, following which it is concluded that in order to fully

---

[360] UNDP- Human Rights and the Millennium Development Goals Making the Link<www.undp.org.Ioslo.centre> accessed 8/12/15.
[361] Emelonye, U., 'Rule of Law and Human Rights Development' <http://www.nigeriabestforum.com/generaltopics/p.72986≥ accessed 22/12/15.
[362] Ibid

protect the rights of PWDs, disability issues must be integrated into all aspects of national planning in Nigeria.

6.1 Human Rights of Persons with Disabilities

While, it is incontrovertible that PWDs are human beings like persons without disabilities, it is a well-known fact that they are denied equal rights with others as human beings. They are often deprived of equal treatment with other human beings, and they also receive negative treatment from the society and from people around them. Supposedly, PWDs are entitled to human rights as human beings. The Constitution of the Federal Republic of Nigeria confers certain rights on all its citizens and, in particular, Chapter IV provides specific rights that are regarded as fundamental to human existence. PWDs, like other Nigerians, are ordinarily entitled to those rights entrenched in the Constitution. Some of the rights include:

Right to Life[363]
Right to Dignity of Human Persons[364]
Right to Personal Liberty[365]
Right to Fair Hearing[366]
Right to Private and Family Life[367]
Right to Freedom of thought, Conscience and Religion[368]
Right to Freedom of Expression and the Press[369]
Right to Peaceful Assembly and association[370]
Right to Freedom of Movement[371]
Right to Freedom from Discrimination[372]

---

[363] Section 33 of 1999 Constitution of Nigeria.
[364] *Ibid* Sec. 34.
[365] *Ibid* Sec. 35.
[366] *Ibid* Sect. 35.
[367] *Ibid* Sec. 37.
[368] *Ibid* Sec. 38.
[369] *Ibid* Sec. 39.
[370] *Ibid* Sec. 40.
[371] *Ibid,* Sec. 41.
[372] *Ibid,* Sec.42.

Right to Acquire and own Immovable Property anywhere in Nigeria[373]
Except in circumstances provided by the Nigeria Constitution, the above rights are inalienable and cannot be deprived. Worthy of note is the fact that the amended 1999 Constitution of Nigeria contains some provisions that indirectly address the issue of PWDs. For instance, Section 42(2) prohibits discrimination based on the circumstances of a person's birth and also Sections 14, 16 and 17 provide for the right to equal and fundamental rights for all.These rights are also entrenched in various regional and international human rights instruments which are extensively discussed in Chapter Four of this book.

The most important of these international instruments is the United Nations Convention on the Rights of Persons with Disabilities. This is because the Convention is a disability specific instrument that clearly defines disability rights, and how PWDs should be protected and treated as human beings. The Convention thus adopts a broad categorization of PWDs and reaffirms that all persons with all types of disabilities and challenges related thereto must enjoy all human rights and fundamental freedom. It also classifies and qualifies all categories of rights of PWDs, and how to protect those rights from being violated. Accordingly, the Convention categorizes the rights of PWDs to include:

i. Equality and non-discrimination.[374]
ii. Right to life.[375]
iii. Liberty and security of persons.[376]
iv. Freedom of torture or cruel, in human or degrading treatment or punishment.[377]
v. Freedom from exploitation, violence and abuse.[378]
vi. Protecting the integrity of the person.[379]
vii. Liberty of movement and nationality.[380]
viii. Living independently and being included in the community.[381]

---

[373] *Ibid*, Sec. 43.
[374] See Article 5 of the UN Convention on the Rights of Persons With Disabilities (CRPD).
[375] *Ibid*, Article 10.
[376] *Ibid*, Article 14.
[377] *Ibid, Article 15.*
[378] *Ibid*, Article 16.
[379] *Ibid*, Article 17.
[380] *Ibid*, Article 18.

ix. Personal mobility.[382]
x. Freedom of expression and opinion, and access to information.[383]
xi. Respect for privacy[384]
xii. Respect for home and the family.[385]

Worthy of note is the thought behind the above provisions. The Preamble to the Convention states:

> Recalling the principles proclaimed in the Charter of the United Nations which recognize the inherent dignity and worth and the equal inalienable rights of all members of the human family as the foundation of freedom, justice and peace in the world; Recognizing that he United Nations in the Universal Declaration of Human Rights and in the International Convention on Human Rights, has proclaimed and agreed that everyone is entitled to all the rights and freedoms set forth therein without distinction of any kind.[386]

Nigeria adopted the CRPD far back in 2007; but it was not domesticated until recently in 2019, thereby raising hope as to the survival of PWDs in the country. Considering the struggles that they pass through, one would conclude that the actualisation of human rights of PWDs is not an easy one. In other words, the enforcement of human rights provisions of PWDs in accordance with the unalloyed commitment of the United Nations to protect the rights of the disabled as enshrined in the Convention is remarkably at the mercies of nation states.

It is imperative at this juncture to examine the challenges in accessing or enjoying some of the above mentioned rights.

6.1.1 *The Right to Life*

The Right to life is most fundamental of all rights, because it is only the living that can assert or demand for other rights. Accordingly, this right

---

[381] *Ibid,* Article 19.
[382] *Ibid,* Article 20.
[383] *Ibid,* Article 21.
[384] *Ibid,* Article 22.
[385] *Ibid,* Article 23.
[386] Preamble to Conventions on the Rights of Persons with Disabilities.

is enshrined in international treaties as well as in municipal laws of states. The Nigerian Constitution provides that, "every person has a right to life, and no one shall be deprived intentionally of his life, save in execution of the sentence of a court in respect of a criminal offence of which he has been found guilty in Nigeria"[387]. The Constitution further provides that:

> A person shall not be regarded as having been deprived of his life in contravention of this section, if he dies as a result of the use, to such extent and in such circumstances as are permitted by law, of such force as are reasonably necessary:
> (a) for the defence of any person or property;
> (b) in order to effect a lawfularrest, or to prevent the escape of a person lawfully detained or;
> (c)for the purpose of suppressing a riot, insurrection or mutiny.[388]

The United Nations Convention on the Rights of Persons with Disabilities also provides that, "States Parties reaffirm that every human being has the inherent right to life and shall take all necessary measures to ensure its effective enjoyment by persons with disabilities on an equal basis with other".[389]

Considering the foregoing provisions, we submit that all other rights are dependent on the right to life, because it is only the living that has a recognizable right. Hence, this right cannot be taken for granted or withheld from anybody, including PWDs. Unfortunately, it is not in doubt that right from birth, the right to life of PWDs is threatened either by their parents with or without the assistance of medical personnel. This could be as a result of ignorance or repugnant cultural practices of some communities. In some cultures, any abnormality noticed in a new born is taken as a taboo and that ends the life of the innocent baby. Also once a trace or traces of disabilities or impairments are noticed, medicals are withdrawn from such persons who die gradually in pains. In some places in Africa, persons with particular forms of disabilities such as albinism or hunch back are a ready target for ritualists. Hence, the disabled are

---

[387] Section 33, 1999 Constitution (as amended).
[388] *Ibid.*
[389] Article 10 CRPD; see also Article 2 of European Convention on Human Rights.

vulnerable to violations that put their lives in serious jeopardy and this remains evident across the developed and developing world[390].

The above fact is buttressed by the writer who in the course of this research discovered that, in some communities, culture and religion associated disability with evil and such evil is punished with death. This history and perceptions of disability are extensively discussed in Chapter two of this book.

Worthy of note is the growing trend in developed countries in recent years regarding the issue of the treatment of low-birth-weight babies, the withdrawing or withholding of medical treatment from adults, or physician-assisted suicide.[391] These practices are not totally alien to Africa or Nigeria in particular, because obnoxious cultural practices have been secretly robbing the disabled of their right to life. What is more, is the religious perspective as no religion, be it Islam or Christianity, allows the taking of life on grounds of disabilities.

Another area where the right to life is threatened and denied is the prevention of birth. Presently, advancement in technology has made it possible that certain medical procedures can dictate an abnormal foetus in the womb and end the growth through evacuation. The question here is; could it be said that right to life has been denied since life starts on conception? We maintain here that this practice amounts to denial of right to life. Again the issue of *euthanasia* or mercy killing (an act of painlessly putting to death persons suffering from painful and incurable disease or incapacitating physical disorder or allowing them to die by withholding treatment or withdrawing artificial life-support measures) comes into question:Could there be any killing that is truly in the interest of the victims? The answer is totally no –it is difficult to consent to life taking as nobody would like to die. Furthermore, the right to life entails the right not to have one's life arbitrarily terminated no matter the situation. Thus the practice of "mercy killing" when it comes to disabled

---

[390] Clements, L. and Read, J. Disabled People and the Right to Life (Routledge: 2008).

[391] *Ibid*, p. 8. The authors further stated that the decision about whether to withhold or limit life sustaining interventions or even actively to end life were made predominantly within the closed boundaries of professional medical discretion. It was not until the 1980s and beyond that such decision making was seen to have bigger dimensions which took it outside the confines of medicine into public domain.

patients is easily prone to abuse as the issue of consent is a key requirement.

In socio-economic terms, the right to life brings with it connotations of state responsibility for both sustaining life (for instance through the development of a health service) and for the quality of that life in terms of challenging environmental harms and destination.[392] In other words, there are certain things and conditions to put in place in order to ensure and protect the right to life. For instance in *Oneryildiz v Turkey*[393] the court held that the CRPD has to be interpreted in such a way as to oblige states to take appropriate steps to safeguard the lives of those within their jurisdiction no matter what the endangering activity could be. Also in *Osman v UK*[394] the commission in reaching its decision considered the effects of disease and environmental factors on life and held that:

> the extent of the obligation to take preventive steps may however increase in relation to the immediacy of the risk to life where there is a real and imminent risk to life to an identified person or group of persons, a failure by state authorities to take appropriate steps may disclose a violation of the rights to protect life by law[395].

It needs to be mentioned that presently in Nigeria and in most African countries, the practical enforcement of right to life is still a mirage, and therefore unrealistic when viewed in relation to conducive environment and healthcare that ensures that the right to life thrives. There are less responses in government on physical and environmental conditions and needs of PWDs. Clearly, all other rights such as health, environment, shelter, adequate food, freedom from torture and inhuman or degrading treatment or punishment, exploitation, violence, abuse, discrimination and others are anecdotes to the right to life. Therefore, the right to life is anchored inthose rights that makelife meaningful and worth living for PWDs.

---

[392] *Ibid*, p. 16.

[393] (2005) Strasbourg Court and Commission.

[394] (1998) Strasbourg Court and Commission the Human Rights Convention in its General Comments 6 & 17 of 1994 (a & b) cautioned against for Ramon an interpretation of the right which states requires to take all possible measures to reduce infant mortality and to increase life expectancy especially in adopting measures to eliminate malnutrition and epidemics.

[395] *Ibid.*

6.1.2 *Right to Freedom From Discrimination*

Undoubtedly, discrimination is a major problem for PWDs. It comes in form of denial, exclusion, restriction or distinction of PWDs from enjoyment and exercise of rights on equal basis with other citizens in society. Remarkably, the prohibition of discrimination is contained within all national, regional and international human rights standards.

One of the fundamental objectives and directive principles of state policy, as enshrined in the 1999 Nigerian Constitution, enjoins the state to carry out its social objectives towards ensuring thatall citizens without discrimination on any group whatsoever have opportunity for securing adequate means of livelihood as well as adequate opportunity to secure suitable employment.[396]Another provision on economic objectives also seeks to ensure that suitable and adequate shelter, suitable and adequate food, reasonable national minimum living wage, old age care and pensions, and unemployment, sick benefits and welfare of the disabled are provided for all citizens.[397]

These are laudable social and economic objectives which presumably seek to protect the rights of all citizens including PWDs. Unfortunately, by virtue of the provisions of Section 6(6) (c) of the same Constitution, the entire provisions of Chapter II on the Fundamental Objectives and Directive Principles of State Policy are non-justiciable; thus, the provisions cannot be enforced in a court of law[398].

Section 42 of the Constitution enshrines the right to freedom from discrimination, and is therefore relevant to the protection of the rights of PWDs. Though it does not specifically mention "persons with disabilities", its provisions are wide enough to accommodate all persons. Accordingly, the section provides that:

---

[396] Section 17(3)(a) 1999 Constitution.

[397] *Ibid*, Section 16(2)(d).

[398] In Archbishop Anthony OlubunmiOkogie& Others v Attorney-General of Lagos State [(1981) 1 NCLR 218, it was held that the directive principles of state policy as enshrined in the Constitution have to conform to and run subsidiary to the fundamental rights provisions in Chapter IV of the Constitution, and that the said directive principles are subject to the legislative powers of the State.

1. A citizen of Nigeria of a particular community, ethnic group, place of origin, sex, religion or political opinion shall not, by reason only that he is such a person,

(a) be subjected either expressly by; or in the practical application of any law in force in Nigerian or any executive or administrative action of the government, to disabilities or restrictions to which citizens of Nigeria of other communities ethnic groups, places of origin, sex, religion or political opinions are not made subject; or

(b) be accorded either expressly by, or in the practical application of, any law in force in Nigeria or any such executive or administrative action, any privilege or advantage that is not accorded to citizens of Nigeria of other communities ethnic groups, places of origin, sex, religious or political opinions.

2. No citizen shall be subjected to any disability or deprivation merely by reason of the circumstances of his birth.

3. Nothing in subsection (1) of this Section shall invalidated any law by reason, only that the law imposes restrictions with respect to the appointment of any persons to any office under the state or as member of the armed forces of the federation or a member of the Nigerian Police or to any office in the service of a body corporate established directly by any law in force in Nigeria.[399]

While we acknowledge that Section 42 above enshrines the right to freedom from discrimination, it is observed that this provision does not include disability as one of the prohibited grounds of discrimination. In other words, if a person with disability suffers any form of discrimination as a result of his disability, he cannot invoke his right under Section 42 of the Constitution. The simple solution is to effect a constitutional amendment to include disability as one of the prohibited grounds of discrimination.

Furthermore, various provisions of the African Charter on Human and People's Rights (African Charter) can be interpreted as conferring on Nigeria a duty to protect such persons from discrimination[400]. For instance, Article 2 provides a general duty of non-discrimination thus:

---

[399] Section 42 (1-3),1999 Constitution of the Federal Republic of Nigeria.

[400] M L Perlin, International Human Rights and Mental Disability Law: When the Silenced Are Heard (Oxford University Press, 2011) 55.

> Every individual shall be entitled to the enjoyment of the rights and freedoms recognized and guaranteed in the present Charter without distinction of any kind such as race, ethnic group, colour, sex, language, religion, political or any other opinion, national and social origin, fortune, birth or other status.[401]

While this provision does not refer specifically to PWDs, when interpreted in conjunction with Article 18 of the Charter, which states that "…the disabled shall also have the right to special measures of protection in keeping with their physical or moral needs",[402] it becomes clear that the rights of PWDs to non-discrimination are accommodated under this general prohibition[403]. This provision is supplemented by Article 28 of the Charter which provides that:

> Every individual shall have the duty to respect and consider his fellow beings without discrimination, and to maintain relations aimed at promoting, safeguarding and reinforcing mutual respect and tolerance.[404]

This provision seems to confer on Signatory States a duty to take positive steps to safeguard the rights of PWDs and to promote the 'tolerance' of such persons within society.

A right of non-discrimination can also be inferred from Article 3 of the Charter, which provides that "Every individual shall be equal before the law…[405]" and that, "Every individual shall be entitled to equal protection of the law…." This principle of equality is further defined in Article 19 of the Charter, and is very important for disability rights because it affirms that PWDs are entitled to the same rights and protections under the law as their able-bodied counterparts[406]. These

---

[401] African Charter on Human and People's Rights 1981, Article 2.

[402] *Ibid*, Article 18.

[403] M Evans and R Murray, The African Charter on Human and Peoples' Rights: The System in Practice 1986-2006 (2nd edition, Cambridge University Press, Cambridge 2008) 178.

[404] African Charter, Article 28.

[405] *Ibid*, Article 4.

[406] A M Cotter, This Ability: An International Legal Perspective of Disability Discrimination (Ashgate
Publishing, Aldershot 2007) 127.

---

rights are broadly consistent with Section 17 of the Constitution of the Federal Republic of Nigeria 1999.

Unlike the other two instruments, the UN Convention on the Rights of Persons With Disabilities contains specific provisions on non-discrimination of PWDs. Thus Article 5 of the Convention provides that:

(1) States Parties recognize that all persons are equal before and under the law and also entitled without any discrimination to the equal protection and equal benefit of the law.

(2) States Parties shall prohibit all discrimination on the basis of disability and guarantee to persons with disabilities equal and effective legal protection against discrimination on all grounds

(3) In other to promote and eliminate discrimination, States Parties shall take all appropriate steps to ensure that reasonable accommodation is provided.

(4) Specific measures which are necessary to accelerate or achieve de facto equality of persons with disabilities shall not be considered discrimination under the terms of the present Convention.[407]

A generation of disability scholars have argued that the greatest hardship in being impaired liesin facing a relentlessly discriminatory society and a pervasively unaccommodating environment.[408] They further stated the fact that a just society would not discriminate, but would rather build the environment for as wide a range of human variation as was technologically feasible.[409]

Notwithstanding the plethora of instruments against discrimination of PWDs, in practice, the issue of discrimination remains a daily experience for PWDs. They are simply not treated equally like others without disabilities and thus suffer social isolation and marginalization. They are often not allowed directly or directly full participation and enjoyment of some rights and are often times not empowered in order to develop their skills and bring out their abilities for the benefit of the society.

---

[407] UN Convention on the Rights of Person with Disabilities.

[408] Clements, L & Read. J. Disabled People and the right to life. The protection and Violation of Disabled People's Most Basic Human Rights p. 41.

[409] *Ibid.*

This situation is very sad because PWDs are created with potential and many of them have the aptitude to contribute meaningfully in the economy of nations. Unfortunately, they are not given the opportunity to do so, or rather, they are denied the enabling environment to showcase their potential. Many of them die with their gifts because they have been excluded in policy making, inventions and other aspects of life. We are mindful of the fact that some PWDs may not be able to work for long hours and some are limited in the type of work they are able to do but there are vast areas of tasks they could do; yet they are denied the opportunities to do them simply because of their physical disabilities.

Remarkably, PWDs suffer discrimination from government in terms of policy making through non-inclusion of disability matters in government decisions and economic planning[410]. PWDs also suffer discrimination from their family members, and their immediate community[411]. There are situations where parents of children with disabilities discriminate against them by depriving them quality education or education at all. They are sometimes excluded from family decision-making. Other times they are hidden, or denied in public by their parents and family members.

Furthermore, the entire society discriminates against them; society sees PWDs as only deserving pity, charity and welfare, rather than equal human beings. All these amount to exclusion, oppression, and discrimination which limitthe rights of PWDs.

6.1.3 *Political Rights of Persons with Disabilities*

The political rights of PWDs are guaranteed under several human rights instruments. For instance, the Preamble to the International Covenant on Civil and Political Rights (ICCPR) provides thus:

Recognizing that, in accordance with the Universal Declaration of Human Rights, the ideal of free human beings, enjoying civil and political freedom and freedom from fear and want can only be achieved if conditions are created whereby everyone may enjoy his civil

---

[410] Lang and Upah, *Supra.*
[411] *Ibid.*

and political rights, as well as his economic, social and cultural rights...[412]

Likewise, Article 29 CRPD provides for participation in political and public life. It provides that State Parties shall guarantee to PWDs political rights and the opportunity to enjoy them on an equal basis with others, and shall undertake:

(a) To ensure that persons with disability can effectively and fully participate in political and public life on an equal basis with others directly or through freely chosen representatives, including the right and opportunity for persons with disabilities to vote and be elected, inter alia by:

(i) Ensuring that voting procedures, facilities and materials are appropriate, accessible and easy to understand and use;

(ii) Protecting the right of persons with disabilities to vote by secret ballot in elections and public referendums without intimidation, and to stand for elections, to effectively hold office and perform all public functions at all levels of government, facilitating the use of assistive and new technologies where appropriate.

(iii) Guaranteeing the free expression of the will of persons with disabilities as electors and to this end where necessary, at their request, allowing assistance in voting a person of their own choice;

(b) To promote actively an environment in which persons with disabilities can effectively and fully participate in the conduct of public affairs, without discrimination and on an equal basis with others, and encourage their participation in public affairs, including

(i) Participation in non-governmental organizations and associations concerned with the public and political life of the country, and in the activities and administration of political parties.

(ii) Forming and joining organizations of persons with disabilities to represent persons with disabilities at international, national, regional and local levels.[413]

It is quite clear in view of the foregoing that the CRPD provides in clear terms that states must guarantee PWDs their political rights; States must equally create the opportunities for them to exercise their political rights

---

[412] ICCPR 1966.

[413] UN Convention on the Right of Persons with Disabilities. See also Chapter VI of the Constitution of the Federal Republic of Nigeria 1999.

on equal basiswith others. The Convention enjoins states to ensure that PWDs are able to fully participate in political and public life, for example to vote and be voted for in elections. In other words, the voting processes and facilities and other materials relating thereto are to be made accessible, and understandable in clear terms and use byPWDs. The question is how far has the political rights of PWDs been actualized in Nigeria, Africa and round the globe? The question is far-fetched in the sense that in most developing countries as Nigeria, PWDs are denied full participation in political affairs and agenda in their countries and immediate communities. For instance, the political environment and system in Nigeria does not give room for the PWDs to fully and effectively exercise their political rights. A very alarming trend is a situation whereby they are denied an enabling environment to help them participate during elections. Hence, you hardly see them coming close to polling booths or stations during elections. This is because the situation of crisis and election violence deters them from going to vote during such period. Aside election violence, those in wheel chair, the blind and the deaf may not have the means to covey themselves to polling stations. Those that manage to find themselves at polling stations may not have access to interpreters to help them cast their votes to the parties and candidates of their choice.

Confronted with the above reality, PWDs are also excluded directly and indirectly in being voted for during elections. This is because political parties are reluctant to field PWDs in their elective position both at state and national levels. With a few exceptions, how many PWDs find their way to the State and National Assembly in Nigeria, Africa and in the whole world? Meanwhile, among these excluded groups are lawyers, engineers, medical doctors, and political scientists, full of ideas, great wisdom and intellect wasting away; their mastery of the act of politics isleft unharnessed and many die with their dreams. They are also excluded in the political administration of politics. One can hardly find one person with disability as INEC official in every one hundred INEC staff. Until such a time we accept their potential, mainstreaming PWDs into the political arena in Nigeria will remain a mirage.

6.1.4 *Economic Rights of Persons With Disabilities*

Indeed, PWDs are entitled to economic rights. These rights are enshrined under the national, regional and international instruments which they are subject to by virtue of their belonging to the human family with equal rights. The Constitution of Nigeria provides under Section 16 that:

1. The State shall, within the context of the ideals and objectives for which provisions are made in this Constitution-
(a) Harness the resources of the nation and promote national prosperity an efficient, a dynamic and self-reliant economy;
(b) Control the national economy in such a manner as to ensure the maximum welfare, freedom and happiness of every citizen on the basis of social justice and equality of status and opportunity; ...
(c) Without prejudice to the right of any person to participate in areas of the economy within the major sector of the economy, protect the right of every citizen to engage in any economic activities outside the major sectors of the economy.
2. The state shall direct its policy towards ensuring-
(a) The promotion of a planned and balanced economic development;
(b) That the material resources of the nation are harnessed and distributed as best as possible to serve the common good;
(c) That suitable and adequate shelter, suitable and adequate foods, reasonable national minimum living wage, old age care and pensions, and unemployment, sick benefits and welfare of the disabled are provided for all citizens...[414]

Furthermore, Article 3 of International Covenant on Economic Social and Cultural Rights (ICESCR) provides that State Parties shall ensure the equal rights of men and women in the enjoyment of all economic, social and cultural rights set forth in the present government.

Article 6 further provides that "State Parties ... recognize the right to work, which includes the right of everyone to the opportunity to gain his living by work which he freely chooses or accepts, and will take appropriate steps to safeguard this right".

It is also entrenched in CRPD that State Parties recognize the right of PWDs to work on an equal basis with others; this includesthe right to

---

[414] ICESCR 1966. See also Articles (2) 7-11.

the opportunity to gain a living by work freely chosen or accepted in a labour market and work environment that is open, inclusive and accessible to persons with disabilities. States parties shall safeguard and promote the realization of the right to work, including for those who acquire a disability during the course of employment.

The above provisions from different legal instruments attest to the fact that PWDs also enjoy economic rights like those without disabilities. Incontestably, PWDs are endowed with skills and knowledge that can contribute to the economy of the society but they are often neglected and relegated to the background. They are not given the opportunity to participate in economic activities and decisions, and they are being denied economic rights such as access to decent work that will help meet their daily needs and attain financial independence. Other times, persons with disabilities are not given the chance to participate in production activities thereby rendering them unproductive and lazy. They are being underrated to the extent that they are not allowed to participate in economic programme, policies, planning and projects no matter how academically qualified they may be. At other times, PWDs are not provided with an enabling environment to project themselves as owners of economy, for instance, to participate in the creation of jobs for others. They lack an enabling environment for self-reliance and empowerment through vocation and training like other people without disabilities.

Given this reality, wherever they find themselves in private employment, they are denied a just and favourable remuneration, equal pay and favourable condition of work. This condition is also experienced by those employed by government. Worthy of note under this discourse is the fact that persons with disabilities are often isolated and excluded in terms of social and environmental barrierssuch as rigid work routines and full hours on the job with other people. Other challenges are:

i.   Unfavourable and personal transportation.
ii.   Unsuitable housing and accommodation.
iii. Lack of modern equipment or aids.
iv.   Unsuitable working environments e.g. non accessibility of high buildings.
v.   Stigmatization at work place by fellow workers who hold negative perceptions of disabilities.

Ideally, mainstreaming PWDs into the economic and social sphere of the society will certainly create a sense of belonging.

6.1.5 *Right to Good Health*

Disability on its own is a health matter. In other words, some types of disabilities occur as a result of inadequate health care either during formation stage through birth. Having earlier dealt with disabilities in this context, this sectionis basically on the health rights of PWDs. It is important to note that each type of disability has specific health needs, and sincehealth is a human right issue, PWDs are entitled to the right to good health.

Accordingly, the CRPD provides that:

> State Parties recognize that persons with disabilities have the right to the enjoyment of the highest attainable standard of health without discrimination on the basis of disability. States Parties shall have all appropriate measures to ensure access for person with disabilities to health services that are gender sensitive, including health-related rehabilitation. In particular, States Parties shall;
>
> (a) Provide persons with disabilities with the same range, quality and standard of free or affordable health care and programmes as provided to other persons, including in the areas of sexual and reproductive health and population based public health programs...[415]

PWDs also have the right to be prevented from impairment. This would be achievable through identification and treatment at an early stage of life. Clearly, the issue of health is vital to PWDs yet they are frequently excluded either directly or indirectly in health programmes. The denials could be in the following ways:

i. No access to affordable health care services.
ii. Lack of access to regular health care in terms of routine check.
iii. Lack of specialized health givers as we can hardly find doctors who specializein matters connected to disabilities.

---

[415] Article 25 (a). See also Articles 25 (b) (E).

iv. Lack of good medical care which often results inunattended health risks.
v. Neglect or lack of attention to medical needs of persons with disabilities by their parents, government and civil society.
vi. Lack of knowledge of the fact of their right to health.

Clearly, the above positions show that the health right of PWDs is no doubt in jeopardy. Worthy of note is the fact that health is affected by environmental factors such as sanitation, poverty and more. Given this reality, the environment may be changed to improve the health condition of PWDs. For instance, there are certain toilet facilities which they cannot access when pressed with nature:this may lead to messy environment thereby resulting inhard health conditions. Therefore, the health right of PWDs is worrisome,unattainable, and inaccessible.

6.1.6 *Right to Education*

Knowledge is power. This means that a person with knowledge or education is endowed with power. Such power could be exercised in various forms to attain many goals. In the present discourse, the right to education is crucial to the aspirations of PWDs in order to enjoy full and equal opportunities with others.

Right to education is entrenched under Article 24 CRPD which provides that:

> State Parties recognize the right of persons with disabilities to education. With a view to realizing this right without discrimination and on the basis of equal opportunity, State Parties shall ensure an inclusive education system at all levels and lifelong leaning directed to:
>
> (a) The full development of human potential and sense of dignity and self-worth, and the strengthening of respect for human rights, fundamental freedoms and human diversity;
> (b) The development by persons with disabilities of their personality, talents and creativity, as well as their mental and physical abilities, to their fullest potentials;...[416]

---

[416] CRPD; see also Article 24 (c-d).

In realizing this right, State Parties shall ensure that:

(a) Persons with disabilities are not excluded from the general education system on the basis of disability, and that children with disabilities are not excluded from free and compulsory primary education, or from secondary education on the basis of disability;

(b) Persons with disabilities can access an inclusive quality and free primary education and secondary education on an equal basis with others in the communities in which they live.[417]

Furthermore, the International Convention on Economic, Social and Cultural Rights (ICESCR)[418] provides for prohibition of discrimination in relation to the provision of, and access to educational facilities and opportunities.

Nigeria's 1999 Constitution makes no direct reference to the right to education. It merely mandates government to "direct its policy towards ensuring that there are equal and adequate educational opportunities at all levels."[419] Worthy of note however is the Nigeria National Policy on Education and its Universal Basic Education (UBE) programme, which mandates government to provide free, compulsory and universal education to every child of primary and junior secondary school age. The program has a penal provision against parents who deny their children basic education. Government also demonstrated political will by legislating the setting aside of 2% of its consolidated revenue fund to finance the program.

From the above provisions, we state that Nigeria has some good laws and policies on education but lacks reliable implementation culture; and the will to properly implement laws and policies is the bane of relevant institutions. Thus, it remains painful to assert that the right to education is denied PWDs, or they receive less education than others. Many do not have the opportunity of formal schooling. Those who are lucky to go to school cannot afford basic learning aids such as brail and others. In certain cases, they do not attend the same school with others. For instance, some schools do not accept children with disabilities into regular classrooms. Even when they are accepted, there may not be a

---

[417] *Ibid* 2 (a)-(b) see also Articles 3(a-c) 4 and 5.
[418] Article 2 of ICESCR.
[419] Constitution of the Federal Republic of Nigeria, Chapter II, Section 18. (1).

sign language interpreter thereby undermining the principle of equality of educational opportunity. It is important to note that the environment also plays a vital role in the realization of the persons with disabilities right to education. For instance, most or school buildings are constructed in a way that prevents persons with disabilities from entering them or accessing the classrooms and other facilities in the school. Furthermore, persons on wheelchair cannot access some hostels or classrooms, and libraries. Over the years, many countries have ignored to take into consideration the right of persons with disabilities in the educational policies even when it is obvious that they are perhaps the largest minority groups in the world. Another painful instance is a situation where the educational qualifications or certificates of PWDs are rejected in place of that of others with lower qualifications. In other words, some employers of labour prefer to engage a school certificate holder rather than a disabled Masters'Degree holder. Thus, most PWDs are often neglected and denied employment opportunities no matter how well educated they may be. We must simply accept the fact that PWDs are denied their right to education either directly or indirectly.

6.1.7 *Reproductive Rights of Persons with Disabilities*

Undoubted, PWDs are entitled to the right to reproduction or procreation as others without disabilities, and these rights are recognized under legal instruments. The CRPD provides that State Parties shall take effective and appropriate measures to eliminate discrimination against persons with disabilities in all matters relating to marriage, family, parenthood and relationships, on an equal basis with others so as to ensure thatthe right of all persons with disabilities who are of age to marry and to found a family on the basis of free and full consent of the intending spouses is recognized thus:

> The rights of persons with disabilities to decide freely and responsibly on the number and spacing of their children and to have access to age-appropriate information, reproductive and family planning education are recognized and the means necessary to enable them to exercise these rights are provided... [420]

---

[420] Article 23 (1) (a) (b) of CRPD.

Equally, the Convention on the Elimination of All Forms of Discrimination Against Women (CEDAW) enjoins State Parties to ensure appropriate services to women in terms of reproduction. These include all aspects of health and reproductive rights, taking care and providing adequate antenatal and neo-natal services to women with disabilities. Other reproductive rights of PWDs are: right to control their fertility i.e. family planning, method of contraception, protection from sexually transmitted diseases such as HIV/AIDs.[421] Generally, the reproductive system and functions of the PWDs are to be taken care of. The Fundamental Objectives and Directive Principles of State Policy provide that the State shall direct its policy towards ensuring, inter alia,adequate medical and health facilities for all persons.[422] As already observed, rights under Chapter II of the Nigerian Constitution, including health and reproductive rights, are indeed justiciable if there are statutes to back them up. Thus, health-related statutes such as the National Health Act 2014, National HIV-AIDS ACT (NACA) 2007, and the HIV-AIDS (Anti-Discrimination) Act 2014 all serve to provide the platform for justiciablity of health rights of citizens in Nigeria.

In 2003, Nigeria adopted the National Reproductive Health Policy which was reviewed in 2016. This policy embodies the following:

(a) To reduce material morbidity and mortality due to pregnancy, childbirth and unsafe abortions.

(b) To reduce the level of unwanted pregnancies in all women of reproductive age.

(c) To eliminate all forms of gender based violence and other practices that are harmful to the health of women and children.

(d) To reduce gender imbalance in availability of reproductive health services.

(e) To promote reproductive health awareness in young children.

(f) To introduce into school curricula (including primary schools) sexuality and family life education.

(g) To increase knowledge of reproductive biology and promote responsible behaviours of adolescents regarding contraception, safe sex and prevention of sexually transmitted infections.

---

[421] Article 14 (2) (c)(h) of CEDAW.
[422] Section 17 (3)(d) of the 1999 Constitution.

(h)   To reduce gender imbalance in all sexual and reproductive health matters.[423]

Undoubtedly, PWDs are entitled to all the above provisions and as already observed in Chapter 4 of this book, rights under Chapter II of the Nigerian Constitution, including health and reproductive rights are indeed justiciable if there are statutes to back them up. Thus, health-related statutes such as the National Health Act 2014, National HIV-AIDS ACT (NACA) 2007, and the HIV-AIDS (Anti-Discrimination) Act 2014 all serve to provide the platform for justiciablity of health rights of citizens in Nigeria including the disabled. However, the reality is that most health services are inaccessible to PWDs. The worse hit are those in rural communities where there are inadequate health facilities and officials to educate them on reproductive matters.

It is also observed that almost all the policies on reproductive health as seen above seem to be tailored towards the reproductive rights of women alone, while researchers and policy makers accord very little attention to the reproductive concerns of men with disabilities. Although we agree that issues pertaining to pregnancy, maternal health, and prenatal care affect women, other reproductive health matters such as knowledge of reproductive biology and responsible behaviour regarding contraception, safe sex and prevention of sexually transmitted infections is imperative for everybody- both male and female.

6.2 Vulnerable Persons with Disabilities

It is imperative to note that among the community of PWDs, there are some that are exceptionally vulnerable. These include women, children and elderly persons living with disabilities. This group of PWDs are considered vulnerable because they are exceptionally weak, and can easily be hurt if their human rights are denied. Because of their weakness, it is virtually impossible to enjoy their rights equally with others without special consideration.

---

[423]   Other relevant policies are National HIV/AIDs Policy, 2001; National Health Policy, 2016; 2016-2020 National HIV Strategy for Adult and Young Persons.

6.2.1 *Women with Disabilities*

The fact that women with disabilities need special protection is not a contentious one. Women in this group are always disadvantaged by virtue of their gender. Under International Human Rights Law, special protection measures that favour vulnerable and disadvantaged groups do not constitute discrimination;[424] conversely, such actions may be needed to protect and stop discrimination. For instance, the Convention provides that:

(1) State Parties recognize that women and girls with disabilities are subject to multiple discrimination and in this regard shall take measures to ensure the full and equal enjoyment by them of all human rights and fundamental freedoms.
(2) State Parties shall take all appropriate measures to ensure the full development, advancement and empowerment of women for the purpose of guaranteeing them the exercise and enjoyment of the human rights and fundamental freedoms set out in the present Convention.[425]

Furthermore, women with disabilities are also protected under the Convention on the Elimination of All Forms of Discrimination against Women (CEDAW).[426] All the instruments call for integrating the resources and needs of women with disabilities into all aspects of programming to assure equitable protection and assistance.

It is however saddening to note that notwithstanding the rights embodied in the CEDAW and other legal instruments, women with disabilities continue to suffer neglect and discrimination. They are also susceptible to all forms of abuses, ranging from domestic violence, sexual violence, emotional blackmail, and physical violence[427]. Women

---

[424] See the document of United Nations Human Rights and Refugee Protection, 2006, p. 7.

[425] See CRPD, 2006.

[426] All the provision made up of 29 Articles are on the need to see women as equal human being with the opposite sex. Other instruments protecting women with disabilities are the ICCPR in its Article 3, the ICESCR also its Article 3. UNHCR Guidelines on Protection of Refugee Women. The UN Guidelines on Sexual and Gender Based Violence Against Women and many more.

[427] Women and Girls with Disabilities, UNITED NATIONS ENABLE,

with disabilities face discrimination on grounds of gender and disability, and often they have less access to essential services such as health care, education and vocational rehabilitation.[428]

Women play the most essential role in procreation and, therefore, need adequate care and attention during such period[429]. One can only imagine the condition and situation of a woman with disability during pregnancy if she cannot access adequate medical care for herself and the baby in her womb simply because of her condition. In this case, those in rural communities suffer most because of unavailability of medical centres, equipment, drugs and personnel[430]. Even in some urban centres, the negative and often disrespectful attitude of health workers towards pregnant women with disabilities is very saddening. Hence most women with disabilities are their own personal physicians in the sense that throughout the gestation period they may not have had access to hospitals, antenatal drugs and gynaecologists. Thus they are often delivered of their babies without the help of doctors and other medical personnel. In such cases, the best alternative is for them to be aided by their neighbours or family members who are not qualified in that line[431].

The situation continues even after delivery because some women with disabilities may not have the physical ability to carry, feed, cuddle and take care of their babies. In this condition, women with disabilities also suffer stigmatization from the opposite sex. This is because they find it difficult to get married; rather, the same men who reject to have them as wives usually rape and abandon them. This situation leads to high infant mortality rate which is prevalent in Nigeria and most African countries[432]. There are situations where women with disabilities lose their

---

[428] <http://www.un.org /disabilities/default.asp?id=1514> accessed 5/5/16. *Ibid.*

[429] Fagbohungbe M., 'Disability and Reproductive Health in   Nigeria', in E. Azinge and C. Ani (Eds.), *The Rights of Persons With Disabilities*, NIALS 2001, p.23.

[430] *Ibid.*

[431] Smith *Supra*, pp.35-46.

[432] WHO (2017), *Levels and Trends in Child Mortality 2017*<www.who.int> accessed 22/2/18. According to the report, five countries accounted for half of all new-born deaths last year, with Nigeria third in the list. These are India (24 per cent), Pakistan (10 per cent), Nigeria (9 per cent), the Democratic Republic of the Congo (4 per cent) and Ethiopia (3 per cent). Most new-born deaths occurred in two regions: Southern Asia (39 per cent) and sub-Saharan Africa (38 per cent).

children to ritualists because they cannot protect them[433]. Additionally, the highest numbers of street beggars in most Nigerian cities are women with disabilities and their children[434]. A very alarming situation is that most of these children have no disability yet they join their disabled mothers to beg for a living.

Notably, the last periodic report on the state of human rights in Nigeria was submitted on 22 October 2013 by the Ministry of Women Affairs and Social Development to the United Nations Working Group on the Universal Periodic Review.[435]Remarkably however, the report failed to provide an update on the human rights situation of PWDs.[436]

6.2.2 *Children with Disabilities*

Children with disabilities are another set of vulnerable group that suffer neglect and rejection in society[437]. Some children with disabilities are born with such impairments. It could be as a result of lack of medical care during the formation stage while in their mother's womb, others could be lack of adequate medical care after birth, for example, failure to immunize against childhood diseases such as polio. Furthermore, it could be as a result of malnutrition as a result of poverty[438]. Some may even be as a result of armed conflicts and domestic violence. For instance, during the Liberia and Serra Leone Civil War, the rebel groups wickedly

---

[433]   Smith, n 481 above.

[434]   *Ibid.*

[435]   All States parties are obliged to submit regular reports on how the rights are being implemented to the Working Group on the Universal Periodic Review (UPR), established in accordance with Human Rights Council resolution 5/1 of 18 June 2007. States must report initially within two years of accepting the Convention and thereafter every four years. The Committee examines each report and shall make recommendations on the report as it may consider appropriate and shall forward these to the State Party concerned.

[436]   See Human Rights Council Twenty-fifth Session, Agenda item 6☐Universal Periodic Review A/HRC/25/6).Article at <http.//www.refworld.org/docid/43fb2cd12html-> accessed 20/12/2016.

[437]   Landsdown G., 'It is Our World Too! A Report on the Lives of Disabled Children', *Disability Awareness in Action*, 2001.

[438]   Document of Western Australian Disability Services Commission<http://www.health.wa.gov.an/.../training- package/fcommand/disability.pdf> accessed 22 March 2016.

amputated some children, both girls and boys, while others were forced to carry arms and become child soldiers. The child soldiers who obviously were not familiar with the use of arms wounded themselves in that process and were permanently disabled[439]. The girls were abducted as sex slaves and equally suffered permanent disabilities therefrom. The same scenario is being experienced in the North East Nigeria where Boko Haram has continued to perpetrate havoc and unleash inhuman acts against adults and children irrespective of religion.

Worthy of note is the provision of CRPD which enjoins State Parties to take all necessary measures to ensure the full enjoyment by children with disabilities of all human rights and fundamental freedoms on an equal basis with other children. Thus in all actions concerning children with disabilities, the best interests of the child shall be a primary consideration; and State Parties shall ensure that children with disabilities have the right to express their views freely on all matters affecting them, their views being given due weight in accordance with their age and maturity on an equal basis with other children, and to be provided with disability and age-appropriate assistance to realize that right.[440]

There is a plethora of rights ascribed to the protection of children under the United Nations Convention on the Rights of the Child, The African Charter on the Rights and Welfare of the Child, the Nigeria Child Rights Act and other regional instruments on the rights of the child. Despite the provisions which to our minds only operate in papers, children with disabilities continue to suffer rejection, neglect, discrimination and exclusion. It is particularly worrisome that children with disabilities suffer the violation of their rights even in the hands of their parents, family members and their immediate communities, thereby worsening their situation. Under such situation, nobody will be there to help them draw the attention of the government on their rights. Such children suffer from trauma and other psychological problems as a result of rejection and discrimination from those that could have given them love, care and hope. Some parents prefer other children to their disabled

---

[439] UNICEF Report, "Childhood under Threat, the State of the World's Children" UNICEF, (2005).

[440] In Nigeria, about 13 States have enacted laws on the protection of children, and even then, the issue of enforcement remains a challenge. Many other states are still reluctant to enact the Child's Rights Laws.

child, and, for this reason, they do not care about their education and their wellbeing[441].

Furthermore, children with disabilities face greater danger in the society. There are situations where they are sexually abused, used for rituals by ritualists; some are even used as beggars by their family members on major streets[442]. Government on their part has failed to recognize the fact that children with disabilities have the right to special protection and treatment given their particular vulnerability to being exposed to the risks of exploitation and death[443]. Children with disabilities are entitled to rights to education, adequate food and the highest attainable standard of health as enshrined under the instruments protecting the right of children.

In Nigeria, most schools are built without considering the interest of children with disabilities. The buildings are not accessible to children with disabilities. Equally, the public transport system to even have access to the schools is not sensitive to the plight of the children with disabilities. Additionally, the number of children with disabilities in mainstream schools is very low, insignificant and at others not even allowed. Rather, most children with disabilities are usually kept in special schools thereby being prevented from having close interaction with other children without disabilities.

There are other cases where the other children without disabilities make jest of them, reject their friendship and treat them as outcasts. At other times parents of those without disabilities discourage their children from socializing with children with disabilities. A lot of teachers equally refrain from specializing in special education. As a result of discrimination, rejection and sometimes fear, children with disabilities abandon their studies for begging. There are many disabled children that cannot attend school due to poverty, and vocational services are not made available to them.

Children with disabilities are equally denied their rights to good medical services. There are situations where the medical facilities are inaccessible because of the nature of their disabilities. This is because in some rural communities, children with disabilities are regarded as a taboo

---

[441] Avoke, M.K., Hayford, S.K., Ikeanacho, I.J., and Ocloo, M.A., Issues in Special Education, (Accra North: The City Publisher, 1998) p. 11.

[442] *Ibid.*

[443] Upah, Supra .

and their parents refuse to take them to health care centres where such areavailable. Furthermore, children with disabilities suffer stigmatization because their parents hide them from public domain thereby denying them access to inclusive and formal education[444]. They are also vulnerable to sexual abuse, sometimes even by close relatives. Remarkably, some disabilities in children may have been prevented and are preventable if adequate medical services were made available to the mother during prenatal stages[445]. Government should bear in mind that children's health is tomorrow's wealth.

6.2.3 *Elderly or Aged Persons with Disabilities*

Elderly persons with disabilities are grouped as vulnerable people. Therefore, they need special care, attention and protection. In many cases, they are excluded from economic and social rights by their immediate society which they contributed in building. For instance, some aged persons with disabilities may have been placed in such a condition as a result of civil war which they participated in as combatants. The same society does not appreciate them because they are no longer strong to contribute meaningfully and their past effort may have been forgotten. Some of such persons are war veterans that fought to keep Nigeria together as a result of which their legs were amputated, and they suffered loss of sight and intellectual impairments. It is worthy of note that there is no specific provision in the CRPD on the protection of the aged with disabilities. That notwithstanding the aged with disabilities could be either women or men; therefore, they are protected as human beings under the Convention. Remarkably the International Convention on Economic, Social and Cultural Rights Committee expressly addresses the economic, social and cultural rights of older persons contained under the General Comment for Older Persons.[446]Similar provisions are African

---

[444]   Filmer, D. (2005) Disability, Poverty and Schooling in Developing Countries: Results from 11Household Surveys. World Bank Discussion Paper.
[445]   UN Women, 2012, 'Report of the Expert Group Meeting on Prevention of Violence against Women and Girls'<http://www.unwomen.org/~/media/Headq uarters/Attachments/Sections/Library/Publications/20111/Report-of-the-EGM-on-Prevention-of-Violence-against-Women-and-Girls.pdf.> accessed 12/3/17
[446]   See General Comment, No 6 CRPS. The inclusion of the other status should be interpreted as including the aged. The aged could be disabled or non-disabled.

Charter on Human and People's Right;[447] Protocol to the African Charter on Human and People's Rights on the Rights of Women in Africa;[448]and Committee on Economic, Social and Cultural Rights.[449] Furthermore, the principle of non-discrimination enshrined in the ICESCR, ICCPR, CEDAW, and CRPD equally prohibits discrimination on grounds of age and, by extension and inclusion, the aged persons with disabilities. The provision of African Charter on Human and Peoples Rights is instructive. It states that: "The aged and the disabled shall also have the right to special measures of protection in keeping with their physical or moral needs"[450].

Remarkably, in Nigeria and Africa as a whole the aged is often neglected talk less of the aged with disabilities. Unlike in the developed countries where the aged and disabled are well taken care of, in Nigeria, many aged persons with disabilities live undignified lives of neglect and discrimination by even their family members[451]. Some of them are seen begging in cities when they have no close relation to take care of them. In this case, the trauma and depression they face, coupled with their age, pose a greater danger to their health. They are invisible and powerless.

Remarkably, Section 14(2)(b) of the Constitution states that, "The security and welfare of its people shall be the primary purpose of the government", and it goes on to promise in Section 16(2)(d) that, "Suitable and adequate shelter and suitable and adequate food, reasonable national minimum living wage, old age care and pensions and unemployment, sick benefits and welfare of the disabled are provided for all citizens." Unfortunately, the government seems to have reneged on these promises as most elderly are not covered by any social security scheme[452]. Consequently, the burden of care in Nigeria squarely rests on

---

[447] *Ibid*, 2000.

[448] Article 18 (4).

[449] Article 22.

[450] Article 18 (4).

[451] Adeniji, D.O. and Oladejo, D.A. (2012) "Developing a Positive Attitude towards De-phasing Elder Abuse
and its Health Implications" in Osinowo, O.O., Moronkola, O.A., and Egunyomi, D.A. (eds.), *The Adults*
and Aged in Nigeria: Issues and Researches. Royal People (Nigeria) Ltd. p. 168.

[452] Cynthia Okafor, "Caring for the Aged: Why Are Homes for the Elderly Still "Taboo" in Nigeria?"<
http://venturesafrica.com/black-panther-is-just-what-it-is/> accessed 23/2/18.

family members, and those who lack caring families suffer exploitation, abuse, and marginalization[453]. It is worthy to note that we might be physically and mentally healthy today, but for any person that attains the age of seventy; age-related disability becomes only a matter of time. This means that every single person is a potential member of this group. Thus the earlier society changes its perception about disability and PWDs, the better for the society at large.

---

[453] Femi Ogunshola, "Caring for the Elderly in Nigeria", Peoples Daily (May 11 2014) <http://www.peoplesdailyng.com/caring-for-the-elderly-in-nigeria/>accessed 23/2/18.

CHAPTER SEVEN

Challenges of Protecting and Enforcing the Rights of Persons Withdisabilities in Nigeria

The growing number of PWDs in Nigeria has continued to present enormous challenges to the nation and to the African Continent. According to WHO, Africa has the high number of PWDs[454] and the major causes of disability in Africa include poor maternal healthcare during preor post-natal stage, accident, poor nutrition at infancy, armed conflict, natural disaster and other social misfortunes[455]. PWDs are always uncertain about their future which leads to depression and hopelessness. This is because they frequently experience discrimination and barriers to freely participate in all aspects of the society. Their rights as human beings are frequently trampled upon thereby subjecting them to a situation of helplessness. Notwithstanding the fact that most of the world has realized the need to protect PWDs and many countries, including Nigeria has put in place policies and programmes to ensure their inclusion in all human affairs, PWDs still face numerous challenges that call for urgent redress. Some of the challenges are discussed hereunder.

7.1 Lack of Awareness on the Existence of Disability Rights

This is one of the greatest challenges facing the PWDs in Nigeria. Despite the plethora of rights, national, regional and international ascribed to PWDs, society has not come to terms with the fact that they have the same rights with others. A great number of people are unaware of the fact that the same rights that protect them also protect PWDs. While others are aware of this fact, they pretend not to know. It is

---

[454] World Health Organization (WHO) & World Bank World Report on Disability (2011) <www.who.int/disabilities/world> accessed 24/2/17.
[455] *Ibid.*

imperative at this junction to underscore the fact that this lack of awareness is due to the structure and the formulation and nature of our legislation. Remarkably, the 1999 Constitution of the Federal Republic of Nigeria[456] does not specify in clear terms or directly mention the word 'disability' throughout its 320 Sections (although the Constitution contains some provisions that are indirectly linked to disability). Furthermore, both Section 42(2), which prohibits discrimination based on the circumstances of a person's birth, and Section 14, 16(1) and 17, which guarantee the right to equality and fundamental rights for all, make no reference to Persons With Disabilities. Therefore, an average literate Nigerian is unaware of the rights of persons with disabilities. Interestingly, in the course of this research, we discovered that even colleagues in academics stand on the same footing of ignorance with other laypersons on the rights of persons with disabilities.

The government department responsible for the promotion and protection of the rights and welfare of PWDs in Nigeria is the Federal Ministry of Women Affairs and Social Development, and the Ministry has not done much in terms of creation of awareness of the rights of PWDs. The issue of disabilities only comes to mind when one encounters a person with disability begging on the street. Similarly, many PWDs are unaware of their legal rights because a majority of them are illiterate. Those who know about their rights cannot access them because of lack of an enforcement mechanism. Furthermore, Nigeria apart from ratifying the United Nations Convention on the Rights of Person with Disabilities, its domestication which was made possible by the enactment of the Discrimination Against Persons with Disabilities (Prohibition) Act, 2018 will project the high level of awareness of rights of persons with disabilities in Nigeria.

Worthy of note is the existence of disability bodies such as the Joint National Association of Persons with Disabilities (JONAPWD), an official body that specifically addresses the violation of the rights of persons with disabilities. The body collaborates with the Nigerian Government in order to promote the rights of persons with disabilities. There is also Association of Comprehensive Empowerment of Nigerians with Disabilities (ASCEND) with an objective aim of integrating persons with disabilities into the society. Having highlighted the powers and

---

[456] *Ibid.*

responsibilities of bodies concerned with the issues disabilities in Nigeria, there is need to create awareness on the existence of disability rights which will go a long way in combating the stigma.

7.2 Weak Enforcement of Existing Laws

It is the same laws that protect persons without disabilities which equally shield persons with disabilities. Apart from the international legal instrument (the CRPD which Nigeria is a signatory to, though not yet domesticated), there are other relevant legal instruments such as the International Covenant on Economic, Social and Cultural Rights (ICESR), the International Covenant on Civil and Political Right (ICCPR), Convention on the Rights of the Child (CRC), Convention on the Elimination of All Forms of Discrimination Against Women (CEDAW), African Charter on Human and Peoples' Rights (ACHPR) and many other regional and international legal instruments on disability rights. It is disheartening that most of the legal instruments fail to provide for enforcement mechanism, a loophole too many. One of the reasons why the laws are unenforceable is that persons with disabilities were not allowed to participate actively at the onset. If they were involved in the drafting of the laws, the gap would not have been because he who wears the shoes feels the pain. In other words, persons with disabilities know that there are certain rights they cannot assert on their own without the help of certain agencies of the government and the civil society. Though some of the documents clarify the human rights of persons with disabilities, it is left for the government to include same in all development efforts. Another cause of weak enforcement is lack of cooperation between national and international community in the realization of the rights of persons with disabilities. Another cause of weak enforcement is that government development programmes and principles are not structured in a way that embraces the realization of human rights standards.

It is noted and appreciated that the agenda of efforts of the United Nations in the need to mainstream disability in development, activities towards the realization of same have often taken place in a compartmentalized and limited manner.[457] Undoubtedly, inclusion of persons with disabilities into the development goals and decisions on matters that affect them will definitely strengthen the enforcement and realization of their rights as entrenched under the existing laws.

7.3 Lack of Political Will

This is another serious challenge bedevilling the protection of the human rights of persons with disabilities in Nigeria and in international community. For instance, the barriers to inclusive education being experienced by persons with disabilities need to be changed, but lack of political will abides as constraint. The Federal Ministry of Education oversees matters relating to education in Nigeria, both formal and vocational. Policies are being formulated for development in all levels of education. Yet inclusive education is far within the reach of persons with disabilities. Clearly speaking, the lack of active engagement of persons with disabilities in matters that concern their wellbeing is another setback in policy decision. Equally, there has been neglect and less commitment on the part of policy makers to come up with an efficient administrative infrastructure for the provision of services on disability matters. There is therefore lack of effective approaches to the implementation of the provisions of the legal instruments and Government policies on human rights implementation to reflect on the culture and environment as they have impact on the effect and experience of persons with disabilities in Nigeria. It is imperative that policy formulation, legitimization, implementation and evaluation be given credence in matters relating to disabilities.

7.4 Culture/Religious Beliefs

It is important to note that religion and culture negatively affect the realization of the rights of persons with disabilities. In other words, they are at the top ladder as barriers to the realization of the rights of people with disabilities. Some cultures are repugnant to natural justice equity

---

[457]   United Nations Development Group p. 13. See also<http://
dsqsds.org/article/view/625/802> accessed20/12/2016.

and good conscience. For instance, some cultures perceive persons with disabilities as evil, carriers of evil, bad luck, ill luck, misfortune, death and curse bearers and carriers. In some Nigerian cultures, if a child is born deformed, such a child is thrown into evil forests and the gods are appeased for cleansing of that family. Those that survive the ordeal are always isolated, marginalized, and not allowed to participate fully in the society. They are not allowed by such communities to enjoythe same rights and privileges, and mingle with others in the community.

Their human dignity is not respected and is often denied. Effects of culture lead to denial, rejection and discrimination of persons with disabilities. In some communities, they are denied access to social amenities, healthcare, same stream or river, buying and selling in the same market. In other communities, they are denied equal participation in cultural activities; some cultures forbid persons with disabilities from appearance in public thereby confining and isolating them in a place which is a breach of fundamental rights to freedom of movement and association. They are forbidden from participation in cultural activities and denied cultural heritage which is against the UN Convention.[458]

Worthy of note is the issue of religion. Some people practice their religion upside down and outside the provisions of the Holy Books, the Bible and the Quran. For instance, some religions adherents wrongly believe that persons with disabilities are in their condition as a result of their sins or that of their parents and forefathers[459]. As a result, they are isolated, rejected and discriminated against. Some people with disabilities are denied access to worship centres because of their condition thereby undermining the realization of the human rights of persons with disabilities.

---

[458] Article 3 of CRPD enjoins the state to have measures that will promote, protect and uphold the cultural rights of persons with disabilities, and the right to enjoy access to participation in cultural life. See Also Preamble to ICESCR.

[459] Nigerian is full of devout Christians and Muslims who have imported traditional beliefs to shape their understanding of disability. Thus for many people, disability is a spiritual sickness or curse that can be healed by prayers, confinement, and in some cases, physical violence.

CHAPTER EIGHT

Concluding Remarks

The protection of the rights of PWDs has consistently posed challenges to the government whose duty is to protect and provide for the well being of its citizens irrespective of status, gender, and ethnicity. This book examined the relevance of human rights in the protection of persons with disabilities in Nigeria by analysing the legal framework and institutional mechanisms relevant for their protection and wellbeing. We evaluated the adequacy of these laws and institutions, by assessing the present plight of persons with disabilities in the country. Challenges that impede the effective protection of the rights of the disabled were considered, and recommendations made for practical measures to be put in place to ensure the protection and fulfilment of these rights.

The key findings of the book based on analysis of existing literature, legislation, and cases, are summarized as follows:

i. There is no uniform and generally accepted definition of what constitutes disability. This makes the issue of protection more difficult and unenforceable because while some of the existing legal instruments on the protection of human rights of PWDs failed to proffer definitions on the word "disability", others restricted or ascribed disability to certain ailments and excluded other forms thereby excluding persons with other forms of disabilities from enjoying their rights. The inability of scholars and legal instruments to come up with a universally accepted definition of disability has restricted the protection available to PWDs. Notably, even the leading international instrument on disability, the CRPD and its Optional Protocol failed to provide definition of the word 'disability.' This again is an omission too many. The 1999 Constitution of the Federal Republic of Nigeria also failed to directly provide for the rights of PWDs and the meaning of the word 'disability'. Conversely, an examination of the word 'disability' indicates that it is capable of multiple meanings as can be seen from the forms and classifications.

It is our view that the difference in meaning should not rob the disabled of their rights or lead to rejection by their immediate environment neither should it be a bar from the mainstreaming of policies and national planning.

ii. Presently, in Nigeria, there is little appreciation that disability is primarily an issue rooted in human rights. Thus, there is lack of awareness among many Nigerians on the existence of the rights of persons with disabilities. Notably, a greater number of PWDs are unaware of the fact that they are entitled to certain rights as human beings and as special beings. The common perception held by policy-makers and the public at large (including persons with disabilities themselves) is that disability issues are charity and welfare matters. Thus, this notion is a major, imbedded factor that negatively affects the social inclusion of disabled people within the country.

Thus, the need for public education on human rights; particularly regarding equality of PWDs and those without disability before the law was made manifest in the book. There should be public awareness through sensitization programmes on disability issues generally, and the need to see disability issues as human rights rather than the generally believed charity issue. These programmes should include radio and television jingles in the major Nigerian Languages. Community and faith-based institutions should also be used as agents to create awareness.

iii. The recent enactment ofDiscrimination Against Persons with Disabilities (Prohibition) Act, 2018, came as a succour with specificity on issues regarding the rights of PWDs; hopefully to complement the existing relevant human rights instruments and conventions that have so far proven weak in their implementation and enforcement.

It is early to comment on the effectiveness of the recent Act, but as time goes on further study will reveal the strength and weakness of the Act.

iv. The existing institutions relevant to the protection of persons with disabilities such as National Human Rights Commission, Public Complaints Commission, Courts and Tribunals, Ministries and Establishments, Non-governmental Organizations and others are clearly weak. They rant on social media and media houses about the theoretical aspects of their duties relating to persons with disabilities, but they lack effective monitoring and evaluation mechanisms to assess or benchmark their utility. Furthermore, most of the above organizations operate only in cities thereby neglecting those in rural communities that host the greatest number of PWDs. There is also the problem of poor funding and corruption which hinders their operation. Admittedly, some states have appointed Special Advisors on Disabilities, but it appears that these advisors are mere political appointees by the state governors. Their roles are not clear, and they are not effective because evidence suggests these advisors adopt a charity/welfare approach to disability by providing cash hand-outs to a very small number of disabled people. This method is not beneficial to long-term sustainable change, which is rooted in the rights-based approach to disability.

With the recent Act establishing the National Commission for Persons with Disabilities (the Commission), it is hoped that government will support it with adequate funding to effectively discharge its mandate.

v. Efforts have been made to trace the historical discrimination and stigmatization to traditional African society where disability was considered a punishment visited upon the family by the gods. Because of such perceptions, PWDs were deprived of human love and dignity and were subjected to inhuman treatment by the society that is supposed to give them protection and love. Interestingly, in some African cultures children born with disabilities were seen as being possessed by supernatural forces and evidence of good luck to the whole community. Some cultures still discriminate against PWDs for they still suffer neglect, rejection, and discrimination in modern society.

Nevertheless, the words of God contained in the holy books, Holy Bible and Holy Qur'an, brought the message of love and compassion for PWDs, thereby discrediting the claims that disabilities occur as a result of sin as envisaged by some cultures. The holy books encourage people to assist and protect the disabled. Emphasis was made on social responsibilities and duties to provide their basic needs.

171

vi. Society is not interested and at the same time is in doubt of the capabilities and the economic acumen of persons with disabilities. They are regarded as incapable of economic participation and contribution in the society. In some communities, they were not allowed to marry or be married for fear of contamination and spread of the curse according to their cultural belief. In the same vein, parents and other family members of PWDs also suffer discrimination, exclusion, marginalization, rejection, stigmatization and many others. In some communities, such parents are accused of being the cause of their children's disabilities. Parents of children with disabilities suffer emotional, economic and financial stress, most especially the poor ones. Conversely, in certain situations, persons with disabilities especially the vulnerable ones suffer rejection, exclusion, hatred, stigmatization and discrimination in the hands of their parents, family members and friends, which often leads to a helpless and suicidal situation. The larger society does not accept them either. They are seen as unproductive, and are neither allowed to exercise their rights nor prove their worth and talents.

The Discrimination Against Persons with Disabilities (Prohibition) Act, 2018 has come to alleviate the sufferings and discrimination against people living with disability. However there is need for government to support the implementation of the Act in order to ensure real progress in terms of disability rights. Also, Persons With Disabilities should be actively involved in the management and activities of the Commission.

vii. Legal scholars and researchers in other fields have made references to the Disability Decree of 1993 as dealing with persons with disabilities in Nigeria and having been promulgated under the military dispensation.

However, the origin, existence or validity of the said legislation is quite controversial. It is not contained in the 2004 Edition of the Laws of the Federation of Nigeria. The present status of that law is not clear, thereby raising questions about its authenticity*ab initio*.

viii. Multiplicity of environmental barriers militate against the social inclusion of persons with disabilities, and that their economic, political, healthy, education, reproductive and social wellbeing are being denied with impunity. These are the aspects of citizen rights which every responsive government strives to promote through policies and programmes aimed at mainstreaming disabilities into the society. Furthermore, it is noted that the situation of vulnerable persons with disabilities such as women, children and the aged are particularly pitiable. Despite their condition they are frequently abused sexually and physically. They suffer double jeopardy, neglect, rejection and discrimination.

The need to raise awareness in society about disability issues is very critical to the protection of the rights of PWDs, and their inclusion into mainstream society.

ix. Sexual and reproductive health of PWDs has been widely and deeply neglected in a historical pattern that includes denied information about sexual and reproductive health, and denied rights to establish relationships and to decide whether, when and with whom to have a family. Yet as human beings, men and women with disabilities have the same desires for intimate relationships, marriage and parenthood as others, and despite popular perceptions of their asexuality, they are indeed sexually active.

Special attention must be given to the reproductive rights of PWDs in terms of ensuring that PWDs are educated on reproductive health and how to make responsible choices. Also, they should be able to access reproductive health facilities for treatments and other services such as family planning, ante-natal and maternity care, etc on equal basis with others.

x. There is no robust and reliable data on disability, and this means that policy makers attempting to design and implement more inclusive disability strategies and programmes are doing this on a background of meagre information scattered among organisations and institutions around the world.

Without reliable data, it is extremely difficult to conduct research necessary to fully understand the status of PWDs, develop cost-effective disability policies and strategies, or evaluate the cost-effectiveness of competing approaches. There is therefore need for a clear, consistent, all-embracing and generally acceptable definition of disability that will form the basis of collecting a comprehensive and reliable data on the number of Nigerians living with disabilities according to their age, sex, and type of disability. This will assist the government in planning suitable and accessible disability policies and programmes.

xi. There is also lack of enforcement mechanisms on the existing laws that protect the rights of persons with disabilities. The much acclaimed CRPD failed to make provisions on the enforcement mechanisms and punishment for non-enforcement. Generally, matters relating to the protection of the rights of PWDs are treated with laxity.

The Disability Act of 2018 makes provision for the establishment of separate agencies at the federal and state levels that will be in charge of disability while at the local government level, a committee should be set up to monitor and evaluate the effectiveness of disability service provisions and also ensure that the provisions are carried out to the letter.

xii. The right to education is an empowerment right. Persons with disabilities should be included in education policies at all levels, and Government should ensure equal educational opportunities without discrimination for children and youth with disabilities. Also, all stakeholders should encourage access to mainstream schooling for children with disabilities by providing easily accessible means of transportation, accessible school environments, and accessible facilities. Similarly, government should champion teacher training in special education at all levels. Schools should be equipped with learning aids to assist teachers and children with disabilities. Most of the learning aids are very expensive and parents of the disabled cannot afford them. This will reduce disparities, encourage equality and enhance non-discrimination thereby promoting the best interest of children with disabilities. There is further need to emphasize the recognition of the qualifications and certificates of persons with disabilities on equal basis with those without disabilities.

xiii. There is need for government to encourage the employment of suitably qualified PWDs in all sectors of the economy, and mandate the private sector to respect the right to work of persons with disabilities. In the same vein, government should encourage PWDs to be self-reliant and empowered by providing them (and their immediate families where necessary) with reasonable and accessible micro-credit schemes in order to alleviate poverty to a certain level. These opportunities should be extended to the PWDs in rural areas where most persons with disabilities are unaware of their rights.

Notably, there is a dearth of domestic jurisprudence on disability, due to the absence of ample referrals regarding disability issues to the courts by PWDs and their family members. This would have formed the basis for this book to delve into in-depth discussion of the duties and activities of caregivers regarding the actualization of the human rights of persons with disabilities. Other related areas not discussed in details for the same reason are the cultural rights of persons with disabilities, and the effect of education in the quality of life of PWDs. There is no doubt that the complex nature of globalization and Information Communication Technology create new challenges that affect persons with disabilities economically and socially. It would also be worthwhile if further research is conducted on a related area such as: the effect of ICT in the realization of Human Rights of Persons with Disabilities. It is contended that such topic would go a long way in filling the gap that exists in this area. Furthermore, there is need to research on the position of law relating to disability caregivers. This is with a view to determining the role they play in the protection of the rights of persons with disabilities. The issue of finance and other resources used to provide right based protection comes into question as to who bears the financial burden.Therefore, the issue of poverty in developing countries is crucial to the enjoyment of human rights of persons with disabilities especially as poverty could also lead to disability.

Taking everything into account, it will be an abdication if we fail to stress that promotion of disability rights should be of concern to every single person,because an "abled" person can fall into the "disabled" category at any time. It could be as a result of accident, disease, conflict, or even due to old age, which is inevitable in the natural circle of life.

WORKS CITED

ARTICLES IN JOURNALS

Ajuwon P. M., "Making Inclusive Education Work in Nigeria: Evaluation of Special Educators' Attitudes" (2012) 32 Disability Studies Quarterly 2, 2012, p.32.

Amudson, R."*Against Normal Function*"[2000](31) *Studies in History and Philosophy of Biological and Biomedical Sciences*, pp. 33-53.

Bayefsky, A.F. "The Principles of Equality and Non-discrimination in International Law" [1990] (II).

Chataika, T., McKenzie, J.A., Swart, E., &Lyner-Cleophas, M., "Access to Education in Africa: Responding to the United Nations Convention on the Rights of the   Persons with Disability" *Disability & Society* Vol. 27, Iss. 3, 2012 pp. 385-398.

ChombaWaMunyi, "Past And Present Perceptions Towards Disability: A Historical Perspective," [2012] (32) (2) *Disability Studies Quarterly* (1/2), pp.1-34.

Kanter A.S., 'The Promise and Challenge of the United Nations on the Rights of the Persons with Disabilities' [2007] (34) *Syracuse Journal of International Law and Commerce*; p. 289.

Lawthers A., Pransky S., Peterson L., and Himmelstein J., "Rethinking quality in the context of persons with disability" (2004) 15 *Int. Journal for Quality in Health Care 4*, 287-99.

Maja, P.A., Mann, W.M., Sing, D., Steyn, A.J. and Naidoo, P., "Employing People with Disabilities in South Africa" *South African Journal of Occupational Therapy* Vol 41, Iss. 1, 2011, pp. 24-32.

Parson, T. "The Sick Role and the Role of the Physician" [1975] (53) *Journal of Health and Society, pp. 257-278.*

Perlin, M.L. "Striking for the Guardians and Protectors of the Mind: The Convention on the Rights of the Persons with Mental Disabilities and the Future of Guardianship Law" (2013) *Penn State Law Review* Vol 117, Iss 4, pp. 1160.

Smith, N., "The Face of Disability In Nigeria: A Disability Survey In Kogi and Niger   States", *The Journal of Disability, CBR and Inclusive Development*, Vol 22, No.1, 2011, p.35-46.

Umeh, Ngozi C; Adeola, Romola. "Nigeria". *African Disability Rights Yearbook* 2013, 2016.

BOOKS

Abang T., *The Exceptional Child: Handbook of Special Education* (Jos: FAB ANIEH Nig. Ltd, 2005).

Abu Dawood 4941; and Tirmidhi 1924.

Akhidenor, C., *Nigerians' Attitudes Toward People with Disabilities* (USA: Pro Quest 2007).

Alkalis H., "Education of the Hard of Hearing: A Forgotten Alternative in Nigeria" in Ozoji E., Umolu J.U, and Olaniyan, S.O., eds., p.42.

Ameh C., "Science and Technology for the Handicapped" in Ozoji E.D, Umolu J.U, and   Olaniyan S.O eds.,p.181.

Arnardóttir, O., A Future of Multidimensional Disadvantage Equality? The Avoke, M.K. et al, Issues in Special Education (The City Publishers, 1998).

Avoke, M.K., Hayford, S.K., Ikeanacho, I.J., andOcloo, M.A., *Issues in Special Education*   (Accra North: The City Publisher, 1998).

Ayodele, A. 'Legal And Institutional Mechanisms For Protecting Persons With Disabilities   In Nigeria', in E. Azinge And C. Ani (Eds), *The Rights Of Persons With Disabilities*, (NIALS 2001), P.127.

Barnes C. and Mercer G. (eds.), *The Social Model of Disability and the Majority World* (Leeds: The disability Press, 2005) pp. 1-16.

Biegon, J., "The Promotion and Protection of Disability Rights in the African Human Rights System," in *Aspects to Disability Law in Africa,* ed. I. Grobbelaar-du Plessis   & T. Van Reene (Pretoria: Pretoria University Law Press 2011).

Blank, P. and Others, Disability Civil Rights and Policy, (Thomson West, 2004) p2.

Blank, P., ed., *Disability Rights* (England: Ashgate Publishing Ltd, 2005).

Bowe, F., Handicapping America: Barriers to Disabled People in Disability Our Challenge, ed., Hourihan, J.P., (New York: A distinguished lecture series sponsored by the project for handicapped college students: Teacher's College, Colombia University, New York).

Charlton, J., *Nothing About Us Without Us: Disability Oppression and Empowerment* (USA: University of California Press, 1998).

Clements, L & Read. J. Disabled People and the right to life. The protection and Violation of Disabled People's Most Basic Human Rights p. 41.

Cotter, A.M., *This Ability: An International Legal Perspective of Disability Discrimination* (Ashgate Publishing, Aldershot 2007).

Degener, T., "International Disability Law-A New Legal Subject on the Rise" (paper delivered at the International Experts' Meeting in Hong Kong, December 13-17- 1999).

Dube. A., *Disability Rights Protection Under the African Human Rights System in the Light of the Conventionon Persons Living with Disabilities* (Deutschland: LAP Lambert Academic Publishing GMBH & Co. KG, 2002).

E. Azinge and C. Ani (Eds), *The Rights of Persons With Disabilities*, NIALS 2011.

Eiesland, N.L., The Disabled God: Towards A Liberatory Theology of Disability (Abingdon Press, 1994).

Elizabeth A. Martin (ed.), Oxford Dictionary of Law, 6th Edition, (Oxford University Press 2004) 2015.

Evans M., and Murray R., *The African Charter on Human and Peoples' Rights: The System in Practice 1986-2006* (2nd edition, Cambridge University Press, Cambridge 2008) 178.

Fagbohungbe M., Disability and Reproductive Health in Nigeria', in E. AzingeAnd C. Ani (Eds), *The Rights Of Persons With Disabilities*, NIALS 2011, p.23.

Filmer, D. (2005) Disability, Poverty and Schooling in Developing Countries: Results from 11 Household Surveys. World Bank Discussion Paper.

Fleischer. Z., *The Disability Rights Movement From Charity to Confrontation*(Philadelphia: Temple University Press, 2001) p. 85.

Gharaibeh N., "Disability in Arab Societies: Poverty and Poor Resources", in *Disabilities – Insights From Across Fields And Around The World*, eds., Catherine Marshall, Elizabeth Kendall, Martha Banks and Mariah Cover (USA: Praeger Publishers, 2009).

Golden, (1978) cited in Abang, T., The Exceptional Child-Handbook of Special Education (Fah Educational Books, 2005) p.17.

Hallahan, D.P, and Kauffman, J.M., *Exceptional Children; Introduction to Special Education* (New York: Prentice Hall Inc., 1982).

Kershaw, "Handicapped Children in the Ordinary School" in *The Handicapped persons in the Community*, eds., David Boswell and Janet Wingrove (London: Tavistock   Publication Ltd, 1974).

Landsdown G., "It is Our World Too! A Report on the Lives of Disabled Children", *Disability Awareness in Action*, 2001.

Lang, R. and Upah, L., *Disability Scoping Study in Nigeria* (Nigeria: DFID 2008) 31.

Longmore, P.K., *Why I Burnt My Book and Other Essays on Disability* (Philadelphia: Temple University Press, 2003).

Marriot, A., and Gooding K., *Social Assistance and Disability in Developing Countries* (West Sussex: Sight Saver International, Hayward's Health, 2007).

Marshall C.A., Kendal E., Banks M., and Gover M., eds., *Disabilities: Legal and Political Frameworks* (USA: Praeger,2009).

Matthew 11:20 (Revised Standard Version).

Ntikidem E.P., "Programmes and Services for the Exceptional Children in the 6-3-3-4 System of Education" in *Contemporary Issues in Mainstreaming the Exceptional Child in Nigeria 6-3-3-4 System of Education (A publication of National Council for Exceptional Children)* eds., UzojiE., Umolu J., &Olaniyan O. (Jos: Ehindero   Press,1991).

Okeke, B.A. Essentials of Special Education (Nsukka, Afro-Orbis Publication Ltd: 2001) 23-24.

Oliver, M., *The Politics of Disablement* (London: Macmillan Press Ltd, 1990).

Oyero, R.O., *An appraisal of the right to dignity of prisoners and detainees with disabilities: a case study of Ghana and Nigeria* (South Africa: University of Pretoria, 2004).

Perlin, M.L., *International Human Rights and Mental Disability Law: When the Silenced are Heard* (Oxford: University Press, Oxford 2011) 55.

Quinn G., and Degener I., "Human Rights and Disability- The Current Use and Future   Potential Use of the United Nations Human Rights Instruments in the Context of Disability" quoted in Dube A., p.33.

R Lang and L Upah, Disability Scoping Study in Nigeria (DFID, Nigeria 2008).

R. G. Barker and Others, *'Adjustment to Physical Handicap and Illness: A Survey of the Social Psychology of Physique and Disability'* (New York: 1953).

Riouxand M., and Basser L., *Critical Perspectives on Human Rights and Disability Law* (The Netherlands: MartinusNijhoff Publishers, 2011).

Sarpong, P., Ghana in Retrospect: Some Aspects of Ghanaian Culture (Accra: TemaPublishing Corp, 1974).

Shakespeare T. D., *Disability Rights and Wrongs* (London: Rutledge, 2006).

Shakespeare, Tom (2006). "The Social Model of Disability". *The Disability Studies Reader*. New York: Routledge. p. 197.

The American Heritage Medical Dictionary,(Houghton Mifflin Company, 2007).

UN Convention on the Rights of Persons with Disabilities: European and Scandinavian   Perspectives (MartinusNijhoff 2009), pp. 41-66.

Wright, B.A., *Physical Disability: A Psychological Approach*, (Harper and BON, 1960).

Reports

"Implementation of the World Programme of Action concerning Disabled Persons: towards a society for all in the twenty-first century, Reportof the Secretary-General," A/60/290.

A/HRC/13/29. *Thematic Study by the United Nations High Commissioner for Human Rights on the Structure and Role of National Mechanisms for the Implementation and Monitoring of the Convention on the Rights of Persons with Disabilities.*<http://www2.ohchr.org/english/bodies/hrcouncil/docs /13session/A-HRC-13-
29.pdf> accessed 3 March 2015.

CLEEN Foundation, *Rights of the Child in Nigeria*(Committee on the Rights of the Child, Geneva 2005).

Committee on Economic, Social and Cultural Rights (CESCR) General Comment 5 (para 14) and Comment 20, para 10.

DFID Report,2005;Disability and Inclusive Development, Barron&Amerena ed., London: Leonard Cheshire International, 2007.

Disability Statistics Database for Microcomputers (DISTAT) Web. (UN, 1990).March 6, 2015 http://unstats.un.org/unsd/demographic/scon cerns/disability/default.htm.

Federal Republic of Nigeria Official Gazette, No 2 Abuja, 2 February 2009.

Final Report of The EU Election Observation Mission, Nigeria General Elections 2015<http://eeas.europa.eu/nigeria/docs/eu-eom-nigeria-2015-final-report_en.pdf>accessed 3 July 2016.

Lang, Raymond and Upah, Lucy "Scoping Study: Disability Issues in Nigeria", April 2008, United Kindgdom Department for International Development <dfid_nigeriareport.pdf> accessed 22 November 2016

MAARDEC, *The Plight of Disabled Nigerians and the Need For Mass Enlightenment* (2013) <http://www.maardec.net > accessed 11 May 2015.

National Baseline Survey on Persons With Disabilities in Nigeria (2010), Document of the Federal Ministry of Women Affairs and Social Development, Available at:<womenaffairs.gov.ng> accessed 9 January 2017.

National population commission Census Priority Table: 2006 Population distribution (April 2010).

Report of the Special Rapporteur on torture and other cruel, inhuman or degrading Treatment or punishment' A/HRC/22/53HRC.22.53.

Report on Disabled Peoples International (DPI) official publication of 1999, vol. 6 page 1.

The Roeher Institute Study (2000), *'Beyond the limits: Mother's Caring for Children with Disabilities'.*

United Nations (1982) *World Programme of Action Concerning Disabled Persons.* A/RES/37/52, New York, United Nations.

WHO (1980) *International Classification of Impairments, Disabilities, and Handicaps: A manual of classification relating to the consequences of disease.* Geneva, World Health Organisation.

WHO (2001) *International Classification of Functioning, Disability and Health.* Geneva, World Health Organisation.

World Bank (1993) *World Development Report.* Washington DC, World Bank.

World Bank (2004) *Disability and HIV/AIDS*<http://www.worldbank.or g/>acceded 24 March 2016..

World Health Organization (WHO) & World Bank (2011) *World Report on Disability,* <http://www.who.int/disabilities/world_report/2011> accessed 24 March 2016.

Newspapers

'12m Nigerians living with learning disability', *The Punch*Online(5/6/14) <http://www.punchngr.com>accessed 21 February 2016.

'Autism: Experts say disability laws will improve access to treatment', *The Punch* (6/4/13) Web. 21 February 2015<http://www .punchngr.com>

"12m Nigerians living with learning disability", *The Punch* (5/6/14) Web. 21 February 2015 http://www.punchngr.com. "INEC Raises the Bar on Electoral Access for People with Disabilities..." <www.thisdaylive.com/articles/inec-raises...disabilities/191049/

"Man sues firm for permanent disability"*Vanguard* (21/3/11)..<http://www.vanguardngr.com> accessed 4 March 2015.

"Protecting Rights of People Living with Disabilities in 2015 Elections ..."<www.thisdaylive.com/articles/protecting...disabilities.../199449 > accessed 4 March 2015.

BarthiolomewMadukwe, "World Human Rights Day: Persons With Disabilities Cry For LSSP Law" available at: <http://www.vanguardngr.com/2014/12/world- human-rights-day persons-disabilities-cry-LSPP-law> accessed 26 November 16.

Equal Rights Trust, Letter to His Excellency, Mr.Goodluck Jonathan regarding the Nigeria Disability Bill (2011)<http://www.equalrightst rust.org/ertdocumentbank/GOODLUCK%20JONATHAN%20SU BMISSION.pdf> accessed 11 May 2013.

Johnson Agbakworu, "Public Complaints Act Breach: Two Heads of Government Agencies, Three Others for Prosecution", The Vanguard of 10/11/13 < vanguardngr.com>accessed 10 November 16.

Punch News of 11/10/16," Public Complaints Commission Workers Protest Slash in Salaries" <pnchng.com>accessed10 November 2016.

Internet Materials

"From Exclusion to Equality: Realizing the rights of Persons with Disabilities", Handbook for Parliamentarians on the Convention on the Rights of

Persons with Disabilities and its Optional Protocol<http://www.ipu.org/PDF/publications/disabilities> accessed17 February 2015.

Adetoro N., "Information and Communications Technology (ICT) As An Access Equalizer of Information: Opportunities And Challenges For Nigeria's Persons With Visual Impairment (2012). 11 May 2013 <http://www.academia.edu> accessed 11 May 2013.

Alexa Josephine, *Social Impact of Disability*<http://www.ehow.com/info_8363316>accessed 19 May 2015.

Amusat N., "Disability Care in Nigeria: The Need for Professional Advocacy(2008)".<http://www.ajol.info/index.php/ajprs/article/viewFile/51 313/39976>accessed 19
May 2015.Building election accessibility in Nigeria<election access.org>accessed 20 November 2016.

BussinessDictionary<http://www.businessdictionary.com/definition/di scrimination.html#ixzz4 Tm7tRhA>accessed 29 March 2016.

Catherine Slater, 'A History of Mental Disability 1000AD to 2000AD: From Idiocy to Intellectual Impairment<http://caslater.freeservers .com/disability3.htm>accessed 1 April 2016.

Dele Alabi, "Legal Aid Council Grapples with Challenges of Logistics, Poor Funding" <legalaidcouncil.gov.ng>accessed 15 November 2016.

Disabilities Rights<http://www.un.org/disabilities>accesed 22 March 2015.

Disability and HIV/AIDS, (World Bank, 2004) <htt://www.worldbank.org>accessed 23 April2015.

Disability History Timeline <htt://www.disabilityhistory.org/timeline-new.html> accessed 21 January 2016.

Disability History Timeline<http://www.disabilityhistory.org/timeline-newhtml>accessed 20 June 2015.

Document of Western Australian Disability Services Commission <http://www.health. wa.gov.an/.../training-package/fcommand/ disability.pdf> accessed 22 March 2016.

Document of Western Australian Disability Services Commission <http://www.health.wa.gov.an/.../trainingpackage/fcommand/disa bility.pdf>accessed 22 March 2016.

Emelonye, U. "Rule of Law and Human Rights Development." <http://www.nigerabestforum.com/geenraltopics/p.72986>accessed 22/12/15.

Equal Rights Trust, Letter to His Excellency, Mr.Goodluck Jonathan regarding the Nigeria Disability Bill (2011)<http.://www.equalrightstrust.org/ertdocument bank> accessed 11 June 2015.

Federal Ministry of Health Website<education.gov.ng> accessed 24 November 2016.

Federal Ministry of Justice<justice.gov.ng> accessed 24 November 2016.

Federal Ministry of Labour and Productivity <labour.gov.ng>accessed 24 November 2016.

Federal Ministry of Women Affairs and Social Development<womenaff airs.gov.ng>accessed 24/11/16.

Final Report of The EU Election Observation Mission, Nigeria General Elections 2015<http://eeas.europa.eu/nigeria/docs/eu-eom-nigeria-2015 final report_>accessed 17 June 2016.

GAATES, Nigeria Passes Law on Discriminating Against Persons With Disabilities (30 April2012)<http://globalaccessibilitynews.com /2012/04/30/nigeria-passes-law- on discriminating-against-persons-with-disabilities/> accessed 11 May 2015

Handicap International Handbook on PRSP (1999), <Error! Hyperlink reference not valid.> accessed 15 March 2015.

Heward, W.L, 'Exceptional Children: An Introduction to Special Education', p.10-11, <http://www.education.com/reference/article/who-exceptional-children/>accessed 18 June 2015.

International Classification of Impairments, Disabilities and Handicaps (ICIDH), General World Health Organization, 1980.<http://www.who.int/classifications/icf/en/>accessed 25 June 2015.

Kaplan, D., 'The Definition of Disability' <http://www.accessiblesociety.org/topics/demographeicsidentity/d kaplaripaper.htm>accessed 22 June 2015.

Lang, R. and Upah, L., Scoping Study; Disability issues in Nigeria, Available at:<https:// www.ucl.ac.uk/lc-ccr/downloads/scopingstudies/dfid_nigeriareport>accessed25 June 2015.

Lansdown, G., "Disabled Children in South Africa: Progress in Implementing the Convention on the Rights of the Child" (being a paper on the rights of disabled children) <http://www.daa.org.uk> accessed 27 October 2015.

MAARDEC, The Plight of Disabled Nigerians and the Need for Mass Enlightenment (2013) <http://www.maardec.net> accessed 11 May 2013.

Nigerians With Disability Decree 1993, Section 3<http://digitalcommons .ilr.cornell.edu/cgi/viewcontent.cgi?article> accessed 6 July 2015.

Odemwingie E, Nigeria: 2011 Elections - A Case for Persons With Disabilities (2010).<http://allafrica.com/stories/201011291728.html.>access ed 11 May 2013.

Oliver, M., The Individual and Social Models of Disability; Paper presented at Joint Workshop of the Living Options Group and the Research of the Royal College of Physicians <leeds.ac.uk > accessed 12 March 2016.

Ozoji, E., Disability Awareness Programme: objectives and Implementation in Nigeria(1993)<http://dspace.unijos.edu.ng /bitstream>accessed 11 May 2013Peter S., Education for All, Including Children With Disabilities. Web. 20 January 2010. http//www/siteresource.org

Plato, The Republic: Concerning The Definition of Justice, (380 B.C.) <http://classics.mit.edu/Plato/republic.html> accessed 1 April 2016.

Quaran 24:61, The Holy Quaran (English Translation by Muhammad Alli) <http://www.aaiil.org/text/hq/trans/ma_list.shtml>Accessed 29 March 2016.

Revised Standard Version of the Holy Bible, John 9:1-3; <https://www.biblegateway.com/versions/Revised-Standard-Version-RSV-Bible> accessed 29 March 2016.

Somorin, O., "ICT for the Physically Challenged", Nigerian Tribune. Web. 3 March2015.<http://www.tribune.com.ng/ news2013/index.php/en/component/k2/itm/10552> accessed 11 February 2018.

The American Heritage Dictionary of the English Language, 4th Edition (Houghton Mifflin Company 2004) <http://dictionary.reference.com/browse/exceptional> accessed18 June 2015.

The UK Loss Information Centre<http://www.himblosinformationcentre.com> accessed 20 March 2016.

Tidy Colin, *'General Learning Disability'<Patient.info>*Accessed 18 March 2015

UK Equality Act 2010, (Section 6)< http://www.legislation.gov.uk /ukpga> Accessed 6 July 2015.

UN Convention on the Rights of Persons with Disabilities, 2006; See also the World Health Assembly Resolution 5823 of May 2005 <www.who.int/disabilities/publications/darworld-report-concept.pdffile>accessed 23/4/15.

UN Women, 2012, 'Report of the Expert Group Meeting on Prevention of Violence against Women and Girls' <http://www.unwomen.org//media/Headquarters/Attachments /Sections/Library/Publications/2012/11/Report-of-the-EGM-on-Prevention-of-Violence-against-Women-and-Girls.pdf.> accessed 12/3/17.

UNDP- Human Rights and the Millennium Development Goals Making the Link. p.8, <www.undp.org.Ioslo.centre> accessed 8/12/15.

United Nations Development Group P. 13. See also <http://dsqsds.org/article/view/625/802>. accessed on 20/12/2016.

United Nations, Office of the United Nations High Commissioner for Human Rights and Inter-Parliamentary Union. *From exclusion to equality: Realizing the rights of persons with disabilities. Handbook for parliamentarians.* <http://www.ipu.org/PDF /publications/ disabilities-e.pdf>.

WHO Health topics /Disabilities < http://www.who.int/topics/disabilities/en/> accessed 23 April 2016.

World Health Organization (WHO) & World Bank World Report on Disability (2011) <www.who.int/disabilities/world> accessed 24 March 2016.

Magazines

Kwenda, S. (2010) "Africa's Disabled will not be Forgotten" *African Renewal* April 2010, p. 18.

Lippman, *UNESCO Braille Courier*, (1972) p.89, UNESCO.

Mary Johnson, "Eastwood Declares Loss a 'Win'," *Ragged Edge* (November-December 2000), 25.

Mental Retardation,' *Psychology Today*<https://www.psychologytoday.com /conditions/mental-retardation> accessed 15 March 2015.

Other Sources

A Manual of Classification Relating to the Consequence of Disease (Geneva: WHO, 1980).

Document of the Federal Republic of Nigeria on National Policy on Education 1981.

Oliver, M., The Individual and Social Models of Disability; Paper presented at Joint Workshop of the Living Options Group and the Research of the Royal College of Physicians <leeds.ac.uk > accessed 12 March 2016.

Sanstitevan, J, *"The Ombudsman Institutions and Accountability in Societies of Transition"*,The Helen Kellogg Institute for International Studies, Notre Dame University, 2003.

UNICEF Report, "Childhood under Threat, the State of the World's Children" UNICEF, (2005).

Appendix 1

DISCRIMINATION AGAINST PERSONS WITH DISABILITIES (PROHIBITION) ACT, 2018

EXPANARORY MEMORANDUM

This Act provides for the full integration of persons with disabilities into the society and establishes the National Commission for Persons with Disabilities and vests the Commission with the responsibilities for their education, health care, social, economic and civil rights.

DISCRIMINATION AGAINST PERSONS WITH DISABILITIES (PROHIBITION) ACT, 2018

EXPANARORY MEMORANDUM

This Act provides for the full integration of persons with disabilities into the society and establishes the National Commission for Persons with Disabilities and vests the Commission with the responsibilities for their education, health care, social, economic and civil rights.

DISCRIMINATION AGAINST PERSONS WITH DISABILITIES (PROHIBITION) ACT, 2018

Arrangement of Sections

Section:

DISCRIMINATION AGAINST PERSONS WITH DISABILITIES (PROHIBITION) ACT, 2018

A Bill

For

An Act to provide for the full integration of persons with disabilities into the society, establish the National Commission for People with Disabilities and vest in the Commission the responsibilities for their education, health care, social, economic and civil rights; and for related matters.

{ } Commencement.

ENACTED by the National Assembly of the Federal Republic of Nigeria -

PART I – PROHIBITION OF DISCRIMINATION, AND AWARENESS PROGRAMMES

1. (1) A person with disability shall not be discriminated against on the ground of his disability by any person or institution in any manner or circumstance.

   Prohibition of discrimination and penalty.

   (2) A person who contravenes subsection (1), commits an offence and is liable on conviction to, if the person is -

       (a) a body corporate, a fine of N1,000,000; and

       (b) an individual, a fine of N100,000 or six months imprisonment or both.

   (3) Notwithstanding the prosecution, conviction or otherwise of any person for any offence under this Act, the person against whom the crime or wrong is committed may maintain a civil action against the person committing the offence or causing the injury, without prejudice to any conviction or acquittal.

2. The Federal Ministry of Information shall make provisions for promotion of awareness regarding the -

   Awareness programmes.

       (a) rights, respect and dignity of persons with disabilities; and

       (b) capabilities, achievements and contributions of persons with disabilities to the society.

PART II – ACCESSIBILTY OF PHYSICAL STRUCTURE

3. A person with disability has the right to access the physical environment and buildings on an equal basis with others.

Right of access to public premises.

4. A public building shall be constructed with the necessary accessibility aids such as lifts (where necessary), ramps and any other facility that shall make them accessible to and usable by persons with disabilities.

Accessibility aids in public building.

5. Road side-walks, pedestrian crossings and all other special facilities as set out in the First Schedule made for public use shall be made accessible to and usable by persons with disabilities including those on wheelchairs and the visually impaired.

Accessibility to roads side-walks and special facilities.

First Schedule.

6. From the date of the commencement of this Act, there shall be a transitory period of five years within which all public buildings and structures, whether immovable, movable or automobile, which were inaccessible to persons with disabilities shall be modified to be accessible to and usable by persons with disabilities including those on wheelchairs.

Transitory Period.

7. (1) Before erecting any public structure, its plan shall be scrutinised by the relevant authority to ensure that the plan conforms with the building code.

Building plan.

(2) A government or government agency, body or individual responsible for the approval of building plans shall not approve the plan of a public building if the plan does not make provision for accessibility facilities in line with the building code.

(3) An officer who approves or directs the approval of a building plan that contravenes the building code, commits an offence and is liable on conviction to a fine of at least N1,000,000 or a term of imprisonment of two years or both.

8. (1) Subject to section 7, in the event of the existence of a state of inaccessibility or barrier to access of a person with disability to an environment that he has a right or duty to access, he may, without prejudice to his right to seek redress in court, notify the relevant authority in charge of the environment of the existence of the state of inaccessibility or barrier to accessibility of the environment, and the relevant authority in charge shall take immediate and necessary steps to remove the barrier and make the environment accessible to the person with disability.

Complaint of inaccessibility.

(2) A relevant authority in charge that receives the notice in subsection (1) but fails to comply, commits an offence and is liable on conviction, if it is-

(a) a corporate body, N10,000 damages payable to the affected person for each day of default; or

PART II – ACCESSIBILTY OF PHYSICAL STRUCTURE

3. A person with disability has the right to access the physical environment and buildings on an equal basis with others.

    Right of access to public premises.

4. A public building shall be constructed with the necessary accessibility aids such as lifts (where necessary), ramps and any other facility that shall make them accessible to and usable by persons with disabilities.

    Accessibility aids in public building.

5. Road side-walks, pedestrian crossings and all other special facilities as set out in the First Schedule made for public use shall be made accessible to and usable by persons with disabilities including those on wheelchairs and the visually impaired.

    Accessibility to roads side-walks and special facilities.

    First Schedule.

6. From the date of the commencement of this Act, there shall be a transitory period of five years within which all public buildings and structures, whether immovable, movable or automobile, which were inaccessible to persons with disabilities shall be modified to be accessible to and usable by persons with disabilities including those on wheelchairs.

    Transitory Period.

7. (1) Before erecting any public structure, its plan shall be scrutinised by the relevant authority to ensure that the plan conforms with the building code.

    Building plan.

    (2) A government or government agency, body or individual responsible for the approval of building plans shall not approve the plan of a public building if the plan does not make provision for accessibility facilities in line with the building code.

    (3) An officer who approves or directs the approval of a building plan that contravenes the building code, commits an offence and is liable on conviction to a fine of at least N1,000,000 or a term of imprisonment of two years or both.

8. (1) Subject to section 7, in the event of the existence of a state of inaccessibility or barrier to access of a person with disability to an environment that he has a right or duty to access, he may, without prejudice to his right to seek redress in court, notify the relevant authority in charge of the environment of the existence of the state of inaccessibility or barrier to accessibility of the environment, and the relevant authority in charge shall take immediate and necessary steps to remove the barrier and make the environment accessible to the person with disability.

    Complaint of inaccessibility.

    (2) A relevant authority in charge that receives the notice in subsection (1) but fails to comply, commits an offence and is liable on conviction, if it is-

    (a) a corporate body, N10,000 damages payable to the affected person for each day of default; or

(b) an individual, N5,000 damages payable to the affected person each day of default or six months imprisonment or both.

PART III — ROAD TRANSPORTATION

9. (1) A person, who whether for payment or not, provides goods or services, or makes facilities available, shall not discriminate against another person with disability by- *Goods, services and facilities.*

    (a) refusing to provide those goods or services or make those facilities available to him;

    (b) the terms or conditions on which the provider provides those goods or services or makes those facilities available to him; or

    (c) the manner in which the provider provides those goods or services or makes those facilities available to him.

10. (1) Government transport services providers shall make provisions for lifts, ramps and other accessibility aids to enhance the accessibility of their vehicles, parks and bus stop to persons with disabilities including those on wheel chairs. *Accessibility of vehicles.*

  (2) Every public vehicle shall have functional audible and visual display of their destination within five years from the commencement of this Act.

11. (1) Transport service providers shall make provisions for lifts, ramps and other accessibility aids to enhance the accessibility of their vehicles, parks and bus stops to persons with disabilities including those on wheelchairs. *Provision of facilities to persons with disabilities.*

  (2) Lifts, ramps and all other accessibility equipment in or for vehicles, and at parks or bus stops shall be maintained in operational condition.

  (3) There shall be regular and frequent maintenance of all accessibility aids and equipment, and defective ones shall be promptly repaired or replaced.

  (4) Before a person with disability boards or alights from a vehicle, the driver shall ensure that the vehicle comes to a stop.

  (5) When a person with disability intends to board a vehicle, all other intending passengers shall wait for him to board before them.

12. (1) At public parking lots, suitable spaces shall be properly marked and reserved for persons with disabilities. *Reserved spaces.*

  (2) For a person with disability to be entitled to the use of the reserved space in subsection (1), his car shall have been properly identified with the necessary insignia.

(3) A person, organisation or corporate body in control of a public parking lot who fails to provide for the reserved spaces in subsection (1), commits an offence and is liable on conviction to a fine of N1, 000 for each day of default.

(4) A person without disability who parks a vehicle in the reserved space in subsection (1), commits an offence and is liable on conviction to a fine of N5,000.

(5) A person who intentionally obstructs the reserved space in subsection (1) commits an offence and is liable on conviction to a fine of N5,000.

(6) Subsection (4) does not apply if a person with disability is a passenger in the vehicle.

PART IV — SEAPORTS, RAILWAYS AND AIRPORT FACILITIES

13. (1) Seaports facilities and vessels shall be made accessible to persons with disabilities.   *Seaports and railways.*

(2) Railway stations, trains and facilities in the trains shall be made accessible to persons with disabilities.

(3) The transitory provision contained in section 6 shall apply to the provisions of this section.

14. (1) All airlines operating in Nigeria shall -   *Assistive service and airline.*

    (a) ensure the accessibility of their aircraft to persons with disabilities;

    (b) make available presentable and functional wheelchairs for the conveyance of persons with disabilities who need them to and from the aircraft;

    (c) ensure that persons with disabilities are assisted to get on and off board in safety and reasonable comfort; and

    (d) ensure that persons with disabilities are accorded priority while boarding and disembarking from the aircraft.

(2) All airports shall make available for the conveyance of persons with disabilities who need presentable and functional assistive and protective devices to and from the aircraft.

15. Any general information shall be translated into the accessible format appropriate to the person with disability present.   *Special safety briefing of person with disabilities.*

PART V — LIBERTY, RIGHT TO EDUCATION, HEALTH AND FIRST
CONSIDERATION IN QUEUES, ACCOMODATION AND IN EMERGENCIES

16.   (1) A person shall not - Prohibition of
use of persons
with disabilities
in soliciting for
alms and
penalty.

      (a) employ, use or involve a person with disability in begging;

      (b) parade persons with disabilities in public with intention of soliciting for alms; or

      (c) use condition of disability as a guise for the purpose of begging in public.

    (2) A person who contravenes subsection (1) commits an offence and is liable on conviction to a fine of N100, 000 or a term of six months imprisonment or both.

17.   (1) A person with disability shall have an unfettered right to education without discrimination or segregation in any form. Right to free
education.

    (2) A person with disability is entitled to free education to secondary school level.

    (3) The Commission shall provide educational assistive devices.

18.   (1) All public schools, whether primary, secondary or tertiary shall be run to be inclusive of and accessible to persons with disabilities, accordingly every school shall have- Inclusiveness of
education.

      (a) at least a trained personnel to cater for the educational development of persons with disabilities; and

      (b) special facilities for the effective education of persons with disabilities.

    (2) Braille, sign language and other skills for communicating with persons with disabilities shall form part of the curricula of primary, secondary and tertiary institutions.

19.   The education of special education personnel shall be highly subsidised. Subsidised
education for
special education
personnel.

20.   Government shall ensure that the education of persons with disabilities, particularly children, who are blind, deaf or with multiple disabilities, is delivered in the most appropriate language, mode and means of communication for the individual, and in environments which maximise academic and social development. Appropriate
mode of
education for
persons with
disabilities.

21. (1) Government shall guarantee that persons with disabilities have unfettered access to adequate health care without discrimination on the basis of disability. *Free healthcare.*

(2) A person with mental disability shall be entitled to free medical and health service in all public institutions.

22. (1) A person with mental disability shall obtain a Permanent Certificate of Disability from the Commission. *Certificate of Disability.*

(2) If a doctor suspects disability in the course of treatment of a person who before was not a person with disability, the doctor may with the approval of the Commission, issue a Temporary Certificate of Disability which shall last for not longer than 180 days.

(3) If the state of disability persists beyond 180 days, the Commission on the recommendation of a doctor, shall issue the person a Permanent Certificate of Disability which shall last for as long as the state of the disability persists.

(4) A person issued with a Permanent Certificate of Disability is entitled to all rights and privileges under this Act.

23. A person who unlawfully issues or obtains a Certificate of Disability, commits an offence and is liable on conviction to a fine of N200,000 or imprisonment for a term of one year or both. *Unlawful procurement of certificate of disability.*

24. A public hospital where a person with communicational disabilities is medically attended to shall make provision for special communication. *Provision of special communication at hospitals.*

25. In all situations of risk, violence, emergencies and the occurrences of natural disasters, the Government shall take all necessary steps to ensure the safety and protection of persons with disabilities taking cognisance of their peculiar vulnerability. *Situation of risk and humanitarian emergencies.*

26. (1) In queues, persons with disabilities shall be given first consideration and, as much as possible, be attended to outside the queue. *Service at queues.*

(2) A person who contravenes this section commits an offence and is liable on conviction to a fine of N50,000.00 or a term of six months imprisonment or both.

27. If accommodation is being provided by schools for their students, employers for their employees, service providers for their customers, organisations for their members, government for the people and in any other circumstance whatsoever, persons with disabilities shall be given first consideration. *Accommodation.*

PART VI – OPPORTUNITY FOR EMPLOYMENT AND PARTICIPATION IN POLITICS AND PUBLIC LIFE

28. (1) A person with disability has the right to work on an equal basis with others and this includes the right to opportunity to gain a living by work freely chosen or accepted in a labour market and work environment that is open.

Equal right to work.

(2) A person who contravenes subsection (1), commits an offence and is liable on conviction to nominal damages of a minimum of N250,000 payable to the affected person with disability.

(3) Where a company contravenes subsection (1) -

    (a) the company commits an offence and is liable to nominal damages of a minimum of N500,000 payable to the affected person with disability; and

    (b) any principal officer of the company involved in the violation is liable to N50,000 damages payable to the affected person with disability.

29. All employers of labour in public organisations shall, as much as possible, have persons with disabilities constituting at least 5% of their employment.

Opportunity for employment.

30. (1) Persons with disabilities shall be encouraged to fully participate in politics and public life.

Participation in politics.

(2) Government shall actively promote an environment in which persons with disabilities can effectively and fully participate in-

    (a) the conduct of public affairs without discrimination;

    (b) non-governmental organisations and associations concerned with the public and political life of the country; and

    (c) activities and administration of political parties.

PART VII — ESTABLISHMENT OF THE NATIONAL COMMISSION FOR PERSONS WITH DISABILITIES

31. (1) There is established the National Commission for Persons with Disabilities (in this Act referred to as "the Commission") to be placed under the Presidency.

Establishment of National Commission for persons with disabilities.

(2) The Commission-

    (a) is a body corporate with –

        (i) perpetual succession,

        (ii) a common seal; and

    (b) may sue and be sued in its corporate name; and

    (c) may acquire, hold and dispose of property, movable or immovable.

(3) The head office of the Commission shall be in the Federal Capital Territory, Abuja.

32. (1) There is established a Governing Council for the Commission (in this Act referred to as the "the Council") which shall conduct the affairs of the Commission. *Establishment and membership of the Governing Council.*

    (2) The Council shall consist of -

        (a) a part time chairman;

        (b) one person with disability from each geopolitical zone;

        (c) a representative each from the Federal Ministry of -

            (i) Education,

            (ii) Health,

            (iii) Sports,

            (iv) Women Affairs,

            (v) Housing,

            (vi) Transport,

            (vii) Environment,

            (viii) Labour and Productivity,

            (ix) Justice, and

            (ix) Finance; and

    (d) a representative each from the National Human Rights Commission and the National Planning Commission.

(3) The Chairman of the Council and one representative each from the 6 geo-political zones, shall be appointed by the President subject to the confirmation of the Senate.

33. The supplementary provisions set out in the Second Schedule to this Act shall have effect with respect to the proceedings of the Council and the other matters contained in the Schedule.

34. The Chairman and members of the Council shall each hold office-

    (a) for a term of four years and may be re-appointed for a further term of four years and no more; and

    (b) on such terms and conditions as may be specified in their letters of appointment.

35. (1) A person ceases to hold office as a member of the Council if he-

    (a) becomes bankrupt, or compounds with his creditors;

    (b) is convicted of a felony or any offence involving dishonesty or fraud;

    (c) is disqualified of his professional qualification;

    (d) is guilty of a serious misconduct in relation to his duties; or

    (e) resigns his appointment by a letter addressed to the President.

(2) If a member of the Council ceases to hold office for any reason whatsoever before the expiration of the term for which he is appointed, another person representing the same interest as that member shall be appointed to the Council for the unexpired term.

(3) A member of the Council shall be removed by the President on the recommendation of the Council if he is satisfied that it is not in the interest of the Commission or the public that the member continues in that office.

36. Members of the Council shall be paid allowances and expenses as the Government may direct

37. The Council shall have power to-

    (a) manage and superintend over the affairs of the Commission;

    (b) make rules and regulations for the effective running of the Commission;

(j) establish and promote inclusive schools, vocational and rehabilitation centres for the development of persons with disabilities;

(k) liaise with the public and private sectors and other bodies to ensure that the peculiar interests of persons with disabilities are taken into consideration in every government policy, programme and activity;

(l) issue insignia of identification with persons with disabilities;

(m) in collaboration with other relevant government agencies and professional bodies in the building industry, enforce compliance of public buildings codes and impose necessary sanctions and make appropriate orders;

(n) receive complaints of persons with disabilities on the violation of their rights;

(o) support an individual's right to seek redress in court, investigation, prosecution or sanctioning, in appropriate cases, the violation of the provision of this Act;

(p) ensure research, development and education on disability issues and disabled persons;

(q) collaborate with the media to make information available in accessible format for persons with disabilities; and

(r) procure assistive devices for all disability types.

39. (1) The Commission shall have power to do any lawful thing, which will facilitate carrying out of its functions and in particular may- *Powers of the Commission.*

(a) enter into contract for the education and welfare of persons with disabilities;

(b) purchase or acquire any assets, business or property considered necessary for the proper conduct of its functions;

(c) sell, let, lease or dispose of any of its property;

(d) undertake or sponsor research where necessary for the performance of its functions; and

(e) train managerial, technical or other category of staff for the purpose of running the affairs of the Commission.

(2) The power conferred on the Commission may be exercised by it or through any of its employees or agent authorised in that behalf by the Commission.

(3) The Commission shall not be subject to a direction, control or suspension by any other authority or person in the performance of its functions under this Act except the President.

PART VIII – APPOINTMENT AND DUTIES OF THE EXECUTIVE SECRETARY AND OTHER STAFF

40. (1) There shall be an Executive Secretary for the Commission who shall -

Appointment and duties of the Executive Secretary of the Commission.

    (a) have such qualification and experience as appropriate for a person required to perform the functions of that office;

    (b) be a person with disability; and

    (c) be responsible to the Council for the execution of the policies and administration of the daily affairs of the Commission.

41. The Council shall appoint for the Commission such number of employees as may, in the opinion of the Council, be expedient and necessary for the proper and efficient performance of the functions of the Commission.

Staff of the commission and their remuneration.

42. (1) The Council may appoint for the Commission, either directly or by secondment from any Public Service of the Federation, such number of employees as may, in the opinion of the Council, be required to assist the Commission in the performance of any of its functions under this Act.

Appointment and secondment from public service.

(2) The person seconded under this section, may elect to be transferred to the service of the Commission, and any previous service the person may have rendered in the Public Service shall count as service to the Commission for the purpose of any pension subsequently payable by the Commission.

43. There shall be established, in the head office of the Commission, such departments as may be deemed necessary for the effective and efficient functioning of the Commission.

Structure of the Commission.

44. The staff of the Commission are entitled to pension, gratuity, and any other retirement benefit in accordance with the Pension Reform Act.

Pension and gratuity.

Act No.4, 2014.

45. (1) The Commission shall establish and maintain a fund into which shall be paid and credited –

Funds of the Commission.

  (a) all subventions and budgetary allocations from the Federal Government of Nigeria; and

  (b) such money as may be granted to the Commission by anybody or institution within or outside Nigeria.

(2) The Commission shall defray all expenditures incurred by it including –

  (a) cost of administration;

  (b) payment of salaries, fees, or other remuneration, allowances, pensions and gratuities payable to members and employees of the Commission; and

  (c) anything done in connection with any of its functions.

(3) The Council shall cause the account of the Commission to be audited quarterly and shall be externally audited once every year.

46. (1) The Commission may accept gift of land, money or other property on such terms and conditions, if any, as may be specified by the person or organisation making the gift, provided such terms and conditions are not inconsistent with any prevailing law.

Power to accept gifts.

(2) The Commission shall not accept any gift if the conditions attached are inconsistent with the functions of the Commission under this Act.

47. The Commission may borrow such money as it may require to execute or complete some special projects of the Commission.

Power to borrow.

48. (1) The Commission shall --

Annual estimate and expenditure.

  (a) cause to be kept accounts and records of transaction and affairs of the Commission; and

  (b) ensure that all payments out of its Fund are correctly made and properly authorised.

(2) The Commission shall ensure that adequate control is maintained over the assets of, or in the custody of, the Commission and over its incurring of liabilities.

49. (1) The Auditor–General for the Federation shall - Audit.

    (a) inspect and audit the account and records of financial transactions of the Commission;

    (b) inspect records relating to assets of the Commission; and

    (c) draw the attention of the Secretary to the Government of the Federation to any irregularities disclosed by the inspection and audit.

(2) The Auditor-General for the Federation may dispense with all or any part of detailed inspection and audit of any account or record referred to in subsection (1).

(3) The auditor or an officer authorised by him is entitled at all reasonable time to a full and free access to all account records, documents and papers of the Commission relating directly or indirectly to the receipt or payment of money by the Commission or to the acquisition received, custody or disposal of assets by the Commission.

50. The Commission shall submit – Annual report.

    (a) an annual report of its activities to the office of the Secretary to the Government of the Federation not later than 30th June of each financial year; and

    (b) a copy of its audited accounts and a copy of the annual report to the National Assembly.

51. The Commission may, subject to the Land Use Act, acquire any land for the purpose of performing its functions. Power to acquire land.
Cap. L5, LFN, 2004.

PART IX — MISCELLANEOUS PROVISIONS

52. A notice, summons or other documents required or authorised to be served upon the Commission under the provisions of this Act, any other law or enactment may be served by delivering it to the Executive Secretary or by sending it by registered post and addressing it to the Executive Secretary at the head office of the Commission. Service of documents.

53. Any such money which may be the judgment of any court awarded against the Commission shall be paid from the Fund of the Commission. Payment of judgment debt.

54. A member of the Council, the Executive Secretary, any officer or employee of the Commission shall be indemnified against any proceeding, whether civil or criminal, in which judgement is given in his favour or in which is acquitted, if any such proceeding is brought against him in his capacity as a member of the Council, the Executive Secretary, officer or the employee of the Commission.

55. (1) To be entitled to the damages specifically provided in this Act, it shall be sufficient for a plaintiff or claimant, as the case may be, in a court proceeding to prove the violation of the relevant section of this Act without specific proof of damages.

(2) Nothing in this Act shall prevent a court from accessing and awarding general and special damages in addition to the normal damages provided for in this Act.

56. The Council may make regulations for the purpose of carrying out or giving full effect to the provisions of this Act.

PART X – INTERPRETATION

57. In this Act-

"accessibility aid" includes any fixture and device that aids accessibility;

"accommodation" in the context of housing, includes residential or business accommodation;

"assistive device" means any device that assists, increases or improves the functional capabilities of persons with disabilities;

"Commission" means National Commission for People with Disabilities established under this Act;

"commission agent" means the person who does work for the Commission as its agent and who is remunerated, whether in whole or in part by the Commission;

"disabled" means having a disability;

"disability" includes long term physical, mental, intellectual or sensory impairment which in interaction with various barriers may hinder full and effective participation in society on equal basis with others;

"discrimination" means differential treatment and its verbs and infinite form, discriminate, to discriminate have the corresponding signification;

"document" includes any book register or other record of information, however compiled, record or stored;

"educational authority" means a body of persons administering an education institution;

"educational institution" means a school college, university or other institution at which education or training is provided;

"employee" includes applicant or prospective employee, commission agent, contract worker, independent contractor, or person applying to the commission agent, contract worker or independent contractor;

"employer" includes prospective employer, principal and a person who engages or proposes to engage a commission agent, contract worker or independent contractor;

"employer of labour" means employer as interpreted by the Employee's Compensation Act No. 13, 2010;

"function" includes duty;

"government employee" means a person who is appointed, employed or engaged in the public service of, or by a public authority of the Federation, a State, the Federal Capital Territory or a local government, or holds an administrative office;

"person" includes natural, artificial, juristic or judicial persons, companies, enterprises firms, organisations, association, government departments, ministries, parastatals;

"person with disabilities" means-

    (a) a person who has received Temporary or Permanent Certificate of Disability to have condition which is expected to continue permanently or for a considerable length of time which can reasonably be expected to limit the person's functional ability substantially, but not limited to seeing, hearing, thinking, ambulating, climbing, descending, lifting, grasping, rising, and includes any related function or any limitation due to weakness or significantly decreased endurance so that he cannot perform his everyday routine, living and working without significantly increased hardship and vulnerability to everyday obstacles and hazards; and

    (b) a person with long term physical, mental, intellectual or sensory impairment which in interaction with various barriers may hinder their full and effective participation in society on equal basis with others;

211

Special Facilities

1. Wheel chairs, clear floors or ground space on wheel chairs, wheel chair passage and turning space

2. Crutches, guide canes etc

3. Hearing Aid

4. Curb ramps

5. Ramps

6. Handrails, grab bars

7. Stain-shopping stairs

8. Elevators or Lifts

9. Windows

10. Entrance doors

11. Drinking fountains and water coolers

12. Toilet facilities

13. Door protective and re-opening devices manoeuvring entrances at doors

14. Parking spaces and passenger loading zones

15. Accessible routes including walk ways, halls, windows, aisles and spaces

16. Alarm -

           (a) audible alarms;

           (b) visual alarms; and

           (c) auxiliary alarms

SUPPLEMENTARY PROVISIONS RELATING TO THE COUNCIL

Proceedings of the Council

1. (1) Subject to this Act and section 27 of the Interpretation Act, the Council may make standing orders regulating its proceedings or those of any of its Committees. Cap. 123, LFN, 2004.

    (2) The quorum of the Council shall be the Chairman or the person presiding at the meeting and five other members of the Council, one of whom shall be an ex-officio member, and the quorum of any committee of the Council shall be as determined by the Council.

2. (1) The Council shall meet whenever it is summoned by the Chairman and if the Chairman is required to do so by notice given to him by at least eight other members, he shall summon a meeting of the Council to be held within 14 days from the date on which the notice was given.

    (2) Where the Council desires to obtain the advice of any person on a particular matter, the Council may co-opt him to the Council for such period as it deems fit, but a person who is in attendance by virtue of this paragraph is not entitled to vote at any meeting of the Council and shall not count towards a quorum.

3. (1) The Council may set up one or more committees to perform, on behalf of the Council, such functions as the Council may determine.

    (2) A committee set up under paragraph (1) shall consider such number of persons as may be determined by the Council and a person shall hold office in the Committee in accordance with the terms of his appointment.

    (3) A decision of a committee of the Council is of no effect until it is confirmed by the Council.

4. (1) The affixing of the seal of the Commission shall be authenticated by the signatures of the Chairman, Executive Secretary or any other member of the Council generally or specifically authorised by the Council to act for that purpose.

    (2) A contract or instrument, which if made or executed by any person not being a body corporate would not be required to be under seal, may be executed on behalf of the Commission by the Executive Secretary or any person generally authorised by the Council to act for that purpose.

    (3) A document purporting to be a document duly executed under the seal of the Commission shall be received in evidence and shall, unless the contrary is proved, be presumed to be so executed.

5. The validity of any proceeding of the Council or Committee shall not be adversely affected by a

First Schedule   Section 5

Special Facilities

1. Wheel chairs, clear floors or ground space on wheel chairs, wheel chair passage and turning space

2. Crutches, guide canes etc

3. Hearing Aid

4. Curb ramps

5. Ramps

6. Handrails, grab bars

7. Stain-shopping stairs

8. Elevators or Lifts

9. Windows

10. Entrance doors

11. Drinking fountains and water coolers

12. Toilet facilities

13. Door protective and re-opening devices manoeuvring entrances at doors

14. Parking spaces and passenger loading zones

15. Accessible routes including walk ways, halls, windows, aisles and spaces

16. Alarm -

        (a) audible alarms;

        (b) visual alarms; and

        (c) auxiliary alarms

(a) vacancy in the membership of the Council or Committee;

(b) defect in the appointment of a member of the Council or Committee; or

(c) reason that a person not entitled to do so took part in the proceedings of the Council or Committee.

FORM 1   Section 38 (m)

COMPLIANCE ORDER

Notice has been taken of the fact that your Programme is not inclusive of Disabilities Issues.

In particular: ....

This contravenes section 38 of Discrimination against Persons with Disabilities (Prohibition) Act, you are hereby ordered to immediately comply with the Act.

Take note that if, after three months from receipt of this order, you still remain in default, your operational licence shall be withdrawn.

Signed

FORM 2 Section 22 (1)

CERTIFICATE OF PERMANENT DISABILITY

This is to certify that ....of ....was examined by me ....on this day of ....and found to be permanently incapacitated.

Signed

CERTIFICATE OF TEMPORARY DISABILITY Section 22 (2)

This is to certify that ....of

...................................was examined by me ....on this day of .... and found to be temporarily incapacitated.

Signed

Appendix 2
United Nations Convention On
The Rights of Persons with Disabilities And
Optional Protocol

Preamble

The States Parties to the present Convention,

(a) Recalling the principles proclaimed in the Charter of the United Nations which recognize the inherent dignity and worth and the equal and inalienable rights of all members of the human family as the foundation of freedom, justice and peace in the world,

(b) Recognizing that the United Nations, in the Universal Declaration of Human Rights and in the International Covenants on Human Rights, has proclaimed and agreed that everyone is entitled to all the rights and freedoms set forth therein, without distinction of any kind,

(c) Reaffirming the universality, indivisibility, interdependence and interrelatedness of all human rights and fundamental freedoms and the need for persons with disabilities to be guaranteed their full enjoyment without discrimination,

(d) Recalling the International Covenant on Economic, Social and Cultural Rights, the International Covenant on Civil and Political Rights, the International Convention on the Elimination of All Forms of Racial Discrimination, the Convention on the Elimination of All Forms of Discrimination against Women, the Convention against Torture and Other Cruel, Inhuman or Degrading Treatment or Punishment, the Convention on the Rights of the Child, and the International Convention on the Protection of the Rights of All Migrant Workers and Members of Their Families,

(e) Recognizing that disability is an evolving concept and that disability results from the interaction between persons with impairments and attitudinal and environmental barriers that hinders their full and effective participation in society on an equal basis with others,

(f) Recognizing the importance of the principles and policy guidelines contained in the World Programme of Action concerning Disabled Persons and in the Standard Rules on the Equalization of Opportunities for Persons with Disabilities in influencing the promotion, formulation and evaluation of the policies, plans, programmes and actions at the national, regional and international levels to further equalize opportunities for persons with disabilities,

(g) Emphasizing the importance of mainstreaming disability issues as an integral part of relevant strategies of sustainable development,

(h) Recognizing also that discrimination against any person on the basis of disability is a violation of the inherent dignity and worth of the human person,

9. (i) Recognizing further the diversity of persons with disabilities,

10. (j) Recognizing the need to promote and protect the human rights of all persons with disabilities, including those who require more intensive support,

(k) Concerned that, despite these various instruments and undertakings, persons with disabilities continue to face barriers in their participation as equal members of society and violations of their human rights in all parts of the world,

(l) Recognizing the importance of international cooperation for improving the living conditions of persons with disabilities in every country, particularly in developing countries,

(m) Recognizing the valued existing and potential contributions made by persons with disabilities to the overall well-being and diversity of their communities, and that the promotion of the full enjoyment by persons with disabilities of their human rights and fundamental freedoms and of full participation by persons with disabilities will result in their enhanced sense of belonging and in significant advances in the human, social and economic development of society and the eradication of poverty,

(n) Recognizing the importance for persons with disabilities of their individual autonomy and independence, including the freedom to make their own choices,

(o) Considering that persons with disabilities should have the opportunity to be actively involved in decision-making processes about policies and programmes, including those directly concerning them,

(p) Concerned about the difficult conditions faced by persons with disabilities who are subject to multiple or aggravated forms of discrimination on the basis of race, colour, sex, language, religion, political or other opinion, national, ethnic, indigenous or social origin, property, birth, age or other status,

(q) Recognizing that women and girls with disabilities are often at greater risk, both within and outside the home, of violence, injury or abuse, neglect or negligent treatment, maltreatment or exploitation,

(r) Recognizing that children with disabilities should have full enjoyment of all human rights and fundamental freedoms on an equal basis with other children, and recalling obligations to that end undertaken by States Parties to the Convention on the Rights of the Child,

(s) Emphasizing the need to incorporate a gender perspective in all efforts to promote the full enjoyment of human rights and fundamental freedoms by persons with disabilities,

(t) Highlighting the fact that the majority of persons with disabilities live in conditions of poverty, and in this regard recognizing the critical need to address the negative impact of poverty on persons with disabilities,

(u) Bearing in mind that conditions of peace and security based on full respect for the purposes and principles contained in the Charter of the United Nations and observance of applicable human rights instruments are indispensable for the full protection of persons with disabilities, in particular during armed conflicts and foreign occupation,

(v) Recognizing the importance of accessibility to the physical, social, economic and cultural environment, to health and education and to information and communication, in enabling persons with disabilities to fully enjoy all human rights and fundamental freedoms,

(w) Realizing that the individual, having duties to other individuals and to the community to which he or she belongs, is under a responsibility to strive for the promotion and observance of the rights recognized in the International Bill of Human Rights,

(x) Convinced that the family is the natural and fundamental group unit of society and is entitled to protection by society and the State, and that persons with disabilities and their family members should receive the necessary protection and assistance to enable families to contribute towards the full and equal enjoyment of the rights of persons with disabilities,

(y) Convinced that a comprehensive and integral international convention to promote and protect the rights and dignity of persons with disabilities will make a significant contribution to redressing the profound social disadvantage of persons with disabilities and promote their participation in the civil, political, economic, social and cultural spheres with equal opportunities, in both developing and developed countries,

Have agreed as follows:

Article 1 Purpose

The purpose of the present Convention is to promote, protect and ensure the full and equal enjoyment of all human rights and fundamental freedoms by all persons with disabilities, and to promote respect for their inherent dignity.

Persons with disabilities include those who have long-term physical, mental, intellectual or sensory impairments which in interaction with various barriers may hinder their full and effective participation in society on an equal basis with others.

Article 2 Definitions

For the purposes of the present Convention:

"Communication" includes languages, display of text, Braille, tactile communication, large print, accessible multimedia as well as written, audio, plain-language, human-reader and augmentative and alternative modes, means and formats of communication, including accessible information and communication technology;

"Language" includes spoken and signed languages and other forms of non spoken languages;

"Discrimination on the basis of disability" means any distinction, exclusion or restriction on the basis of disability which has the purpose or effect of impairing or nullifying the recognition, enjoyment or exercise, on an equal basis with others, of all human rights and fundamental freedoms in the political, economic, social, cultural, civil or any other field. It includes all forms of discrimination, including denial of reasonable accommodation;

"Reasonable accommodation" means necessary and appropriate modification and adjustments not imposing a disproportionate or undue burden, where needed in a particular case, to ensure to persons with disabilities the enjoyment or exercise on an equal basis with others of all human rights and fundamental freedoms;

"Universal design" means the design of products, environments, programmes and services to be usable by all people, to the greatest extent possible, without the need for adaptation or specialized design. "Universal design" shall not exclude assistive devices for particular groups of persons with disabilities where this is needed.

Article 3 General principles

The principles of the present Convention shall be:
(a) Respect for inherent dignity, individual autonomy including the freedom to make one's own choices, and independence of persons;
(b)
(c)
(d) as part of
(e) (f) (g)
Non-discrimination;
Full and effective participation and inclusion in society;
Respect for difference and acceptance of persons with disabilities human diversity and humanity;
Equality of opportunity; Accessibility;
Equality between men and women;
(h)
and respect for the right of children with disabilities to preserve their identities.
Respect for the evolving capacities of children with disabilities

Article 4 General obligations

1. States Parties undertake to ensure and promote the full realization of all human rights and fundamental freedoms for all persons with disabilities without discrimination of any kind on the basis of disability. To this end, States Parties undertake:

(a) To adopt all appropriate legislative, administrative and other measures for the implementation of the rights recognized in the present Convention;

(b) To take all appropriate measures, including legislation, to modify or abolish existing laws, regulations, customs and practices that constitute discrimination against persons with disabilities;

(c) To take into account the protection and promotion of the human rights of persons with disabilities in all policies and programmes;

(d) To refrain from engaging in any act or practice that is inconsistent with the present Convention and to ensure that public authorities and institutions act in conformity with the present Convention;

(e) To take all appropriate measures to eliminate discrimination on the basis of disability by any person, organization or private enterprise;

(f) To undertake or promote research and development of universally designed goods, services, equipment and facilities, as defined in article 2 of the present Convention, which should require the minimum possible adaptation and the least cost to meet the specific needs of a person with disabilities, to promote their availability and use, and to promote universal design in the development of standards and guidelines;

(g) To undertake or promote research and development of, and to promote the availability and use of new technologies, including information and communications technologies, mobility aids, devices and assistive technologies, suitable for persons with disabilities, giving priority to technologies at an affordable cost;

(h) To provide accessible information to persons with disabilities about mobility aids, devices and assistive technologies, including new technologies, as well as other forms of assistance, support services and facilities;

(i) To promote the training of professionals and staff working with persons with disabilities in the rights recognized in the present Convention so as to better provide the assistance and services guaranteed by those rights.

2. With regard to economic, social and cultural rights, each State Party undertakes to take measures to the maximum of its available resources and, where needed, within the framework of international cooperation, with a view to achieving progressively the full realization of these rights, without prejudice to those obligations contained in the present

Convention that are immediately applicable according to international law.

3. In the development and implementation of legislation and policies to implement the present Convention, and in other decision-making processes concerning issues relating to persons with disabilities, States Parties shall closely consult with and actively involve persons with disabilities, including children with disabilities, through their representative organizations.

4. Nothing in the present Convention shall affect any provisions which are more conducive to the realization of the rights of persons with disabilities and which may be contained in the law of a State Party or international law in force for that State. There shall be no restriction upon or derogation from any of the
human rights and fundamental freedoms recognized or existing in any State Party to the present Convention pursuant to law, conventions, regulation or custom on the pretext that the present Convention does not recognize such rights or freedoms or that it recognizes them to a lesser extent.

5. The provisions of the present Convention shall extend to all parts of federal States without any limitations or exceptions.

Article 5

Equality and non-discrimination
1. States Parties recognize that all persons are equal before and under the law and are entitled without any discrimination to the equal protection and equal benefit of the law.
2. States Parties shall prohibit all discrimination on the basis of disability and guarantee to persons with disabilities equal and effective legal protection against discrimination on all grounds.
3. In order to promote equality and eliminate discrimination, States Parties shall take all appropriate steps to ensure that reasonable accommodation is provided.
4. Specific measures which are necessary to accelerate or achieve de facto equality of persons with disabilities shall not be considered discrimination under the terms of the present Convention.

Article 6 Women with disabilities

1. States Parties recognize that women and girls with disabilities are subject to multiple discrimination, and in this regard shall take measures to ensure the full and equal enjoyment by them of all human rights and fundamental freedoms.

2. States Parties shall take all appropriate measures to ensure the full development, advancement and empowerment of women, for the purpose of guaranteeing them the exercise and enjoyment of the human rights and fundamental freedoms set out in the present Convention.

Article 7 Children with disabilities

1. States Parties shall take all necessary measures to ensure the full enjoyment by children with disabilities of all human rights and fundamental freedoms on an equal basis with other children.

2. In all actions concerning children with disabilities, the best interests of the child shall be a primary consideration.

3. States Parties shall ensure that children with disabilities have the right to express their views freely on all matters affecting them, their views being given due weight in accordance with their age and maturity, on an equal basis with other children, and to be provided with disability and age-appropriate assistance to realize that right.

Article 8 Awareness-raising

1. States Parties undertake to adopt immediate, effective and appropriate measures:

(a) To raise awareness throughout society, including at the family level, regarding persons with disabilities, and to foster respect for the rights and dignity of persons with disabilities;

(b) To combat stereotypes, prejudices and harmful practices relating to persons with disabilities, including those based on sex and age, in all areas of life;

(c) To promote awareness of the capabilities and contributions of persons with disabilities.

2. Measures to this end include:

(a) Initiating and maintaining effective public awareness campaigns designed:

1.   (i) To nurture receptiveness to the rights of persons with disabilities;

2.   (ii) To promote positive perceptions and greater social awareness towards persons with disabilities;

(iii) To promote recognition of the skills, merits and abilities of persons with disabilities, and of their contributions to the workplace and the labour market;

(b) Fostering at all levels of the education system, including in all children from an early age, an attitude of respect for the rights of persons with disabilities;

(c) Encouraging all organs of the media to portray persons with disabilities in a manner consistent with the purpose of the present Convention;

(d) Promoting awareness-training programmes regarding persons with disabilities and the rights of persons with disabilities.

Article 9 Accessibility

1. To enable persons with disabilities to live independently and participate fully in all aspects of life, States Parties shall take appropriate measures to ensure to persons with disabilities access, on an equal basis with others, to the physical environment, to transportation, to information and communications, including information and communications technologies and systems, and to other facilities and services open or provided to the public, both in urban and in rural areas. These measures, which shall include the identification and elimination of obstacles and barriers to accessibility, shall apply to, inter alia:

(a) Buildings, roads, transportation and other indoor and outdoor facilities, including schools, housing, medical facilities and workplaces;

(b) Information, communications and other services, including electronic services and emergency services.

2. States Parties shall also take appropriate measures:

(a) To develop, promulgate and monitor the implementation of minimum standards and guidelines for the accessibility of facilities and services open or provided to the public;

(b) To ensure that private entities that offer facilities and services which are open or provided to the public take into account all aspects of accessibility for persons with disabilities;

(c) To provide training for stakeholders on accessibility issues facing persons with disabilities;

(d) To provide in buildings and other facilities open to the public signage in Braille and in easy to read and understand forms;

(e) To provide forms of live assistance and intermediaries, including guides, readers and professional sign language interpreters, to facilitate accessibility to buildings and other facilities open to the public;

(f) To promote other appropriate forms of assistance and support to persons with disabilities to ensure their access to information;

(g) To promote access for persons with disabilities to new information and communications technologies and systems, including the Internet;

(h) To promote the design, development, production and distribution of accessible information and communications technologies and systems at an early stage, so that these technologies and systems become accessible at minimum cost.

Article 10 Right to life

States Parties reaffirm that every human being has the inherent right to life and shall take all necessary measures to ensure its effective enjoyment by persons with disabilities on an equal basis with others.

Article 11

Situations of risk and humanitarian emergencies
States Parties shall take, in accordance with their obligations under international law, including international humanitarian law and international human rights law, all necessary measures to ensure the protection and safety of persons with disabilities in situations of risk, including situations of armed conflict, humanitarian emergencies and the occurrence of natural disasters.

Article 12

Equal recognition before the law
1. States Parties reaffirm that persons with disabilities have the right to recognition everywhere as persons before the law.
2. States Parties shall recognize that persons with disabilities enjoy legal capacity on an equal basis with others in all aspects of life.
3. States Parties shall take appropriate measures to provide access by persons with disabilities to the support they may require in exercising their legal capacity.
4. States Parties shall ensure that all measures that relate to the exercise of legal capacity provide for appropriate and effective safeguards to prevent abuse in accordance with international human rights law. Such safeguards shall ensure that measures relating to the exercise of legal capacity respect the rights, will and preferences of the person, are free of conflict of interest and undue influence, are proportional and tailored to the person's circumstances, apply for the shortest time possible and are subject to regular review by a competent, independent and impartial authority or judicial body. The safeguards shall be proportional to the degree to which such measures affect the person's rights and interests.
5. Subject to the provisions of this article, States Parties shall take all appropriate and effective measures to ensure the equal right of persons with disabilities to own or inherit property, to control their own financial affairs and to have equal access to bank loans, mortgages and other forms of financial credit, and shall ensure that persons with disabilities are not arbitrarily deprived of their property.

Article 13 Access to justice

1. States Parties shall ensure effective access to justice for persons with disabilities on an equal basis with others, including through the provision of procedural and age-appropriate accommodations, in order to facilitate their effective role as direct and indirect participants, including as witnesses, in all legal proceedings, including at investigative and other preliminary stages.
2. In order to help to ensure effective access to justice for persons with disabilities, States Parties shall promote appropriate training for those

working in the field of administration of justice, including police and prison staff.

Article 14

Liberty and security of person
1. States Parties shall ensure that persons with disabilities, on an equal basis with others:
1. (a) Enjoy the right to liberty and security of person;
2. (b) Are not deprived of their liberty unlawfully or arbitrarily, and that
any deprivation of liberty is in conformity with the law, and that the existence of a disability shall in no case justify a deprivation of liberty.
2. States Parties shall ensure that if persons with disabilities are deprived of their liberty through any process, they are, on an equal basis with others, entitled to guarantees in accordance with international human rights law and shall be treated in compliance with the objectives and principles of the present Convention, including by provision of reasonable accommodation.

Article 15

Freedom from torture or cruel, inhuman or degrading treatment or punishment
1. No one shall be subjected to torture or to cruel, inhuman or degrading treatment or punishment. In particular, no one shall be subjected without his or her free consent to medical or scientific experimentation.
2. States Parties shall take all effective legislative, administrative, judicial or other measures to prevent persons with disabilities, on an equal basis with others, from being subjected to torture or cruel, inhuman or degrading treatment or punishment.

Article 16

Freedom from exploitation, violence and abuse
1. States Parties shall take all appropriate legislative, administrative, social, educational and other measures to protect persons with

disabilities, both within and outside the home, from all forms of exploitation, violence and abuse, including their gender-based aspects.

2. States Parties shall also take all appropriate measures to prevent all forms of exploitation, violence and abuse by ensuring, inter alia, appropriate forms of gender- and age-sensitive assistance and support for persons with disabilities and their families and caregivers, including through the provision of information and education on how to avoid, recognize and report instances of exploitation, violence and abuse. States Parties shall ensure that protection services are age-, gender- and disability-sensitive.

3. In order to prevent the occurrence of all forms of exploitation, violence and abuse, States Parties shall ensure that all facilities and programmes designed to serve persons with disabilities are effectively monitored by independent authorities.

4. States Parties shall take all appropriate measures to promote the physical, cognitive and psychological recovery, rehabilitation and social reintegration of persons with disabilities who become victims of any form of exploitation, violence or abuse, including through the provision of protection services. Such recovery and reintegration shall take place in an environment that fosters the health, welfare, self-respect, dignity and autonomy of the person and takes into account gender- and age-specific needs.

5. States Parties shall put in place effective legislation and policies, including women- and child-focused legislation and policies, to ensure that instances of exploitation, violence and abuse against persons with disabilities are identified, investigated and, where appropriate, prosecuted.

Article 17

Protecting the integrity of the person
Every person with disabilities has a right to respect for his or her physical and mental integrity on an equal basis with others.
Article 18
Liberty of movement and nationality
1. States Parties shall recognize the rights of persons with disabilities to liberty of movement, to freedom to choose their residence and to a

nationality, on an equal basis with others, including by ensuring that persons with disabilities:

(a) Have the right to acquire and change a nationality and are not deprived of their nationality arbitrarily or on the basis of disability;

(b) Are not deprived, on the basis of disability, of their ability to obtain, possess and utilize documentation of their nationality or other documentation of identification, or to utilize relevant processes such as immigration proceedings, that may be needed to facilitate exercise of the right to liberty of movement;

(c) Are free to leave any country, including their own;

(d) Are not deprived, arbitrarily or on the basis of disability, of the right to enter their own country.

2. Children with disabilities shall be registered immediately after birth and shall have the right from birth to a name, the right to acquire a nationality and, as far as possible, the right to know and be cared for by their parents.

Article 19

Living independently and being included in the community

States Parties to the present Convention recognize the equal right of all persons with disabilities to live in the community, with choices equal to others, and shall take effective and appropriate measures to facilitate full enjoyment by persons with disabilities of this right and their full inclusion and participation in the community, including by ensuring that:

(a) Persons with disabilities have the opportunity to choose their place of residence and where and with whom they live on an equal basis with others and are not obliged to live in a particular living arrangement;

(b) Persons with disabilities have access to a range of in-home, residential and other community support services, including personal assistance necessary to support living and inclusion in the community, and to prevent isolation or segregation from the community;

(c) Community services and facilities for the general population are available on an equal basis to persons with disabilities and are responsive to their needs.

Article 20 Personal mobility

States Parties shall take effective measures to ensure personal mobility with the greatest possible independence for persons with disabilities, including by:
(a) Facilitating the personal mobility of persons with disabilities in the manner and at the time of their choice, and at affordable cost;
(b) Facilitating access by persons with disabilities to quality mobility aids, devices, assistive technologies and forms of live assistance and intermediaries, including by making them available at affordable cost;
(c) Providing training in mobility skills to persons with disabilities and to specialist staff working with persons with disabilities;
(d) Encouraging entities that produce mobility aids, devices and assistive technologies to take into account all aspects of mobility for persons with disabilities.

Article 21

Freedom of expression and opinion, and access to information
States Parties shall take all appropriate measures to ensure that persons with disabilities can exercise the right to freedom of expression and opinion, including the freedom to seek, receive and impart information and ideas on an equal basis with others and through all forms of communication of their choice, as defined in article 2 of the present Convention, including by:
(a) Providing information intended for the general public to persons with disabilities in accessible formats and technologies appropriate to different kinds of disabilities in a timely manner and without additional cost;
(b) Accepting and facilitating the use of sign languages, Braille, augmentative and alternative communication, and all other accessible means, modes and formats of communication of their choice by persons with disabilities in official interactions;
(c) Urging private entities that provide services to the general public, including through the Internet, to provide information and services in accessible and usable formats for persons with disabilities;

(d) Encouraging the mass media, including providers of information through the Internet, to make their services accessible to persons with disabilities;

(e) Recognizing and promoting the use of sign languages. Article 22

Respect for privacy

1. No person with disabilities, regardless of place of residence or living arrangements, shall be subjected to arbitrary or unlawful interference with his or her privacy, family, home or correspondence or other types of communication or to unlawful attacks on his or her honour and reputation. Persons with disabilities have the right to the protection of the law against such interference or attacks.

2. States Parties shall protect the privacy of personal, health and rehabilitation information of persons with disabilities on an equal basis with others.

Article 23

Respect for home and the family

1. States Parties shall take effective and appropriate measures to eliminate discrimination against persons with disabilities in all matters relating to marriage, family, parenthood and relationships, on an equal basis with others, so as to ensure that:

(a) The right of all persons with disabilities who are of marriageable age to marry and to found a family on the basis of free and full consent of the intending spouses is recognized;

(b) The rights of persons with disabilities to decide freely and responsibly on the number and spacing of their children and to have access to age-appropriate information, reproductive and family planning education are recognized, and the means necessary to enable them to exercise these rights are provided;

(c) Persons with disabilities, including children, retain their fertility on an equal basis with others.

2. States Parties shall ensure the rights and responsibilities of persons with disabilities, with regard to guardianship, wardship, trusteeship, adoption of children or similar institutions, where these concepts exist in national legislation; in all cases the best interests of the child shall be paramount. States Parties shall render appropriate assistance to persons with disabilities in the performance of their child-rearing responsibilities.

3. States Parties shall ensure that children with disabilities have equal rights with respect to family life. With a view to realizing these rights, and to prevent concealment, abandonment, neglect and segregation of children with disabilities, States Parties shall undertake to provide early and comprehensive information, services and support to children with disabilities and their families.

4. States Parties shall ensure that a child shall not be separated from his or her parents against their will, except when competent authorities subject to judicial review determine, in accordance with applicable law and procedures, that such separation is necessary for the best interests of the child. In no case shall a child be separated from parents on the basis of a disability of either the child or one or both of the parents.

5. States Parties shall, where the immediate family is unable to care for a child with disabilities, undertake every effort to provide alternative care within the wider family, and failing that, within the community in a family setting.

Article 24 Education

1. States Parties recognize the right of persons with disabilities to education. With a view to realizing this right without discrimination and on the basis of equal opportunity, States Parties shall ensure an inclusive education system at all levels and lifelong learning directed to:

(a) The full development of human potential and sense of dignity and self-worth, and the strengthening of respect for human rights, fundamental freedoms and human diversity;

(b) The development by persons with disabilities of their personality, talents and creativity, as well as their mental and physical abilities, to their fullest potential;

(c) Enabling persons with disabilities to participate effectively in a free society.

2. In realizing this right, States Parties shall ensure that:

(a) Persons with disabilities are not excluded from the general education system on the basis of disability, and that children with disabilities are not excluded from free and compulsory primary education, or from secondary education, on the basis of disability;

(b) Persons with disabilities can access an inclusive, quality and free primary education and secondary education on an equal basis with others in the communities in which they live;

(c) Reasonable accommodation of the individual's requirements is provided;

(d) Persons with disabilities receive the support required, within the general education system, to facilitate their effective education;

(e) Effective individualized support measures are provided in environments that maximize academic and social development, consistent with the goal of full inclusion.

3. States Parties shall enable persons with disabilities to learn life and social development skills to facilitate their full and equal participation in education and as members of the community. To this end, States Parties shall take appropriate measures, including:

(a) Facilitating the learning of Braille, alternative script, augmentative and alternative modes, means and formats of communication and orientation and mobility skills, and facilitating peer support and mentoring;

(b) Facilitating the learning of sign language and the promotion of the linguistic identity of the deaf community;

(c) Ensuring that the education of persons, and in particular children, who are blind, deaf or deafblind, is delivered in the most appropriate languages and modes and means of communication for the individual, and in environments which maximize academic and social development.

4. In order to help ensure the realization of this right, States Parties shall take appropriate measures to employ teachers, including teachers with disabilities, who are qualified in sign language and/or Braille, and to train professionals and staff who work at all levels of education. Such training shall incorporate disability awareness and the use of appropriate augmentative and alternative modes, means and formats of communication, educational techniques and materials to support persons with disabilities.

5. States Parties shall ensure that persons with disabilities are able to access general tertiary education, vocational training, adult education and lifelong learning without discrimination and on an equal basis with others. To this end, States Parties shall ensure that reasonable accommodation is provided to persons with disabilities.

Article 25 Health

States Parties recognize that persons with disabilities have the right to the enjoyment of the highest attainable standard of health without discrimination on the basis of disability. States Parties shall take all appropriate measures to ensure access for persons with disabilities to health services that are gender-sensitive, including health-related rehabilitation. In particular, States Parties shall:

(a) Provide persons with disabilities with the same range, quality and standard of free or affordable health care and programmes as provided to other persons, including in the area of sexual and reproductive health and population-based public health programmes;

(b) Provide those health services needed by persons with disabilities specifically because of their disabilities, including early identification and intervention as appropriate, and services designed to minimize and prevent further disabilities, including among children and older persons;

(c) Provide these health services as close as possible to people's own communities, including in rural areas;

(d) Require health professionals to provide care of the same quality to persons with disabilities as to others, including on the basis of free and informed consent by, inter alia, raising awareness of the human rights, dignity, autonomy and needs of persons with disabilities through training and the promulgation of ethical standards for public and private health care;

(e) Prohibit discrimination against persons with disabilities in the provision of health insurance, and life insurance where such insurance is permitted by national law, which shall be provided in a fair and reasonable manner;

(f) Prevent discriminatory denial of health care or health services or food and fluids on the basis of disability.

Article 26 Habilitation and rehabilitation

1. States Parties shall take effective and appropriate measures, including through peer support, to enable persons with disabilities to attain and maintain maximum independence, full physical, mental, social and vocational ability, and full inclusion and participation in all aspects of life. To that end, States Parties shall organize, strengthen and extend comprehensive habilitation and rehabilitation services and programmes,

particularly in the areas of health, employment, education and social services, in such a way that these services and programmes:

(a) Begin at the earliest possible stage, and are based on the multidisciplinary assessment of individual needs and strengths;

(b) Support participation and inclusion in the community and all aspects of society, are voluntary, and are available to persons with disabilities as close as possible to their own communities, including in rural areas.

2. States Parties shall promote the development of initial and continuing training for professionals and staff working in habilitation and rehabilitation services.

3. States Parties shall promote the availability, knowledge and use of assistive devices and technologies, designed for persons with disabilities, as they relate to habilitation and rehabilitation.

Article 27

Work and employment

1. States Parties recognize the right of persons with disabilities to work, on an equal basis with others; this includes the right to the opportunity to gain a living by work freely chosen or accepted in a labour market and work environment that is open, inclusive and accessible to persons with disabilities. States Parties shall safeguard and promote the realization of the right to work, including for those who acquire a disability during the course of employment, by taking appropriate steps, including through legislation, to, inter alia:

(a) Prohibit discrimination on the basis of disability with regard to all matters concerning all forms of employment, including conditions of recruitment, hiring and employment, continuance of employment, career advancement and safe and healthy working conditions;

(b) Protect the rights of persons with disabilities, on an equal basis with others, to just and favourable conditions of work, including equal opportunities and equal remuneration for work of equal value, safe and healthy working conditions, including protection from harassment, and the redress of grievances;

(c) Ensure that persons with disabilities are able to exercise their labour and trade union rights on an equal basis with others;

(d) Enable persons with disabilities to have effective access to general technical and vocational guidance programmes, placement services and vocational and continuing training;

(e) Promote employment opportunities and career advancement for persons with disabilities in the labour market, as well as assistance in finding, obtaining, maintaining and returning to employment;

(f) Promote opportunities for self-employment, entrepreneurship, the development of cooperatives and starting one's own business;

7. (g) Employ persons with disabilities in the public sector;

8. (h) Promote the employment of persons with disabilities in the private sector through appropriate policies and measures, which may include affirmative action programmes, incentives and other measures;

(i) Ensure that reasonable accommodation is provided to persons with disabilities in the workplace;

(j) Promote the acquisition by persons with disabilities of work experience in the open labour market;

(k) Promote vocational and professional rehabilitation, job retention and return-to-work programmes for persons with disabilities.

2. States Parties shall ensure that persons with disabilities are not held in slavery or in servitude, and are protected, on an equal basis with others, from forced or compulsory labour.

Article 28

Adequate standard of living and social protection

1. States Parties recognize the right of persons with disabilities to an adequate standard of living for themselves and their families, including adequate food, clothing and housing, and to the continuous improvement of living conditions, and shall take appropriate steps to safeguard and promote the realization of this right without discrimination on the basis of disability.

2. States Parties recognize the right of persons with disabilities to social protection and to the enjoyment of that right without discrimination on the basis of disability, and shall take appropriate steps to safeguard and promote the realization of this right, including measures:

(a) To ensure equal access by persons with disabilities to clean water services, and to ensure access to appropriate and affordable services, devices and other assistance for disability-related needs;

(b) To ensure access by persons with disabilities, in particular women and girls with disabilities and older persons with disabilities, to social protection programmes and poverty reduction programmes;

(c) To ensure access by persons with disabilities and their families living in situations of poverty to assistance from the State with disability-related expenses, including adequate training, counselling, financial assistance and respite care;

(d) To ensure access by persons with disabilities to public housing programmes;

(e) To ensure equal access by persons with disabilities to retirement benefits and programmes.

Article 29

Participation in political and public life

States Parties shall guarantee to persons with disabilities political rights and the opportunity to enjoy them on an equal basis with others, and shall undertake:

(a) To ensure that persons with disabilities can effectively and fully participate in political and public life on an equal basis with others, directly or through freely chosen representatives, including the right and opportunity for persons with disabilities to vote and be elected, inter alia, by:

(i) Ensuring that voting procedures, facilities and materials are appropriate, accessible and easy to understand and use;

(ii) Protecting the right of persons with disabilities to vote by secret ballot in elections and public referendums without intimidation, and to stand for elections, to effectively hold office and perform all public functions at all levels of government, facilitating the use of assistive and new technologies where appropriate;

(iii) Guaranteeing the free expression of the will of persons with disabilities as electors and to this end, where necessary, at their request, allowing assistance in voting by a person of their own choice;

(b) To promote actively an environment in which persons with disabilities can effectively and fully participate in the conduct of public affairs, without discrimination and on an equal basis with others, and encourage their participation in public affairs, including:

(i) Participation in non-governmental organizations and associations concerned with the public and political life of the country, and in the activities and administration of political parties;

(ii) Forming and joining organizations of persons with disabilities to represent persons with disabilities at international, national, regional and local levels.

Article 30

Participation in cultural life, recreation, leisure and sport
1. States Parties recognize the right of persons with disabilities to take part on an equal basis with others in cultural life, and shall take all appropriate measures to ensure that persons with disabilities:
1.   (a) Enjoy access to cultural materials in accessible formats;
2.   (b) Enjoy access to television programmes, films, theatre and other cultural activities, in accessible formats;
(c) Enjoy access to places for cultural performances or services, such as theatres, museums, cinemas, libraries and tourism services, and, as far as possible, enjoy access to monuments and sites of national cultural importance.
2. States Parties shall take appropriate measures to enable persons with disabilities to have the opportunity to develop and utilize their creative, artistic and intellectual potential, not only for their own benefit, but also for the enrichment of society.
3. States Parties shall take all appropriate steps, in accordance with international law, to ensure that laws protecting intellectual property rights do not constitute an unreasonable or discriminatory barrier to access by persons with disabilities to cultural materials.
4. Persons with disabilities shall be entitled, on an equal basis with others, to recognition and support of their specific cultural and linguistic identity, including sign languages and deaf culture.
5. With a view to enabling persons with disabilities to participate on an equal basis with others in recreational, leisure and sporting activities, States Parties shall take appropriate measures:
(a) To encourage and promote the participation, to the fullest extent possible, of persons with disabilities in mainstream sporting activities at all levels;

(b) To ensure that persons with disabilities have an opportunity to organize, develop and participate in disability-specific sporting and recreational activities and, to this end, encourage the provision, on an equal basis with others, of appropriate instruction, training and resources;

(c) To ensure that persons with disabilities have access to sporting, recreational and tourism venues;

(d) To ensure that children with disabilities have equal access with other children to participation in play, recreation and leisure and sporting activities, including those activities in the school system;

(e) To ensure that persons with disabilities have access to services from those involved in the organization of recreational, tourism, leisure and sporting activities.

Article 31 Statistics and data collection

1. States Parties undertake to collect appropriate information, including statistical and research data, to enable them to formulate and implement policies to give effect to the present Convention. The process of collecting and maintaining this information shall:

(a) Comply with legally established safeguards, including legislation on data protection, to ensure confidentiality and respect for the privacy of persons with disabilities;

(b) Comply with internationally accepted norms to protect human rights and fundamental freedoms and ethical principles in the collection and use of statistics.

2. The information collected in accordance with this article shall be disaggregated, as appropriate, and used to help assess the implementation of States Parties' obligations under the present Convention and to identify and address the barriers faced by persons with disabilities in exercising their rights.

3. States Parties shall assume responsibility for the dissemination of these statistics and ensure their accessibility to persons with disabilities and others.

Article 32 International cooperation

1. States Parties recognize the importance of international cooperation and its promotion, in support of national efforts for the realization of the purpose and objectives of the present Convention, and will

undertake appropriate and effective measures in this regard, between and among States and, as appropriate, in partnership with relevant international and regional organizations and civil society, in particular organizations of persons with disabilities. Such measures could include, inter alia:

(a) Ensuring that international cooperation, including international development programmes, is inclusive of and accessible to persons with disabilities;

(b) Facilitating and supporting capacity-building, including through the exchange and sharing of information, experiences, training programmes and best practices;

(c) Facilitating cooperation in research and access to scientific and technical knowledge;

(d) Providing, as appropriate, technical and economic assistance, including by facilitating access to and sharing of accessible and assistive technologies, and through the transfer of technologies.

2. The provisions of this article are without prejudice to the obligations of each State Party to fulfil its obligations under the present Convention.

Article 33

National implementation and monitoring

1. States Parties, in accordance with their system of organization, shall designate one or more focal points within government for matters relating to the implementation of the present Convention, and shall give due consideration to the establishment or designation of a coordination mechanism within government to facilitate related action in different sectors and at different levels.

2. States Parties shall, in accordance with their legal and administrative systems, maintain, strengthen, designate or establish within the State Party, a framework, including one or more independent mechanisms, as appropriate, to promote, protect and monitor implementation of the present Convention. When designating or establishing such a mechanism, States Parties shall take into account the principles relating to the status and functioning of national institutions for protection and promotion of human rights.

3. Civil society, in particular persons with disabilities and their representative organizations, shall be involved and participate fully in the monitoring process.

Article 34

ommittee on the Rights of Persons with Disabilities
1. There shall be established a Committee on the Rights of Persons with Disabilities (hereafter referred to as "the Committee"), which shall carry out the functions hereinafter provided.
2. The Committee shall consist, at the time of entry into force of the present Convention, of twelve experts. After an additional sixty ratifications or accessions to the Convention, the membership of the Committee shall increase by six members, attaining a maximum number of eighteen members.
3. The members of the Committee shall serve in their personal capacity and shall be of high moral standing and recognized competence and experience in the field covered by the present Convention. When nominating their candidates, States Parties are invited to give due consideration to the provision set out in article 4, paragraph 3, of the present Convention.
4. The members of the Committee shall be elected by States Parties, consideration being given to equitable geographical distribution, representation of the different forms of civilization and of the principal legal systems, balanced gender representation and participation of experts with disabilities.
5. The members of the Committee shall be elected by secret ballot from a list of persons nominated by the States Parties from among their nationals at meetings of the Conference of States Parties. At those meetings, for which two thirds of States Parties shall constitute a quorum, the persons elected to the Committee shall be those who obtain the largest number of votes and an absolute majority of the votes of the representatives of States Parties present and voting.
6. The initial election shall be held no later than six months after the date of entry into force of the present Convention. At least four months before the date of each election, the Secretary-General of the United Nations shall address a letter to the States Parties inviting them to submit the nominations within two months. The Secretary-General shall

subsequently prepare a list in alphabetical order of all persons thus nominated, indicating the State Parties which have nominated them, and shall submit it to the States Parties to the present Convention.

7. The members of the Committee shall be elected for a term of four years. They shall be eligible for re-election once. However, the term of six of the members elected at the first election shall expire at the end of two years; immediately after the first election, the names of these six members shall be chosen by lot by the chairperson of the meeting referred to in paragraph 5 of this article.

8. The election of the six additional members of the Committee shall be held on the occasion of regular elections, in accordance with the relevant provisions of this article.

9. If a member of the Committee dies or resigns or declares that for any other cause she or he can no longer perform her or his duties, the State Party which nominated the member shall appoint another expert possessing the qualifications and meeting the requirements set out in the relevant provisions of this article, to serve for the remainder of the term.

10. The Committee shall establish its own rules of procedure.

11. The Secretary-General of the United Nations shall provide the necessary staff and facilities for the effective performance of the functions of the Committee under the present Convention, and shall convene its initial meeting.

12. With the approval of the General Assembly of the United Nations, the members of the Committee established under the present Convention shall receive emoluments from United Nations resources on such terms and conditions as the Assembly may decide, having regard to the importance of the Committee's responsibilities.

13. The members of the Committee shall be entitled to the facilities, privileges and immunities of experts on mission for the United Nations as laid down in the relevant sections of the Convention on the Privileges and Immunities of the United Nations.

Article 35 Reports by States Parties

1. Each State Party shall submit to the Committee, through the Secretary- General of the United Nations, a comprehensive report on measures taken to give effect to its obligations under the present Convention and on the progress made in that regard, within two years

after the entry into force of the present Convention for the State Party concerned.

2. Thereafter, States Parties shall submit subsequent reports at least every four years and further whenever the Committee so requests.

3. The Committee shall decide any guidelines applicable to the content of the reports.

4. A State Party which has submitted a comprehensive initial report to the Committee need not, in its subsequent reports, repeat information previously provided. When preparing reports to the Committee, States Parties are invited to consider doing so in an open and transparent process and to give due consideration to the provision set out in article 4, paragraph 3, of the present Convention.

5. Reports may indicate factors and difficulties affecting the degree of fulfilment of obligations under the present Convention.

Article 36 Consideration of reports

1. Each report shall be considered by the Committee, which shall make such suggestions and general recommendations on the report as it may consider appropriate and shall forward these to the State Party concerned. The State Party may respond with any information it chooses to the Committee. The Committee may request further information from States Parties relevant to the implementation of the present Convention.

2. If a State Party is significantly overdue in the submission of a report, the Committee may notify the State Party concerned of the need to examine the implementation of the present Convention in that State Party, on the basis of reliable information available to the Committee, if the relevant report is not submitted within three months following the notification. The Committee shall invite the State Party concerned to participate in such examination. Should the State Party respond by submitting the relevant report, the provisions of paragraph 1 of this article will apply.

3. The Secretary-General of the United Nations shall make available the reports to all States Parties.

4. States Parties shall make their reports widely available to the public in their own countries and facilitate access to the suggestions and general recommendations relating to these reports.

5. The Committee shall transmit, as it may consider appropriate, to the specialized agencies, funds and programmes of the United Nations, and other competent bodies, reports from States Parties in order to address a request or indication of a need for technical advice or assistance contained therein, along with the Committee's observations and recommendations, if any, on these requests or indications.

Article 37

Cooperation between States Parties and the Committee
1. Each State Party shall cooperate with the Committee and assist its members in the fulfilment of their mandate.
2. In its relationship with States Parties, the Committee shall give due consideration to ways and means of enhancing national capacities for the implementation of the present Convention, including through international cooperation.

Article 38

Relationship of the Committee with other bodies
In order to foster the effective implementation of the present Convention and to encourage international cooperation in the field covered by the present Convention:
(a) The specialized agencies and other United Nations organs shall be entitled to be represented at the consideration of the implementation of such provisions of the present Convention as fall within the scope of their mandate. The Committee may invite the specialized agencies and other competent bodies as it may consider appropriate to provide expert advice on the implementation of the Convention in areas falling within the scope of their respective mandates. The Committee may invite specialized agencies and other United Nations organs to submit reports on the implementation of the Convention in areas falling within the scope of their activities;
(b) The Committee, as it discharges its mandate, shall consult, as appropriate, other relevant bodies instituted by international human rights treaties, with a view to ensuring the consistency of their respective reporting guidelines, suggestions and general recommendations, and avoiding duplication and overlap in the performance of their functions.

Article 39

Report of the Committee
The Committee shall report every two years to the General Assembly and to the Economic and Social Council on its activities, and may make suggestions and general recommendations based on the examination of reports and information received from the States Parties. Such suggestions and general recommendations shall be included in the report of the Committee together with comments, if any, from States Parties.

Article 40 Conference of States Parties

1. The States Parties shall meet regularly in a Conference of States Parties in order to consider any matter with regard to the implementation of the present Convention.
2. No later than six months after the entry into force of the present Convention, the Conference of States Parties shall be convened by the Secretary-General of the United Nations. The subsequent meetings shall be convened by the Secretary-General biennially or upon the decision of the Conference of States Parties.

Article 41 Depositary

The Secretary-General of the United Nations shall be the depositary of the present Convention.

Article 42 Signature

The present Convention shall be open for signature by all States and by regional integration organizations at United Nations Headquarters in New York as of 30 March 2007.

Article 43 Consent to be bound

The present Convention shall be subject to ratification by signatory States and to formal confirmation by signatory regional integration organizations. It shall be open for accession by any State or regional integration organization which has not signed the Convention.

Article 44

Regional integration organizations

1. "Regional integration organization" shall mean an organization constituted by sovereign States of a given region, to which its member States have transferred competence in respect of matters governed by the present Convention. Such organizations shall declare, in their instruments of formal confirmation or accession, the extent of their competence with respect to matters governed by the present Convention. Subsequently, they shall inform the depositary of any substantial modification in the extent of their competence.

2. References to "States Parties" in the present Convention shall apply to such organizations within the limits of their competence.

3. For the purposes of article 45, paragraph 1, and article 47, paragraphs 2 and 3, of the present Convention, any instrument deposited by a regional integration organization shall not be counted.

4. Regional integration organizations, in matters within their competence, may exercise their right to vote in the Conference of States Parties, with a number of votes equal to the number of their member States that are Parties to the present Convention. Such an organization shall not exercise its right to vote if any of its member States exercises its right, and vice versa.

Article 45 Entry into force

1. The present Convention shall enter into force on the thirtieth day after the deposit of the twentieth instrument of ratification or accession.

2. For each State or regional integration organization ratifying, formally confirming or acceding to the present Convention after the deposit of the twentieth such instrument, the Convention shall enter into force on the thirtieth day after the deposit of its own such instrument.

Article 46 Reservations

1. Reservations incompatible with the object and purpose of the present Convention shall not be permitted.

2. Reservations may be withdrawn at any time.

Article 47 Amendments

1. Any State Party may propose an amendment to the present Convention and submit it to the Secretary-General of the United Nations. The Secretary- General shall communicate any proposed amendments to States Parties, with a request to be notified whether they favour a conference of States Parties for the purpose of considering and deciding upon the proposals. In the event that, within four months from the date of such communication, at least one third of the States Parties favour such a conference, the Secretary-General shall convene the conference under the auspices of the United Nations. Any amendment adopted by a majority of two thirds of the States Parties present and voting shall be submitted by the Secretary-General to the General Assembly of the United Nations for approval and thereafter to all States Parties for acceptance.

2. An amendment adopted and approved in accordance with paragraph 1 of this article shall enter into force on the thirtieth day after the number of instruments of acceptance deposited reaches two thirds of the number of States Parties at the date of adoption of the amendment. Thereafter, the amendment shall enter into force for any State Party on the thirtieth day following the deposit of its own instrument of acceptance. An amendment shall be binding only on those States Parties which have accepted it.

3. If so decided by the Conference of States Parties by consensus, an amendment adopted and approved in accordance with paragraph 1 of this article which relates exclusively to articles 34, 38, 39 and 40 shall enter into force for all States Parties on the thirtieth day after the number of instruments of acceptance deposited reaches two thirds of the number of States Parties at the date of adoption of the amendment.

Article 48 Denunciation

A State Party may denounce the present Convention by written notification to the Secretary-General of the United Nations. The denunciation shall become effective one year after the date of receipt of the notification by the Secretary-General.

Article 49 Accessible format

The text of the present Convention shall be made available in accessible formats.
Article 50 Authentic texts
The Arabic, Chinese, English, French, Russian and Spanish texts of the present Convention shall be equally authentic.
IN WITNESS THEREOF the undersigned plenipotentiaries, being duly authorized thereto by their respective Governments, have signed the present Convention.

Optional Protocol to the Convention on the Rights of Persons with Disabilities

The States Parties to the present Protocol have agreed as follows:

Article 1

1. A State Party to the present Protocol ("State Party") recognizes the competence of the Committee on the Rights of Persons with Disabilities ("the Committee") to receive and consider communications from or on behalf of individuals or groups of individuals subject to its jurisdiction who claim to be victims of a violation by that State Party of the provisions of the Convention.
2. No communication shall be received by the Committee if it concerns a State Party to the Convention that is not a party to the present Protocol.

Article 2

The Committee shall consider a communication inadmissible when:
1. (a) The communication is anonymous;
2. (b) The communication constitutes an abuse of the right of submission of such communications or is incompatible with the provisions of the Convention;
3. (c) The same matter has already been examined by the Committee or
has been or is being examined under another procedure of international investigation or settlement;

261

4. (d) All available domestic remedies have not been exhausted. This shall not be the rule where the application of the remedies is unreasonably prolonged or unlikely to bring effective relief;

5. (e) It is manifestly ill-founded or not sufficiently substantiated; or when

6. (f) The facts that are the subject of the communication occurred prior to the entry into force of the present Protocol for the State Party concerned unless those facts continued after that date.

Article 3

Subject to the provisions of article 2 of the present Protocol, the Committee shall bring any communications submitted to it confidentially to the attention of the State Party. Within six months, the receiving State shall submit to the Committee written explanations or statements clarifying the matter and the remedy, if any, that may have been taken by that State.

Article 4

. At any time after the receipt of a communication and before a determination on the merits has been reached, the Committee may transmit to the State Party concerned for its urgent consideration a request that the State Party take such interim measures as may be necessary to avoid possible irreparable damage to the victim or victims of the alleged violation.

2. Where the Committee exercises its discretion under paragraph 1 of this article, this does not imply a determination on admissibility or on the merits of the communication.

Article 5

The Committee shall hold closed meetings when examining communications under the present Protocol. After examining a communication, the Committee shall forward its suggestions and recommendations, if any, to the State Party concerned and to the petitioner.

Article 6

1. If the Committee receives reliable information indicating grave or systematic violations by a State Party of rights set forth in the Convention, the Committee shall invite that State Party to cooperate in the examination of the information and to this end submit observations with regard to the information concerned.

2. Taking into account any observations that may have been submitted by the State Party concerned as well as any other reliable information available to it, the Committee may designate one or more of its members to conduct an inquiry and to report urgently to the Committee. Where warranted and with the consent of the State Party, the inquiry may include a visit to its territory.

3. After examining the findings of such an inquiry, the Committee shall transmit these findings to the State Party concerned together with any comments and recommendations.

4. The State Party concerned shall, within six months of receiving the findings, comments and recommendations transmitted by the Committee, submit its observations to the Committee.

5. Such an inquiry shall be conducted confidentially and the cooperation of the State Party shall be sought at all stages of the proceedings.

Article 7

1. The Committee may invite the State Party concerned to include in its report under article 35 of the Convention details of any measures taken in response to an inquiry conducted under article 6 of the present Protocol.

2. The Committee may, if necessary, after the end of the period of six months referred to in article 6, paragraph 4, invite the State Party concerned to inform it of the measures taken in response to such an inquiry.

Article 8

Each State Party may, at the time of signature or ratification of the present Protocol or accession thereto, declare that it does not recognize the competence of the Committee provided for in articles 6 and 7.

Article 9

The Secretary-General of the United Nations shall be the depositary of the present Protocol.

Article 10

The present Protocol shall be open for signature by signatory States and regional integration organizations of the Convention at United Nations Headquarters in New York as of 30 March 2007.

Article 11

The present Protocol shall be subject to ratification by signatory States of the present Protocol which have ratified or acceded to the Convention. It shall be subject to formal confirmation by signatory regional integration organizations of the present Protocol which have formally confirmed or acceded to the Convention. It shall be open for accession by any State or regional integration organization which has ratified, formally confirmed or acceded to the Convention and which has not signed the Protocol.

Article 12

1. "Regional integration organization" shall mean an organization constituted by sovereign States of a given region, to which its member States have transferred competence in respect of matters governed by the Convention and the present Protocol. Such organizations shall declare, in their instruments of formal confirmation or accession, the extent of their competence with respect to matters governed by the Convention and the present Protocol.
Subsequently, they shall inform the depositary of any substantial modification in the extent of their competence.
2. References to "States Parties" in the present Protocol shall apply to such organizations within the limits of their competence.
3. For the purposes of article 13, paragraph 1, and article 15, paragraph 2, of the present Protocol, any instrument deposited by a regional integration organization shall not be counted.
4. Regional integration organizations, in matters within their competence, may exercise their right to vote in the meeting of States Parties, with a number of votes equal to the number of their member States that are Parties to the present Protocol. Such an organization shall

not exercise its right to vote if any of its member States exercises its right, and vice versa.

Article 13

1. Subject to the entry into force of the Convention, the present Protocol shall enter into force on the thirtieth day after the deposit of the tenth instrument of ratification or accession.
2. For each State or regional integration organization ratifying, formally confirming or acceding to the present Protocol after the deposit of the tenth such instrument, the Protocol shall enter into force on the thirtieth day after the deposit of its own such instrument.

Article 14

1. Reservations incompatible with the object and purpose of the present Protocol shall not be permitted.
2. Reservations may be withdrawn at any time.

Article 15

1. Any State Party may propose an amendment to the present Protocol and submit it to the Secretary-General of the United Nations. The Secretary- General shall communicate any proposed amendments to States Parties, with a request to be notified whether they favour a meeting of States Parties for the purpose of considering and deciding upon the proposals. In the event that, within four months from the date of such communication, at least one third of the States Parties favour such a meeting, the Secretary-General shall convene the meeting under the auspices of the United Nations. Any amendment adopted by a majority of two thirds of the States Parties present and voting shall be submitted by the Secretary-General to the General Assembly of the United Nations for approval and thereafter to all States Parties for acceptance.
2. An amendment adopted and approved in accordance with paragraph 1 of this article shall enter into force on the thirtieth day after the number of instruments of acceptance deposited reaches two thirds of the number of States Parties at the date of adoption of the amendment. Thereafter,

the amendment shall enter into force for any State Party on the thirtieth day following the deposit of its own instrument of acceptance. An amendment shall be binding only on those States Parties which have accepted it.

Article 16

A State Party may denounce the present Protocol by written notification to the Secretary-General of the United Nations. The denunciation shall become effective one year after the date of receipt of the notification by the Secretary- General.

Article 17

The text of the present Protocol shall be made available in accessible formats.

Article 18

The Arabic, Chinese, English, French, Russian and Spanish texts of the present Protocol shall be equally authentic.
IN WITNESS THEREOF the undersigned plenipotentiaries, being duly authorized thereto by their respective Governments, have signed the present Protocol.

Appendix 3

Universal Declaration of Human Rights

Preamble

Whereas recognition of the inherent dignity and of the equal and inalienable rights of all members of the human family is the foundation of freedom, justice and peace in the world,

Whereas disregard and contempt for human rights have resulted in barbarous acts which have outraged the conscience of mankind, and the advent of a world in which human beings shall enjoy freedom of speech and belief and freedom from fear and want has been proclaimed as the highest aspiration of the common people,

Whereas it is essential, if man is not to be compelled to have recourse, as a last resort, to rebellion against tyranny and oppression, that human rights should be protected by the rule of law,

Whereas it is essential to promote the development of friendly relations between nations,

Whereas the peoples of the United Nations have in the Charter reaffirmed their faith in fundamental human rights, in the dignity and worth of the human person and in the equal rights of men and women and have determined to promote social progress and better standards of life in larger freedom,

Whereas Member States have pledged themselves to achieve, in cooperation with the United Nations, the promotion of universal respect for and observance of human rights and fundamental freedoms,

Whereas a common understanding of these rights and freedoms is of the greatest importance for the full realization of this pledge,

Now, therefore,The General Assembly,Proclaims this Universal Declaration of Human Rights as a common standard of achievement for all peoples and all nations, to the end that every individual and every organ of society, keeping this Declaration constantly in mind, shall strive by teaching and education to promote respect for these rights and freedoms and by progressive measures, national and international, to secure their universal and effective recognition and observance, both among the peoples of Member States themselves and among the peoples of territories under their jurisdiction.

Article I

All human beings are born free and equal in dignity and rights. They are endowed with reason and conscience and should act towards one another in a spirit of brotherhood.

Article 2

Everyone is entitled to all the rights and freedoms set forth in this Declaration, without distinction of any kind, such as race, colour, sex, language, religion, political or other opinion, national or social origin, property, birth or other status. Furthermore, no distinction shall be made on the basis of the political, jurisdictional or international status of the country or territory to which a person belongs, whether it be independent, trust, non-self-governing or under any other limitation of sovereignty.

Article 3

Everyone has the right to life, liberty and the security of person.

Article 4

No one shall be held in slavery or servitude; slavery and the slave trade shall be prohibited in all their forms.

Article 5

No one shall be subjected to torture or to cruel, inhuman or degrading treatment or punishment.

Article 6

Everyone has the right to recognition everywhere as a person before the law.

Article 7

All are equal before the law and are entitled without any discrimination to equal protection of the law. All are entitled to equal protection against any discrimination in violation of this Declaration and against any incitement to such discrimination.

Article 8

Everyone has the right to an effective remedy by the competent national tribunals for acts violating the fundamental rights granted him by the constitution or by law.

Article 9

No one shall be subjected to arbitrary arrest, detention or exile.

Article 10

Everyone is entitled in full equality to a fair and public hearing by an independent and impartial tribunal, in the determination of his rights and obligations and of any criminal charge against him.

Article 11

1. Everyonechargedwithapenaloffencehastherighttobepresumed innocent until proved guilty according to law in a public trial at which he has had all the guarantees necessary for his defence.
2. Nooneshallbeheldguiltyofanypenaloffenceonaccountofanyactor omission which did not constitute a penal offence, under national or international law, at the time when it was committed. Nor shall a heavier penalty be imposed than the one that was applicable at the time the penal offence was committed.

Article 12

No one shall be subjected to arbitrary interference with his privacy, family, home or correspondence, nor to attacks upon his honour and reputation. Everyone has the right to the protection of the law against such interference or attacks.

Article 13

1.   Everyonehastherighttofreedomofmovementandresidencewithinthe borders of each State.
2.   Everyonehastherighttoleaveanycountry,includinghisown,andto return to his country.

Article 14

1.   Everyone has the right to seek and to enjoy in other countries asylum from persecution.
2.   Thisrightmaynotbeinvokedinthecaseofprosecutionsgenuinely   arising from non-political crimes or from acts contrary to the purposes and principles of the United Nations.

Article 15

1.   Everyonehastherighttoanationality.
2.   Nooneshallbearbitrarilydeprivedofhisnationalitynordeniedtherightto change his nationality.

Article 16

1.   Men and women of full age, without any limitation due to race, nationality or religion, have the right to marry and to found a family. They are entitled to equal rights as to marriage, during marriage and at its dissolution.
2.   Marriageshallbeenteredintoonlywiththefreeandfullconsentofthe intending spouses.
3.   The family is the natural and fundamental group unit of society and is entitled to protection by society and the State.

Article 17

1. Everyonehastherighttoownpropertyaloneaswellasinassociationwith others.
2. Nooneshallbearbitrarilydeprivedofhisproperty.

Article 18

Everyone has the right to freedom of thought, conscience and religion; this right includes freedom to change his religion or belief, and freedom, either alone or in community with others and in public or private, to manifest his religion or belief in teaching, practice, worship and observance.

Article 19

Everyone has the right to freedom of opinion and expression; this right includes freedom to hold opinions without interference and to seek, receive and impart information and ideas through any media and regardless of frontiers.

Article 20

1. Everyonehastherighttofreedomofpeacefulassemblyandassociation.
2. Noonemaybecompelledtobelongtoanassociation.

Article 21

1. Everyonehastherighttotakepartinthegovernmentofhiscountry, directly or through freely chosen representatives.
2. Everyonehastherighttoequalaccesstopublicserviceinhiscountry.
3. Thewillofthepeopleshallbethebasisoftheauthorityofgovernment;this will shall be expressed in periodic and genuine elections which shall be by universal and equal suffrage and shall be held by secret vote or by equivalent free voting procedures.

Article 22

Everyone, as a member of society, has the right to social security and is entitled to realization, through national effort and international co-operation and in accordance with the organization and resources of each State, of the economic, social and cultural rights indispensable for his dignity and the free development of his personality.

Article 23

1. Everyone has the right to work, to free choice of employment, to just and favourable conditions of work and to protection against unemployment.
2. Everyone,withoutanydiscrimination,hastherighttoequalpayforequal work.
3. Everyonewhoworkshastherighttojustandfavourableremuneration ensuring for himself and his family an existence worthy of human dignity, and supplemented, if necessary, by other means of social protection.
4. Everyonehastherighttoformandtojointradeunionsfortheprotectionof his interests.

Article 24

Everyone has the right to rest and leisure, including reasonable limitation of working hours and periodic holidays with pay.

Article 25

1. Everyonehastherighttoastandardoflivingadequateforthehealthand well-being of himself and of his family, including food, clothing, housing and medical care and necessary social services, and the right to security in the event of unemployment, sickness, disability, widowhood, old age or other lack of livelihood in circumstances beyond his control.
2. Motherhoodandchildhoodareentitledtospecialcareandassistance.All children, whether born in or out of wedlock, shall enjoy the same social protection.

Article 26

1.   Everyonehastherighttoeducation.Educationshallbefree,atleastinthe elementary and fundamental stages. Elementary education shall be compulsory. Technical and professional education shall be made generally available and higher education shall be equally accessible to all on the basis of merit.

2.   Educationshallbedirectedtothefulldevelopmentofthehuman personality and to the strengthening of respect for human rights and fundamental freedoms. It shall promote understanding, tolerance and friendship among all nations, racial or religious groups, and shall further the activities of the United Nations for the maintenance of peace.

3.   Parents have a prior right to choose the kind of education that shall be given to their children.

Article 27

1. Everyonehastherightfreelytoparticipateintheculturallifeofthe community, to enjoy the arts and to share in scientific advancement and its benefits.

2.   Everyonehastherighttotheprotectionofthemoralandmaterialinterests resulting from any scientific, literary or artistic production of which he is the author.

Article 28

Everyone is entitled to a social and international order in which the rights and freedoms set forth in this Declaration can be fully realized.

Article 29

1.   Everyonehasdutiestothecommunityinwhichalonethefreeandfull development of his personality is possible.

2.   Intheexerciseofhisrightsandfreedoms,everyoneshallbesubjectonly   to such limitations as are determined by law solely for the purpose of securing due recognition and respect for the rights and freedoms of others and of meeting the just requirements of morality, public order and the general welfare in a democratic society.

3.   These rights and freedoms may in no case be exercised contrary to the purposes and principles of the United Nations.

Article 30

Nothing in this Declaration may be interpreted as implying for any State, group or person any right to engage in any activity or to perform any act aimed at the destruction of any of the rights and freedoms set forth herein.

Appendix 4

African (Banjul) Charter on Human and Peoples' Rights

(Adopted 27 June 1981, OAU Doc. CAB/LEG/67/3 rev. 5, 21 I.L.M. 58 (1982), entered into force 21 October 1986)

Preamble

The African States members of the Organization of African Unity, parties to the present convention entitled "African Charter on Human and Peoples' Rights",

Recalling Decision 115 (XVI) of the Assembly of Heads of State and Government at its Sixteenth Ordinary Session held in Monrovia, Liberia, from 17 to 20 July 1979 on the preparation of a "preliminary draft on an African Charter on Human and Peoples' Rights providing inter alia for the establishment of bodies to promote and protect human and peoples' rights";

Considering the Charter of the Organization of African Unity, which stipulates that "freedom, equality, justice and dignity are essential objectives for the achievement of the legitimate aspirations of the African peoples";

Reaffirming the pledge they solemnly made in Article 2 of the said Charter to eradicate all forms of colonialism from Africa, to coordinate and intensify their cooperation and efforts to achieve a better life for the peoples of Africa and to promote international cooperation having due regard to the Charter of the United Nations. and the Universal Declaration of Human Rights;

Taking into consideration the virtues of their historical tradition and the values of African civilization which should inspire and characterize their reflection on the concept of human and peoples' rights;

Recognizing on the one hand, that fundamental human rights stem from the attributes of human beings which justifies their national and international protection and on the other 1 hand that the reality and respect of peoples rights should necessarily guarantee human rights;

Considering that the enjoyment of rights and freedoms also implies the performance of duties on the part of everyone; Convinced that it is henceforth essential to pay a particular attention to the right to development and that civil and political rights cannot be dissociated from economic, social and cultural rights in their conception as well as universality and that the satisfaction of economic, social and cultural rights ia a guarantee for the enjoyment of civil and political rights;

Conscious of their duty to achieve the total liberation of Africa, the peoples of which are still struggling for their dignity and genuine independence, and undertaking to eliminate colonialism, neo-colonialism, apartheid, zionism and to dismantle aggressive foreign military bases and all forms of discrimination, particularly those based on race, ethnic group, color, sex. language, religion or political opinions;

Reaffirming their adherence to the principles of human and peoples' rights and freedoms contained in the declarations, conventions and other instrument adopted by the Organization of African Unity, the Movement of Non-Aligned Countries and the United Nations;

Firmly convinced of their duty to promote and protect human and people' rights and freedoms taking into account the importance traditionally attached to these rights and freedoms in Africa;

Have agreed as follows:

Part I: Rights and Duties

Chapter I: Human and Peoples' Rights

Article 1

The Member States of the Organization of African Unity parties to the present Charter shall recognize the rights, duties and freedoms enshrined in this Chapter and shall undertake to adopt legislative or other measures to give effect to them.

Article 2

Every individual shall be entitled to the enjoyment of the rights and freedoms recognized and guaranteed in the present Charter without distinction of any kind such as race, ethnic group, color, sex, language, religion, political or any other opinion, national and social origin, fortune, birth or other status.

Article 3

1. Every individual shall be equal before the law.
2. Every individual shall be entitled to equal protection of the law.

Article 4

Human beings are inviolable. Every human being shall be entitled to respect for his life and the integrity of his person. No one may be arbitrarily deprived of this right.

Article 5

Every individual shall have the right to the respect of the dignity inherent in a human being and to the recognition of his legal status. All forms of exploitation and degradation of man particularly slavery, slave trade, torture, cruel, inhuman or degrading punishment and treatment shall be prohibited.

Article 6

Every individual shall have the right to liberty and to the security of his person. No one may be deprived of his freedom except for reasons and conditions previously laid down by law. In particular, no one may be arbitrarily arrested or detained.

Article 7

1. Every individual shall have the right to have his cause heard. This comprises: (a) the right to an appeal to competent national organs against acts of violating his fundamental rights as recognized and guaranteed by conventions, laws, regulations and customs in force; (b) the right to be presumed innocent until proved guilty by a competent court or tribunal; (c) the right to defense, including the

right to be defended by counsel of his choice; (d) the right to be tried within a reasonable time by an impartial court or tribunal.

2. No one may be condemned for an act or omission which did not constitute a legally punishable offence at the time it was committed. No penalty may be inflicted for an offence for which no provision was made at the time it was committed. Punishment is personal and can be imposed only on the offender.

Article 8

Freedom of conscience, the profession and free practice of religion shall be guaranteed. No one may, subject to law and order, be submitted to measures restricting the exercise of these freedoms.

Article 9

1. Every individual shall have the right to receive information.
2. Every individual shall have the right to express and disseminate his opinions within the law.

Article 10

1. Every individual shall have the right to free association provided that he abides by the law.
2. Subject to the obligation of solidarity provided for in 29 no one may be compelled to join an association.

Article 11

Every individual shall have the right to assemble freely with others. The exercise of this right shall be subject only to necessary restrictions provided for by law in particular those enacted in the interest of national security, the safety, health, ethics and rights and freedoms of others.

Article 12

1. Every individual shall have the right to freedom of movement and residence within the borders of a State provided he abides by the law.

2. Every individual shall have the right to leave any country including his own, and to return to his country. This right may only be subject to restrictions, provided for by law for the protection of national security, law and order, public health or morality.
3. Every individual shall have the right, when persecuted, to seek and obtain asylum in other countries in accordance with laws of those countries and international conventions.
4. A non-national legally admitted in a territory of a State Party to the present Charter, may only be expelled from it by virtue of a decision taken in accordance with the law.
5. The mass expulsion of non-nationals shall be prohibited. Mass expulsion shall be that which is aimed at national, racial, ethnic or religious groups.

Article 13

1. Every citizen shall have the right to participate freely in the government of his country, either directly or through freely chosen representatives in accordance with the provisions of the law.
2. Every citizen shall have the right of equal access to the public service of his country.
3. Every individual shall have the right of access to public property and services in strict equality of all persons before the law.

Article 14

The right to property shall be guaranteed. It may only be encroached upon in the interest of public need or in the general interest of the community and in accordance with the provisions of appropriate laws.

Article 15

Every individual shall have the right to work under equitable and satisfactory conditions, and shall receive equal pay for equal work.

Article 16

1. Every individual shall have the right to enjoy the best attainable state of physical and mental health.
2. States parties to the present Charter shall take the necessary measures to protect the health of their people and to ensure that they receive medical attention when they are sick.

Article 17

1. Every individual shall have the right to education.
2. Every individual may freely, take part in the cultural life of his community.
3. The promotion and protection of morals and traditional values recognized by the community shall be the duty of the State.

Article 18

1. The family shall be the natural unit and basis of society. It shall be protected by the State which shall take care of its physical health and moral.
2. The State shall have the duty to assist the family which is the custodian or morals and traditional values recognized by the community.
3. The State shall ensure the elimination of every discrimination against women and also ensure the protection of the rights of the woman and the child as stipulated in international declarations and conventions.
4. The aged and the disabled shall also have the right to special measures of protection in keeping with their physical or moral needs.

Article 19

All peoples shall be equal; they shall enjoy the same respect and shall have the same rights. Nothing shall justify the domination of a people by another.

Article 20

1. All peoples shall have the right to existence. They shall have the unquestionable and inalienable right to self- determination. They shall freely determine their political status and shall pursue their economic and social development according to the policy they have freely chosen.
2. Colonized or oppressed peoples shall have the right to free themselves from the bonds of domination by resorting to any means recognized by the international community.
3. All peoples shall have the right to the assistance of the States parties to the present Charter in their liberation struggle against foreign domination, be it political, economic or cultural.

Article 21

1. All peoples shall freely dispose of their wealth and natural resources. This right shall be exercised in the exclusive interest of the people. In no case shall a people be deprived of it.
2. In case of spoliation the dispossessed people shall have the right to the lawful recovery of its property as well as to an adequate compensation.
3. The free disposal of wealth and natural resources shall be exercised without prejudice to the obligation of promoting international economic cooperation based on mutual respect, equitable exchange and the principles of international law.
4. States parties to the present Charter shall individually and collectively exercise the right to free disposal of their wealth and natural resources with a view to strengthening African unity and solidarity.
5. States parties to the present Charter shall undertake to eliminate all forms of foreign economic exploitation particularly that practiced by international monopolies so as to enable their peoples to fully benefit from the advantages derived from their national resources.

Article 22

1. All peoples shall have the right to their economic, social and cultural development with due regard to their freedom and identity and in the equal enjoyment of the common heritage of mankind.
2. States shall have the duty, individually or collectively, to ensure the exercise of the right to development.

Article 23

1. All peoples shall have the right to national and international peace and security. The principles of solidarity and friendly relations implicitly affirmed by the Charter of the United Nations and reaffirmed by that of the Organization of African Unity shall govern relations between States.
2. For the purpose of strengthening peace, solidarity and friendly relations, States parties to the present Charter shall ensure that: (a) any individual enjoying the right of asylum under 12 of the present Charter shall not engage in subversive activities against his country of origin or any other State party to the present Charter; (b) their territories shall not be used as bases for subversive or terrorist activities against the people of any other State party to the present Charter.

Article 24

All peoples shall have the right to a general satisfactory environment favorable to their development.

Article 25

States parties to the present Charter shall have the duty to promote and ensure through teaching, education and publication, the respect of the rights and freedoms contained in the present Charter and to see to it that these freedoms and rights as well as corresponding obligations and duties are understood.
Article 26
States parties to the present Charter shall have the duty to guarantee the independence of the Courts and shall allow the establishment

and improvement of appropriate national institutions entrusted with the promotion and protection of the rights and freedoms guaranteed by the present Charter.

Chapter II: Duties

Article 27

1.   Every individual shall have duties towards his family and society, the State and other legally recognized communities and the international community.
2.   The rights and freedoms of each individual shall be exercised with due regard to the rights of others, collective security, morality and common interest.

Article 28

Every individual shall have the duty to respect and consider his fellow beings without discrimination, and to maintain relations aimed at promoting, safeguarding and reinforcing mutual respect and tolerance.

Article 29 The individual shall also have the duty:

1.   To preserve the harmonious development of the family and to work for the cohesion and respect of the family; to respect his parents at all times, to maintain them in case of need;
2.   To serve his national community by placing his physical and intellectual abilities at its service;
3.   Not to compromise the security of the State whose national or resident he is;
4.   To preserve and strengthen social and national solidarity, particularly when the latter is threatened;
5.   To preserve and strengthen the national independence and the territorial integrity of his country and to contribute to its defense in accordance with the law;
6.   To work to the best of his abilities and competence, and to pay taxes imposed by law in the interest of the society;

7. To preserve and strengthen positive African cultural values in his relations with other members of the society, in the spirit of tolerance, dialogue and consultation and, in general, to contribute to the promotion of the moral well being of society;
8. To contribute to the best of his abilities, at all times and at all levels, to the promotion and achievement of African unity.

Part II: Measures of Safeguard

Chapter I: Establishment and Organization of the African Commission on Human and Peoples' Rights

Article 30

An African Commission on Human and Peoples' Rights, hereinafter called "the Commission", shall be established within the Organization of African Unity to promote human and peoples' rights and ensure their protection in Africa.

Article 31

1. The Commission shall consist of eleven members chosen from amongst African personalities of the highest reputation, known for their high morality, integrity, impartiality and competence in matters of human and peoples' rights; particular consideration being given to persons having legal experience.
2. The members of the Commission shall serve in their personal capacity.

Article 32

The Commission shall not include more than one national of the same state.

Article 33

The members of the Commission shall be elected by secret ballot by the Assembly of Heads of State and Government, from a list of persons nominated by the States parties to the present Charter.

Article 34

Each State party to the present Charter may not nominate more than two candidates. The candidates must have the nationality of one of the States party to the present Charter. When two candidates are nominated by a State, one of them may not be a national of that State.

Article 35

1. The Secretary General of the Organization of African Unity shall invite States parties to the present Charter at least four months before the elections to nominate candidates;
2. The Secretary General of the Organization of African Unity shall make an alphabetical list of the persons thus nominated and communicate it to the Heads of State and Government at least one month before the elections.

Article 36

The members of the Commission shall be elected for a six year period and shall be eligible for re-election. However, the term of office of four of the members elected at the first election shall terminate after two years and the term of office of three others, at the end of four years.

Article 37

Immediately after the first election, the Chairman of the Assembly of Heads of State and Government of the Organization of African Unity shall draw lots to decide the names of those members referred to in Article 36.

Article 38

After their election, the members of the Commission shall make a solemn declaration to discharge their duties impartially and faithfully.

Article 39

1. In case of death or resignation of a member of the Commission the Chairman of the Commission shall immediately inform the Secretary General of the Organization of African Unity, who shall declare the seat vacant from the date of death or from the date on which the resignation takes effect.
2. If, in the unanimous opinion of other members of the Commission, a member has stopped discharging his duties for any reason other than a temporary absence, the Chairman of the Commission shall inform the Secretary General of the Organization of African Unity, who shall then declare the seat vacant.
3. In each of the cases anticipated above, the Assembly of Heads of State and Government shall replace the member whose seat became vacant for the remaining period of his term unless the period is less than six months.

Article 40

Every member of the Commission shall be in office until the date his successor assumes office.

Article 41

The Secretary General of the Organization of African Unity shall appoint the Secretary of the Commission. He shall also provide the staff and services necessary for the effective discharge of the duties of the Commission. The Organization of African Unity shall bear the costs of the staff and services.

Article 42

1. The Commission shall elect its Chairman and Vice Chairman for a two-year period. They shall be eligible for re-election.
2. The Commission shall lay down its rules of procedure.
3. Seven members shall form the quorum.
4. In case of an equality of votes, the Chairman shall have a casting vote.

5. The Secretary General may attend the meetings of the Commission. He shall not participate in deliberations nor shall he be entitled to vote. The Chairman of the Commission may, however, invite him to speak.

Article 43

In discharging their duties, members of the Commission shall enjoy diplomatic privileges and immunities provided for in the General Convention on the Privileges and Immunities of the Organization of African Unity.

Article 44

Provision shall be made for the emoluments and allowances of the members of the Commission in the Regular Budget of the Organization of African Unity.
Chapter II -- Mandate of the Commission

Article 45 the functions of the Commission shall be:

1. To promote Human and Peoples' Rights and in particular:
1. (a) To collect documents, undertake studies and researches on African problems in the field of human and peoples' rights, organize seminars, symposia and conferences, disseminate information, encourage national and local institutions concerned with human and peoples' rights, and should the case arise, give its views or make recommendations to Governments.
2. (b) To formulate and lay down, principles and rules aimed at solving legal problems relating to human and peoples' rights and fundamental freedoms upon which African Governments may base their legislations.
3. (c) Co-operate with other African and international institutions concerned with the promotion and protection of human and peoples' rights.
2. Ensure the protection of human and peoples' rights under conditions laid down by the present Charter.

3. Interpret all the provisions of the present Charter at the request of a State party, an institution of the OAU or an African Organization recognized by the OAU.
4. Perform any other tasks which may be entrusted to it by the Assembly of Heads of State and Government.
    Chapter III -- Procedure of the Commission

Article 46

The Commission may resort to any appropriate method of investigation; it may hear from the Secretary General of the Organization of African Unity or any other person capable of enlightening it.
Communication from States

Article 47

If a State party to the present Charter has good reasons to believe that another State party to this Charter has violated the provisions of the Charter, it may draw, by written communication, the attention of that State to the matter. This communication shall also be addressed to the Secretary General of the OAU and to the Chairman of the Commission. Within three months of the receipt of the communication, the State to which the communication is addressed shall give the enquiring State, written explanation or statement elucidating the matter. This should include as much as possible relevant information relating to the laws and rules of procedure applied and applicable, and the redress already given or course of action available.

Article 48

If within three months from the date on which the original communication is received by the State to which it is addressed, the issue is not settled to the satisfaction of the two States involved through bilateral negotiation or by any other peaceful procedure, either State shall have the right to submit the matter to the Commission through the Chairman and shall notify the other States involved.

Article 49

Notwithstanding the provisions of 47, if a State party to the present Charter considers that another State party has violated the provisions of the Charter, it may refer the matter directly to the Commission by addressing a communication to the Chairman, to the Secretary General of the Organization of African Unity and the State concerned.

Article 50

The Commission can only deal with a matter submitted to it after making sure that all local remedies, if they exist, have been exhausted, unless it is obvious to the Commission that the procedure of achieving these remedies would be unduly prolonged.

Article 51

1. The Commission may ask the States concerned to provide it with all relevant information.
2. When the Commission is considering the matter, States concerned may be represented before it and submit written or oral representation.

Article 52

After having obtained from the States concerned and from other sources all the information it deems necessary and after having tried all appropriate means to reach an amicable solution based on the respect of Human and Peoples' Rights, the Commission shall prepare, within a reasonable period of time from the notification referred to in 48, a report stating the facts and its findings. This report shall be sent to the States concerned and communicated to the Assembly of Heads of State and Government.

Article 53

While transmitting its report, the Commission may make to the Assembly of Heads of State and Government such recommendations as it deems useful.

Article 54

The Commission shall submit to each ordinary Session of the Assembly of Heads of State and Government a report on its activities.
Other Communications

Article 55

1. Before each Session, the Secretary of the Commission shall make a list of the communications other than those of States parties to the present Charter and transmit them to the members of the Commission, who shall indicate which communications should be considered by the Commission.
2. A communication shall be considered by the Commission if a simple majority of its members so decide.

Article 56

Communications relating to human and peoples' rights referred to in 55 received by the Commission, shall be considered if they:
1. Indicate their authors even if the latter request anonymity,
2. Are compatible with the Charter of the Organization of African Unity or with the present Charter,
3. Are not written in disparaging or insulting language directed against the State concerned and its institutions or to the Organization of African Unity,
4. Are not based exclusively on news discriminated through the mass media,
5. Are sent after exhausting local remedies, if any, unless it is obvious that this procedure is unduly prolonged,

6. Are submitted within a reasonable period from the time local remedies are exhausted or from the date the Commission is seized of the matter, and
7. Do not deal with cases which have been settled by these States involved in accordance with the principles of the Charter of the United Nations, or the Charter of the Organization of African Unity or the provisions of the present Charter.

Article 57

Prior to any substantive consideration, all communications shall be brought to the knowledge of the State concerned by the Chairman of the Commission.

Article 58

1. When it appears after deliberations of the Commission that one or more communications apparently relate to special cases which reveal the existence of a series of serious or massive violations of human and peoples' rights, the Commission shall draw the attention of the Assembly of Heads of State and Government to these special cases.
2. The Assembly of Heads of State and Government may then request the Commission to undertake an in-depth study of these cases and make a factual report, accompanied by its findings and recommendations.
3. A case of emergency duly noticed by the Commission shall be submitted by the latter to the Chairman of the Assembly of Heads of State and Government who mayrequest an in-depth study.

Article 59

1. All measures taken within the provisions of the present Charter shall remain confidential until such a time as the Assembly of Heads of State and Government shall otherwise decide.
2. However, the report shall be published by the Chairman of the Commission upon the decision of the Assembly of Heads of State and Government.
3. The report on the activities of the Commission shall be published by its Chairman after it has been considered by the Assembly of Heads of State and Government.

Chapter IV -- Applicable Principles

Article 60

The Commission shall draw inspiration from international law on human and peoples' rights, particularly from the provisions of various African instruments on human and peoples' rights, the Charter of the United Nations, the Charter of the Organization of African Unity, the Universal Declaration of Human Rights, other instruments adopted by the United Nations and by African countries in the field of human and peoples' rights as well as from the provisions of various instruments adopted within the Specialized Agencies of the United Nations of which the parties to the present Charter are members.

Article 61

The Commission shall also take into consideration, as subsidiary measures to determine the principles of law, other general or special international conventions, laying down rules expressly recognized by member states of the Organization of African Unity, African practices consistent with international norms on human and people's rights, customs generally accepted as law, general principles of law recognized by African states as well as legal precedents and doctrine.

Article 62

Each state party shall undertake to submit every two years, from the date the present Charter comes into force, a report on the legislative or other measures taken with a view to giving effect to the rights and freedoms recognized and guaranteed by the present Charter.

Article 63

1. The present Charter shall be open to signature, ratification or adherence of the member
   states of the Organization of African Unity.

2. The instruments of ratification or adherence to the present Charter shall be deposited with the Secretary General of the Organization of African Unity.
3. The present Charter shall come into force three months after the reception by the Secretary General of the instruments of ratification or adherence of a simple majority of the member states of the Organization of African Unity.
Part III: General Provisions

Article 64

1. After the coming into force of the present Charter, members of the Commission shall be elected in accordance with the relevant Articles of the present Charter.
2. The Secretary General of the Organization of African Unity shall convene the first meeting of the Commission at the Headquarters of the Organization within three months of the constitution of the Commission. Thereafter, the Commission shall be convened by its Chairman whenever necessary but at least once a year.

Article 65

For each of the States that will ratify or adhere to the present Charter after its coming into force, the Charter shall take effect three months after the date of the deposit by that State of its instrument of ratification or adherence.

Article 66

Special protocols or agreements may, if necessary, supplement the provisions of the present Charter.

Article 67

The Secretary General of the Organization of African Unity shall inform member states of the Organization of the deposit of each instrument of ratification or adherence.

Article 68

The present Charter may be amended if a State party makes a written request to that effect to the Secretary General of the Organization of African Unity. The Assembly of Heads of State and Government may only consider the draft amendment after all the States partieshave been duly informed of it and the Commission has given its opinion on it at the request of the sponsoring State. The amendment shall be approved by a simple majority of the States parties. It shall come into force for each State which has accepted it in accordance with its constitutional procedure three months after the Secretary General has received notice of the acceptance.
Adopted by the eighteenth Assembly of Heads of State and Government June 1981 – Nairobi, Kenya

www.ingramcontent.com/pod-product-compliance
Lightning Source LLC
Chambersburg PA
CBHW021553210326
41599CB00010B/420